# PUBLIC IN NAME ONLY

D1569707

A VOLUME IN THE SERIES
*Studies in Print Culture and the History of the Book*

EDITED BY
Greg Barnhisel, Joan Shelley Rubin, and Michael Winship

# PUBLIC
## IN NAME
# ONLY

The 1939 Alexandria Library
Sit-In Demonstration

## BRENDA MITCHELL-POWELL

UNIVERSITY OF MASSACHUSETTS PRESS

*Amherst and Boston*

Copyright © 2022 by University of Massachusetts Press
All rights reserved
Printed in the United States of America

ISBN 978-1-62534-657-5 (paper); 658-2 (hardcover)

Designed by Deste Roosa
Set in Deepdene and Futura
Printed and bound by Books International, Inc.

Cover design by Frank Gutbrod
Cover photo: Unknown photographer, *Sit-In Demonstrators Escorted from the Alexandria Library Under Police Arrest. August 21, 1939.* Courtesy of the Collection of the Alexandria Black History Museum, City of Alexandria, Virginia. https://www.alexandriava.gov/historic/blackhistory/default.aspx?id=73256.

Library of Congress Cataloging-in-Publication Data

Names: Mitchell-Powell, Brenda, author.
Title: Public in name only : the 1939 Alexandria Library sit-in demonstration / Brenda Mitchell-Powell.
Other titles: Studies in print culture and the history of the book.
Description: Amherst : University of Massachusetts Press, 2022. | Series: Studies in print culture and the history of the book | Includes bibliographical references and index.
Identifiers: LCCN 2021054537 (print) | LCCN 2021054538 (ebook) | ISBN 9781625346575 (paperback) | ISBN 9781625346582 (hardcover) | ISBN 9781613769355 (ebook) | ISBN 9781613769362 (ebook)
Subjects: LCSH: Alexandria Library (Alexandria, Va.)—History. | Civil rights demonstrations—Virginia—Alexandria—History. | Tucker, Samuel Wilbert, 1913–1990. | Public libraries—Virginia—Alexandria—History. | African Americans and libraries—Virginia—Alexandria. | Segregation—Virginia—Alexandria.
Classification: LCC Z733.A37 M58 2022 (print) | LCC Z733.A37 (ebook) | DDC 027.4755/296—dc23/eng/20211203
LC record available at https://lccn.loc.gov/2021054537
LC ebook record available at https://lccn.loc.gov/2021054538

British Library Cataloguing-in-Publication Data
A catalog record for this book is available from the British Library.

Portions of chapters seven and eight were previously published as "The 1939 Alexandria, Virginia, Public Library Sit-In Demonstration," in *Libraries—Traditions and Innovations: Papers from the Library History Seminar XIII*, eds. Melanie A. Kimball and Katherine M. Wisser (Munich: De Gruyter Saur, 2017), 70–99. Used with permission from De Gruyter Saur.

To Cal for patience and to Michèle for constancy

I am . . . concerned . . . that the Negro shall not be content simply with demanding a share in the existing system. [H]is fundamental responsibility and historical challenge is . . . to make sure that the system which shall survive in the United States of America . . . shall be a system which guarantees justice and freedom for everyone.

—Charles Hamilton Houston

# CONTENTS

# PREFACE AND ACKNOWLEDGMENTS

*Public in Name Only* is a microhistory of one of the lesser-known sit-in demonstrations, a 1939 event orchestrated by Black Alexandrian attorney Samuel Wilbert Tucker and put into action by five protesters, with the goal of integrating the public library in Alexandria, Virginia. This early demonstration challenged entrenched and systemic segregation and expanded civil rights venues, which to this point had been limited to graduate and professional schools. The Alexandria Library protest was among the rare recorded efforts to confront Jim Crow segregation directly rather than merely to demand better allocations of public accommodations or services.[1] It was also the first recorded instance of using a staged sit-in as a strategy to compel a municipality to provide Black citizens with library access that predated the access initiatives of the 1940s, 1950s, and 1960s. The protest thus prefigured the histories of American public libraries and twentieth-century American social and civil rights. Tucker's grassroots campaign was an attempt to subsume the national priorities and tactics of organizations such as the National Association for the Advancement of Colored People (NAACP) into the microcosmic civil rights objectives of a local Black community. Such linkages serve to illustrate how early local strategies to secure equality in library access were an integral part of a larger context of civil rights activities. They also show that studying local microhistories may help us to understand the complexities of the long, ongoing struggle for Black civil rights.

*Public in Name Only* had its genesis in my historical research into the city of Alexandria, which I began after my husband and I decided to retire there. While doing that work, I learned about the 1939 library sit-in. None of my previous studies into Black history, American social history, civil rights history, or library and information science had included any information about this protest, which surprised and disappointed me. I could not fathom how such a significant early event could have remained unchronicled in the professional literature. My curiosity was piqued, and I plunged headlong into research on this unsung protest and its aftermath.

The account of the Alexandria protest is important to me because libraries and librarians have always been important to me. My love affair with libraries began many years ago. My parents were avid readers, and they wanted me to love books and learning, too. During my childhood, I eagerly anticipated my weekly visits with my mother to our local public library. Even at a young age, I viewed the library as a place of wonderment and possibilities. Sensing my delight in the library and its treasures, the librarian nurtured my interest and became one of the most important people in my world. One of the proudest moments in my life was acquiring my first library card at the age of four or five. This meant that not only was I growing up but also that I now possessed my own key to the world of reading, learning, and entertainment. In middle and high school, the library became a safe haven from the taunts of my less studious peers. In college, I spent so much time in the stacks that the security guard reserved a study space there for me. Decades later, when my career as an editor required near constant contact with members of the professional library community, my admiration for those individuals and for the field of library and information science increased exponentially. Eventually, I enrolled in a master's program in the field and then continued on to earn my doctoral degree in archives management.

As a Black woman, I have been extremely lucky compared to some of my Black colleagues and acquaintances.[2] Throughout my time in libraries and with librarians, I have never had to face the degradation, humiliation, and dehumanization of overt racism that barred me from entry or denied me access to materials. Yet I do not take my good fortune for granted. In my work, I have struggled to grasp the paradox of southern librarians' professional ethics versus the discriminatory attitudes and lifeways that prompted them to prohibit knowledge acquisition based solely on race. I learned to recognize the societal mores and institutionalized racism that engendered the paradox, but I have never accepted either. I have had even greater difficulty understanding the discrimination evinced by the American Library Association (ALA), the professional organization charged with encouraging and defending information access, whose actions and attitudes gave the lie to the ethos of professional librarianship.

Thankfully, the raw pain of my day-to-day experiences with racist microaggressions has been comparatively bearable. Only once have I been subjected to overt racism in a library context: when an elderly White patron disapproved of my presence there. Still, I can imagine the weight of unending, systemic racial oppression that characterized southern libraries and life during Jim Crow. To immerse myself in that experience, I read the accounts of numerous Black patrons and librarians who were faced with segregated libraries and racist colleagues. I also reread one of my favorite books, Richard Wright's *Black Boy: A Record of Childhood and Youth*, which details his heartrending and courageous efforts to obtain a book—any book—by H. L. Mencken from his local Whites-only public library. With savvy race management, he used the library regulations and Whites' societal norms against them and succeeded in his mission. Reading his narrative, I recalled a personal story. Years ago, I borrowed a book from my local public library: *The Black Experience: An Anthology of American Literature for the 1970s*, by Francis Edward Kearns. After I brought the book home and began to read it, I noticed that someone had drawn a swastika on one of the opening pages. When I returned the book to the library, I reported the defacement to the librarian, who responded, "I'm so sorry about that. But it's okay. I'll use Wite-Out to cover it up." I have always wondered if she grasped the humor of her words.[3]


This book would not have been possible without the assistance and encouragement of a network of educators, librarians, archivists, and editors. Michèle V. Cloonan, professor and dean emerita of the Simmons University School of Library and Information Science, read early drafts of the manuscript, showed boundless patience with my questions and revisions, and provided expert counsel, a keen editorial eye, and much needed humor. She also offered guidance and independence, constructive criticism and praise and is a cherished friend, advisor, and mentor whose many kindnesses have enriched my life and bolstered my spirit. I can never repay the debt I owe her. Krystyn R. Moon, professor of history and director of the American studies program at the University of Mary Washington, provided vital data on lynching history, residential housing segregation, and lifeway discrimination in Alexandria during Jim Crow. Martha Claire Catlin, historian for the Alexandria Monthly Meeting of the Religious Society of Friends, generously shared details about the Meeting's history and activities. Her counsel has been invaluable. Wayne A. Wiegand, F. William Summers professor of library and information studies emeritus, School of Information, Florida State University, offered professional counsel and early and consistent support for my work.

My deepest gratitude to the staff of the Alexandria Library Special Collections, including George K. Combs, Patricia Walker, Leslie Anderson, Mark Zoeter, Gregory Pierce, Brian Sando, Jeff Flannery, and, especially, Julia M. Downie, whose contributions to this book are immeasurable. Jackie Cohan, records administrator and archivist for the Office of Historic Alexandria, helped me locate pertinent city council meeting notes and the city's annual reports and familiarized me with Alexandria's records retention and access policies. Rebecca Schneider at the Library of Virginia; Lisa Robinson at the Slover Library in Norfolk, Virginia; and Sybil E. Moses, Elizabeth L. Brown, and Megan Halsband at the Library of Congress shared their research expertise. Linda Rudd at the Charles E. Beatley, Jr., Central Library supplied collection data for the Kate Waller Barrett Branch. Clifford L. Muse, Jr., of Howard University's Moorland-Spingarn Research Center shared information about the university's student sit-ins of 1934 and 1943–44. Michele Casto and Maya Thompson of the People's Archive at the District of Columbia Public Library provided research assistance, as did Catherine Weinraub of Beth El Hebrew Congregation in Alexandria.

Audrey P. Davis, the director of the Alexandria Black History Museum, has been a supportive colleague, ally, and friend since my internship at her institution. She graciously allowed me to process the Samuel Wilbert Tucker Collection, which supplied important early insights into the themes of this book, and she shared images from the museum's photographic archives. Thanks also to Bryan L. Porter, the

Commonwealth's attorney for the city of Alexandria; Justin M. Wilson, mayor of Alexandria, and Mark McHugh, mayoral aide; and Kristin B. Lloyd, the curator and acting director of Alexandria History Museum at The Lyceum, for their contributions.

The staff of the University of Massachusetts Press provided exemplary assistance with this book. I am deeply grateful to the editorial board and the peer readers, whose invaluable comments, suggestions, and recommended resources greatly enhanced it. A few individuals deserve special acknowledgment. Boundless thanks to the editors Brian Halley and Rachael DeShano for their kindness, patience, professionalism, encouragement, and constructive feedback and for expertly shepherding the book through publication. Thanks, too, to Madison Karpiej for her assistance with note formatting, Dawn Potter for her meticulous copyediting skills, Deste Roosa for gorgeous interior design and for being such a fine compositor, Frank Gutbrod for an ideal cover design, and to Courtney Andree for her professional marketing expertise. Though an independent contractor, I also want to thank Sandy Sadow for her exacting indexing.

I offer special appreciation to the people I interviewed for this book. Sadly, four of them—Ferdinand T. Day, Dorothy Evans Turner, Gladys Howard Davis, and Barbara Ann Rowan, —are now deceased. I send my thanks to them in absentia as well as to all of the others who shared their critical insights: Audrey P. Davis, Julie B. Perry, Matthew Dull, Lillian S. Patterson, Lovell A. Lee, Shirley M. Lee, Deborah Thomas-McSwain, Howard G. Cooley, Clifford L. Muse, Jr., and Daniel Lee.

The librarian, author, and researcher Nancy Noyes Silcox and the videographer, podcaster, and researcher Matt Spangler were extremely generous with their time, attention, personal contacts, research resources, and support. I am deeply indebted to them for their indispensable contributions.

A doctoral dissertation requires emotional as well as intellectual sustenance. I am grateful for the support and encouragement of my dear friends Patricia Bell-Scott, Gloria Alter, Sandy Berman, and Florence and Roger Canaff. Pamela A. Quarles and Mary A. Halas continue to enable possibilities.

My husband, Cal Powell, served as my in-house computer guru, and his troubleshooting expertise saved me from a pencil-and-paper project. He also generously provided research assistance and helpful comments on the manuscript. His patience, tolerance, and good humor never cease to amaze me. I remain deeply appreciative of his ongoing support for me and the project.

# PUBLIC IN NAME ONLY

# Alexandria as Microcosm

In 1937 when Alexandria, Virginia's, first public library was constructed just a few blocks from his home, Samuel Wilbert Tucker, a
young, Black, native Alexandrian attorney, was enraged that he could
not use the municipal facility solely because of his race.[1] As his frustration intensified, he became increasingly motivated to oppose segregation in public library access through proactive legal recourse.[2] Inspired
by the 1930s legal successes achieved by the NAACP attorneys in
higher-education discrimination cases, Tucker decided to extend those
accomplishments to the arena of public library discrimination because
he understood that libraries were also centers for educational access
and intellectual development that should be available to all citizens,
regardless of race. He knew that, as sites of American democracy, libraries
not only supported individual and communal intellectual growth and
development but also enabled citizens to prepare for participation in
civic life. Moreover, he realized that the act of reading created agency
in individuals' everyday lives. Reading empowers us to construct community and to generate meanings from books that have unique significance for our lives. This is especially true for recreational reading, when
personal agency empowers us to envision and imagine new experiences
and horizons.[3]

Tucker decided to organize a sit-in demonstration at the library to
compel the board and city council to desegregate the facility.[4] His motivation for that decision as well as the date he chose for the event were linked
to several factors, one of which was the thirtieth annual conference of the
National Association for the Advancement of Colored People (NAACP),
held in July 1939 in Richmond, Virginia. At the conference, attendees
approved several resolutions that became priorities for the organization,
two of which had special bearing on Tucker's library protest. Resolution V,
Civil Rights, concerned discrimination because of race, creed, or color

by people or places operated for the public and paid for with public as well as private funds. The new Alexandria Library was such a place: a municipal facility financed with taxes collected from all of the city's citizens. Resolution VI, Education, states, "The NAACP favors universal education, equality in school terms, teachers' salaries, and school facilities. Where separate schools are maintained, the standards should be the same." Tucker's protest was motivated primarily because Blacks paid taxes to subsidize a library they could not use. He thus acted similarly to many talented Howard University Law School alumni, who, inspired by the NAACP resolutions, embraced opportunities to force Virginia courts to uphold the Fourteenth Amendment to the U.S. Constitution and mandate equal protection under the law.

Tucker's strategy to desegregate the Alexandria Library was two-pronged. He began by enlisting a friend, a retired army sergeant named George Wilson, to accompany him to the library and request an application for a library card. Wilson's application was immediately rejected, and the men were told that use of the library was reserved for Whites. Tucker then filed a writ of mandamus ordering the librarian to accept Wilson's application. While he waited for a ruling on the writ, he organized the second component of his desegregation strategy: a library sit-in demonstration.[5] He engaged five young men from the Black community—Otto Lee Tucker, Morris L. Murray, Clarence Strange, Edward Gaddis, and William "Buddy" Evans, who ranged in age from nineteen to twenty-two—to take part in the protest. At his law office he thoroughly trained all of the men in the nonviolent, civil-disobedience techniques he had learned from his mentor, Dr. Howard Thurman, a chaplain at Howard University. Then, on August 21, 1939, as instructed by Tucker, the men entered the library one by one and requested library-card applications. When they were refused, each, in turn, went to the library shelves, selected a book at random, and seated himself at an unoccupied library table. Their presence at separate tables ensured that the men would not converse so they could not be accused of disorderly conduct. Tucker expected the men to be arrested, and he intended to serve as their attorney at their hearings, so he did not participate in the sit-in or go to the site of the demonstration.

Library operations were briefly disturbed, but only because the curious White patrons were busy watching the unfolding drama as the library staff attempted to get the protesters to leave. After the protesters had spent about an hour in the library, the police quietly escorted them out. Library operations for White patrons then continued as usual, without disturbance or interruption. The men were arraigned that same day and were initially charged with trespassing, though the charge was later changed to disorderly conduct. Hearings took place on August 22, August 29, and September 1. After the first and second hearings, the police court judge, James Reese Duncan, who also served on the library board and city council, issued continuances to Armistead Lloyd Boothe, the prosecuting attorney, who was also the city's attorney, vice president of the library board, and a member of the city council.[6] At the third hearing, Judge Duncan did not hear arguments for or against the protesters, and the case was allowed to lapse. It is unclear if Boothe's and Duncan's connections with the library board and the city council were technically and legally a conflict of interest. However, as a matter of protocol, both men should have recused themselves from cases simultaneously involving the two entities because their dual roles certainly had the appearance of a conflict of interest. The men were members of Alexandria's White elite, which wielded tremendous control over city affairs, and their concurrent service was a clear consolidation of power.

On January 10, 1940, Judge William Pape Woolls of Alexandria's corporation court ruled on the George Wilson writ, stating that library privileges had been denied because Tucker had competed Wilson's application on his behalf and Wilson had not properly identified himself as a resident of Alexandria.[7] Yet Woolls also stated that no official rule barred Blacks from the library, thus opening the door for African Americans to submit library-card applications. To circumvent desegregation of the Alexandria Library, the city hastily constructed the Robert H. Robinson Library, a separate-and-unequal Black branch library. On January 30, 1940, Tucker and Wilson returned to the main library to resubmit library-card applications. Instead of accepting them, the librarian offered them cards to be used exclusively at the Black branch.

While some Black residents were heartened by the prospect of their own library, others, like Tucker, were incensed about the main library's continuing policy of Black exclusion and never patronized the new Jim Crow library. Instead, Tucker intended to pursue further legal action. Tucker's commitment to legal and interpersonal respect later extended into educational and social justice issues, moving his civil rights work beyond the library system of Alexandria to include the public-school systems that served Black students throughout Virginia.

In 1867, following the Civil War, Congress passed the military reconstruction acts that divided the South into five military districts overseen by former Union generals.[8] Virginia comprised the First Military District. To be readmitted to the Union, the southern states were required to hold new elections, organize a new constitutional convention, and pass the Thirteenth and Fourteenth amendments to the U.S. Constitution. The Commonwealth of Virginia held its constitutional convention, also known as the Underwood Convention, in Richmond, Virginia, between December 3, 1867, and April 17, 1868, with twenty-four Black delegates and other Radical Republicans taking the majority of seats in the general assembly. The convention and its new constitution, sometimes referred to as the Underwood Constitution, were named after its president, John Curtiss Underwood, who was a federal judge as well as a Radical Republican. Approved by the convention and signed by Underwood on April 17, 1868, the constitution introduced a number of major reforms. The general assembly was required to create a form of local government modeled on the structure of a New England township and to implement a new commonwealth-wide segregated system of public education for Black and White students. The document included a provision allowing the governor to veto legislation passed by the general assembly, and it enfranchised all Black and White males over the age of twenty-one, with the exception of former Confederate supporters. This last provision, the disenfranchisement of former Confederates, stymied ratification, and voters ultimately rejected it, thanks to a campaign of White-initiated misinformation. Eventually, the Underwood Constitution was ratified in 1869.[9]

During the last two decades of the nineteenth century and the first decade of the twentieth century, southern states enacted new constitutions that reversed many of the reforms introduced by Radical Republicans and their Reconstruction Era governments. The Commonwealth of Virginia enacted its new constitution in 1902 after the Democrats regained control of the government. The document included numerous changes to the reforms in the 1869 Underwood Constitution. In addition to reinstating voting laws and legislation conceived to disenfranchise Blacks and block their ability to hold political office, the new constitution contained strict Jim Crow laws conceived to control the lives and activities of Black citizens. Under the terms of the Underwood Constitution, public schools for Black and White children were already segregated, but the 1902 version curtailed the freedoms and rights of African Americans as legislated by the Thirteenth, Fourteenth, and Fifteenth amendments to the U.S. Constitution, thus creating de jure mandates for the segregation of Blacks in virtually all aspects of daily life.[10]

Between 1924 and 1930, as pseudo-sciences such as eugenics became popular excuses for racial and social control, and Virginia's general assembly passed the Racial Integrity Laws: that included the Racial Integrity Act (RIA) of 1924 (also known as the Code of 1924 and, later, the Code of 1930) and the Public Assemblages Act of 1926. The RIA was conceived to maintain separation of the races and to ensure the purity of Anglo-Saxon bloodlines; it prohibited interracial marriages and codified the definition of Black as any person who was one-sixteenth African American. This "one-drop" rule, which was also added to the 1930 amendments, was the strictest definition of Black in the nation. The Public Assemblages Act, also known as the Massenburg Bill, mandated "the separation of white and colored persons at public halls, theaters, opera houses, motion picture shows and places of public entertainment and public assemblages." The bill was introduced into the general assembly by Alvin Massenburg on January 20, 1926, and enacted on March 22, 1926, without the signature of Governor Harry F. Byrd, Sr. In *Managing White Supremacy*, historian J. Douglas Smith writes, "the Massenburg Bill . . . was the first of its kind in the United States; it defined segregation in Virginia for four decades to come."[11]

Black citizens were not the only people to be affected by these laws. In colonial America and the early Republic, many Indigenous people had been enslaved throughout the English colonies, particularly in South Carolina, but in 1806 Virginia outlawed this policy and defined Native Americans as "perfectly white." In 1924, however, the implementation of the RIA redefined the Indigenous population as "Colored," thus relegating them to the same racially subordinated category as mixed-race Blacks. This status change defined Indigenous people as anyone who was one-fourth Native American.[12]

Public libraries were among the meeting places affected by the Public Assemblages Act, and the legislated segregation of Blacks went far beyond the matter of restricted access. It was also a foundational testament that White supremacy and hegemonic dynamics were more important than the principles of intellectual freedom, which Whites reserved for themselves. In addition, restricted access was evidence that White librarians and White library boards supported, and were complicit in, institutionalized racism. This was especially apparent in public libraries, whose collections and services were funded by municipal tax dollars paid by all citizens but were reserved for a select group of users. With very few exceptions, White librarians routinely denied Blacks' rights to information access.[13] Their attitudes and behaviors reflected the discriminatory core values of the southern communities they served. In Virginia communities such as Alexandria, where Jim Crow reigned supreme, White librarians and White library boards enforced the Public Assemblages Act's segregationist policies not because of new de jure mandates but because of normative policies of racial discrimination originally established during Black enslavement. In effect, the de jure mandates merely codified established de facto practices. While a few librarians in other communities occasionally defied segregationist policies, Blacks were routinely barred from White libraries throughout the South.

Historian Patterson Toby Graham argues that racial segregation posed a conflict between librarians' professional ethics and the values of the communities they served. He contends that these librarians "were constrained by local racial customs, Jim Crow laws, and, often by their own racial attitudes," and they knew that defying segregationists could be dangerous. While Graham acknowledges that public library segregation ended because of Black activists' efforts, not thanks to the ethical impulses of White librarians, he maintains that the few White librarians who did defy racial mores were proof that they had the potential to be change agents. Yet as late as 1961, Rosemary Ruhig Du Mont, reporting the results of a public library access study conducted for the American Library Association (ALA), found that problems with library segregation remained acute in the South: "This survey of the actions of the library profession shows the limited nature of past attempts to provide freedom of access to library service for black patrons." More recent scholarship continues to provide evidence that the library profession has been and continues to be complicit in a system of racial protectionism.[14]

The ALA was not immune from discriminatory biases, though a number of notable members, association chapters, editors, and publications did lobby for full integration of American libraries.[15] But the association hesitated to take a firm stand against segregation in American libraries until 1961—twenty-two years after the 1939 Alexandria Library sit-in demonstration and seven years after the Supreme Court ruling in Brown v. Board of Education—when its "Library Bill of Rights" was amended to include the right of all patrons to access, regardless of race (see appendix A and appendix B).

The new article was added to the "Library Bill of Rights" eight years after the Westchester Conference of the ALA and the American Book Publishers Council produced their "Freedom to Read" statement, on May 2–3, 1953.[16] The statement was conceived to combat censorship but did not address issues of race or patron access to libraries. Not until June 19, 1962, did the ALA's council approve the association's "Statement on Individual Membership, Chapter Status, and Institutional Membership," which urged its chapters to eliminate segregation from libraries and professional institutions. If, within a period of three years, they could not "certify that they [had] extended fundamental membership rights to all without regard to race, belief, or political views," they would be "asked to withdraw'" from membership. At this time, however, ALA neither required the chapters to eliminate segregation from libraries and professional institutions nor mandated withdrawal from membership if the terms of the statement were not met (see appendix C).[17] Almost sixty years later, on June 26, 2020, amid worldwide protests against systemic racism in American police departments and the resulting deaths of George Perry Floyd and other Black victims of police brutality, the ALA released a news notice informing its members, staff, and library workers that the association "accepts and acknowledges its role in upholding unjust systems of racism and discrimination against Black, Indigenous, and People of Color (BIPOC) within the association and the profession." The ALA notice also expressed the organization's commitment to the core values of equity, diversity, and inclusion and vowed to develop "a plan toward becoming the inclusive association we aspire to be."[18]

Race and racial categorizations are social constructs rather than biological ones, and they are used to differentiate individuals and groups based on White hierarchical power dynamics that originated in colonial domination and exploitation. Whiteness, with its subconscious presumption of superiority and prepotency, is promulgated as the social and cultural norm to which all non-White individuals and groups are subordinated. Blackness, on the other hand, is the difference or otherness against which Whiteness juxtaposes and extols itself. Control, power, dominance, wealth, and authority are assets that accrue with what George Lipsitz terms "a possessive investment in whiteness," a creation of "public policy and private prejudice . . . that is responsible for the racialized hierarchies of our society." As Richard Dyer remarks, "white power secures its dominance by seeming not to be anything in particular . . . as if it is the natural, inevitable, ordinary way of being human." Charles W. Mills writes that "much of the power of the racial contract arises from its invisibility to the Whites who benefit from it." In effect, Whites regard themselves simply as humans, but they name, differentiate, and racialize all non-Whites. In addition, as Dyer maintains, while Whiteness crosscuts certain particularities, such as gender and class constructions, it exists only in combination with other sociocultural inflections. Lipsitz comments, "As the unmarked category against which difference is constructed, whiteness never has to speak its name, never has to acknowledge its role as an organizing principle in social and cultural relations."[19]

Those constructs about race and racialization ground this book's narrative, as does critical race theory, which, in combination with object relations theory, frames the study's qualitative data. Both theories are used to address Alexandria's race-based hierarchies of dominance, power, and control and the social boundary issues epitomized by the exclusion of Blacks from the physical place and social space of the city's first municipal library.[20] Critical race theory, which evolved from the critical legal studies movement, also incorporates elements of critical theory, feminist perspectives, and traditional civil rights scholarship. Although it initially addressed issues associated solely with jurisprudence, it has since influenced many other fields of scholarship. Critical race theory posits that White privilege and supremacy were institutionalized over time, in part through legal means, to perpetuate racial inequality and marginalization. These inequitable power dynamics continue to affect and inform public civic institutions, such as libraries, as well as daily life. Writing about critical race theory, Richard Delgado and Jean Stefancic explain:

> The movement considers many of the same issues that conventional civil rights and ethnic studies discourses take up, but places them in a broader perspective that includes economics, history, context, group- and self-interest, and even feelings and the unconscious. However, unlike traditional civil rights, which stresses incrementalism and step-by-step progress, [critical race theory] questions the very foundations of the liberal order, including equality theory, legal reasoning, Enlightenment rationalism, and neutral principles of constitutional law.[21]

The first tenet of critical race theory is that racism is ordinary rather than aberrational, and this ordinariness makes racism difficult to identify and acknowledge. The second tenet, sometimes called *interest convergence*, is that racial hierarchies serve two distinct yet related purposes: psychological, which endows working-class Whites with perceived power and authority over Blacks; and material, which gives elite Whites the power and authority to manipulate and control both Blacks and working-class Whites. The usefulness of interest convergence for reinforcing and managing diverse communities of Whites complicates and compounds efforts to eradicate racism. The third tenet is that race and racial categorizations are social constructions devised to endow individuals and groups with particular characteristics, such as the categorization of Blacks as subordinate others, which are then used as needed to support or defend opinions, attitudes, and policies.[22]

According to David Sibley, object relations theory addresses the physical, spatial, and social boundary processes that distinguish and separate groups, which are part of a system of social control activated and maintained by dominant groups to impose and perpetuate constraints in physical, spatial, and social settings. Such constraints enable dominant-group members to exclude individuals and groups perceived as different or objectionable from desirable environments because they have been characterized as "deviant, imperfect[,] marginal" or "discrepant" outsiders. Sibley argues that, "to expose oppressive practices, it is necessary to examine the assumptions about inclusion and exclusion which are implicit in the design of spaces and places." Recognizing the importance of outsider viewpoints for complete subject understanding, he also notes that explanations of exclusion require not only an examination of applicable legal systems and the policies of social control agencies but also of various barriers, prohibitions, and constraints from the perspective of those who are excluded from particular environments. His arguments offer insight into the importance of alternative points of view—for instance, the perspectives and motivations of those who participated in the Alexandria Library sit-in. Thus, in writing this book, I incorporated the memories of a number of interviewees, who contributed details about the sit-in demonstration as well as information about prevailing racial attitudes, local social norms, and the place of public libraries in the life of the community. In some cases, they supplied unexpected information that supplemented my understanding of the context and the rationale for the sit-in demonstration as well as of Alexandria's social and cultural communities.[23] The interviewees include both Black and White Alexandrians, among them the family members of Samuel Wilbert Tucker and William "Buddy" Evans, the daughter of Armistead Lloyd Boothe, employees and patrons of the Alexandria Library System, the director of the Alexandria Black History Museum, and Black Alexandrians with knowledge about the city, the protest, or its participants.

Sibley contends that the arguments used to explicate the inclusion and exclusion of certain individuals and groups in social spaces can also be applied to knowledge studies. He refers specifically to the documentation of the roles of race and academic points of view in the 1890s-era social studies conducted by W. E. B. Du Bois, notably in his monograph *The Philadelphia Negro.* According to Sibley, concepts that are perceived as constituting academic knowledge (which gains acceptability, popularity, and influence through published books and articles) are contingent on power relations that circumscribe the boundaries of knowledge. As a result, concepts and authors who diverge from those boundaries are excluded as dangerous or threatening. The resulting "neglect" of Black academics and their perspectives in social studies of human geography further attests to their categorization as diminished others whose "problems [are] defined in terms of a white world-view."[24]

The 1937 establishment of the Alexandria Library as a free public library in a stand-alone edifice was a paradigmatic shift for the city's elite Whites, who had previously governed and managed a subscription library for an exclusive base of elite, White patrons. In other words, library use had been limited not only by race but also by economics: only Whites (primarily men) with leisure time and financial means were able to take advantage of the facility. Nonetheless, the subscription library was perpetually in need of operating capital, and the new public facility benefited from municipal tax appropriations, a necessary exchange for the obligation to open its stacks to White Alexandrians of all ages, genders, and classes.

For the first time, working-class Whites, regardless of their socioeconomic status, had free access to a site of collected knowledge, but the new public library was also a sign of their perceived parity with elite Whites. For Blacks, however, the new library was an unmistakable symbol of exclusion, Jim Crow discrimination, institutionalized racism, and municipal disregard. The pain of this slight was exacerbated because their municipal taxes contributed to the subsidy of a public library they were not allowed to use.

The Alexandria Library's board and the city council had discussed the issue of Black access to the new public library before the facility opened but decided its use would be limited to Whites and no alternative provisions would be made for Black citizens. This decision, coupled with a preexisting dearth of secondary-school opportunities, exemplified a norm of exclusion in the city, conceived and executed as a way to dictate acceptable racial standards of social behavior in an environment of managed White supremacy. These standards enabled elite and working-class Whites to affirm belief in their own social, cultural, intellectual, and moral superiority; justify Black subordination; and control patterns of everyday interracial interactions. In other words, the selectiveness of the library as a public place and social space mirrored the environment of the municipality in a world guided by the Public Assemblages Act's mandates for racial separation. Though state laws and municipal ordinances ordered the segregation of Blacks and Whites in public facilities, library authorities' total exclusion of Blacks was technically illegal. Exclusionary policies could be legally imposed when the library was a private institution; but as a municipal facility it was required to abide by laws of racial separation, not exclusion. Nevertheless, throughout the South, racial separation often manifested as racial exclusion. The case of the Alexandria Library, therefore, was not unique.

Constructed spaces serve as spatial and social demarcations in specific places, and they are also components of a city's ecology. John E. Buschman and Gloria J. Leckie write:

> Libraries are a type of social and cultural institution, fitting within
> a larger context of other institutions . . . and other socially created
> entities. [A] wide variety of people . . . visit libraries, bringing

their individual values, beliefs, expectations, assumptions, daily practices, and cultural awareness. How does this complicated set of characteristics, including elements from the personal, the private, the public, the physical, the intellectual, and the cultural, coalesce into the space or place that we call the library?[25]

For elite and working-class Whites as well as Blacks, the Alexandria Library was a potent symbol of racial, cultural, and intellectual dominance and of physical, spatial, and social control. These controls were applicable not only in the specific place and space occupied by the edifice but also in the larger community, where normative practices of racial discrimination and segregation were standardized. Whites interpreted Blacks' disregard for this controlled dominance as a boundary transgression in (borrowing Gill Valentine's term) the "social geography" of space and society. White and Black Alexandrians navigated the contested social and cultural terrain of the new library within the normative Jim Crow standards that applied to all municipal institutions. Whites never expected Blacks to challenge these norms; Blacks knew they were not welcome in the library and that defiance of established norms could have serious consequences. Sibley writes, "In the interaction of people and the built environment, it is a truism that space is contested but relatively trivial conflicts can provide clues about power relations and the role of space in social control." The Alexandria Library sit-in demonstration was therefore not simply a singular event situated in a specific time, place, and space. It was also an early struggle for social justice and racial equality waged through civil rights activism in a local community.[26]

For a full and accurate interpretation of human history, we must recognize the pivotal role of race in physical, spatial, social, cultural, and historical interactions. Such an understanding is particularly important in studies of the southern states, where hierarchies of power, dominance, and control were traditionally based on race. In their discussion of causality, Martha Howell and Walter Prevenier refer to "the historical importance of racism" noting that "'race' [is] a historical category, an issue that has seemed to some historians a crucial element of any equation explaining historical change."[27]

Historical change often provided opportunities for southerners to implement or strengthen race-based de jure restrictions. The Civil War and Reconstruction brought dramatic changes to interracial relations, especially in the South, as Blacks achieved many of the freedoms they had previously been denied. However, southern White hostility toward the new order and race-based discrimination against African Americans who asserted their rights continued to exist. The persistence of entrenched southern racism, coupled with northern acquiescence to the South's racial imperatives, underscored the dynamic power and enduring force of White supremacy. Federal authorities left Virginia in 1870 after the Commonwealth signed a new constitution, and that departure, in Virginia and elsewhere in the South, ultimately assured the enactment of segregationist legislation. Significant historical change also followed the 1896 U.S. Supreme Court ruling in *Plessy v. Ferguson*, which legalized the concept of "separate but equal," thereby justifying the provision of segregated and, more often than not, inequitable services and institutions for Blacks. In its 1898 ruling in *Williams v. Mississippi*, the U.S. Supreme Court upheld the Mississippi Supreme Court ruling when it decided that the imposition of literacy tests and poll taxes did not bar Black citizens from voting. In addition, the Court ruled that the Fourteenth Amendment had not been violated in the case of Henry Williams, who had been indicted for murder. In fact, however, these judgments effectively disenfranchised African Americans and gave them no legal recourse to oppose the Court's decisions. Some historical change did benefit Blacks—for instance, the biracial coalition that comprised the Readjuster Party (1877–83), which endeavored to end implementation of Virginia's segregationist policies. However, defeat of the Readjusters by the Democrats in 1883 curtailed anti-segregationist platforms and enabled the new power structure to devise the 1902 constitution that reestablished legislation and policies predicated on White supremacy and racial hierarchies. To ensure compliance with White supremacist imperatives, extrajudicial mob violence in the form of lynchings was used to terrorize and intimidate Blacks. Such violence was not limited to the South, though the vast majority of incidents occurred there, and victims included Black men, women, and children as well as some

Whites. According to the Equal Justice Initiative, 4,743 racial-terror lynchings were reported nationwide between 1882 and 1968. Among them were a hundred Black Virginians: two took place in Alexandria. "More than 300 victims [were] killed outside the former Confederacy between 1877 and 1950. More than one in 15 documented racial-terror lynching victims were killed outside the South." Lynching was not typically punished by state or local authorities, although almost two hundred antilynching bills were introduced in Congress between 1882 and 1968. The *New York Times* reported that on March 29, 2022, President Joseph R. Biden signed a bill that finally made lynching a federal crime. More often than not, therefore, historical change has resulted in race-based social and de jure policies of oppression rather than in benefits for Blacks.[28]

The story of Samuel Tucker and his civil rights initiative does not appear in most macrohistories of libraries and social and cultural communities. However, the reduction of scale that characterizes microhistories is well suited for an in-depth analysis of the sit-in and its architect, protesters, and outcomes. Microhistory is characterized by its attention to lesser-known or ordinary events, individuals, and communities on the margins of power and influence. Charles Joyner refers to this process as "asking large questions in small places," and Georg G. Iggers describes it as "a multifaceted flow with many individual centers. Not history but histories, or, better, stories." Situating the importance of local history and place within the comprehensive story of regional and national interests, Joseph A. Amato writes, "The historian offers the music—the rhythm and the beat—of a linking narrative. Narrative alone affords an understanding through stories and tales of what a place was, where it stood in the process of becoming, and how it exists in the folds of memory and the unfolding layers of interpretation."[29] I have chosen to take a microhistorical approach in my investigation of the impact of the 1939 Alexandria Library sit-in demonstration on the development of library services to White and Black Alexandrians and on the course of library integration and desegregation in the United States. I also use microhistory to explore and analyze the role of human agency in the evolution of library history, because Tucker's personal agency conceived, planned, and implemented the activities associated with the sit-in, and it is the communal agency of the five protesters that made it possible to carry out his plan.

Why does one historical event lead to change while another changes nothing and is forgotten? A microhistorical focus on a singular event in a specific locale at a particular time is a way to analyze both the symbolic meaning and the structural dynamics of historical change. Iggers contends that microhistory is "a rediscovery of culture and the individuality of persons and small groups as agents of historical change"—a description personified by Tucker, the protesters, and the sit-in initiative.[30] Finally, a microhistorical focus is also a way to illustrate the confluence of the four social science contexts in which this work is situated: American library history, American social and southern histories, and civil rights history.

In the microcosmic environment of Alexandria, as in the macro-scale environment of the South, historical experiences that defined and shaped the traditions from the past also dominate every aspect of the present. As Joyner points out, "the region's history can be only partly understood in isolation from the culture within which it was experienced." Historian Eliza Atkins Gleason suggests a link between historical experiences and the management policies of Alexandria's new public library. Commenting on the fact that Whites felt Blacks had no need for library access, she writes, "The institution of chattel slavery carried with it the implication that the Negro was subhuman and incapable of the attainments and devoid of the sensibilities of the white man. The persistence of this general attitude after the abolition of slavery may be taken for granted." In 1913, William F. Yust described a sentiment that persisted decades later: "It may be said . . . that there are still people who think that the negro is incapable of education and that it actually unfits him for usefulness. Uncle Remus has a saying, 'When you put a book into a negro's hand you spoil a good plow hand.' This notion still lurks in the minds of a surprisingly large number of people."[31] The Alexandria Library and, later, the Robert H. Robinson Library epitomized socially and culturally constructed physical places and social spaces that affirmed and perpetuated hegemonic standards and controls. They were places and spaces that symbolized the ways in which Whites and Blacks navigated contested social and cultural systems and institutions that had been conceived to ensure both their disengagement and their interdependence.

In this book I strive to answer three questions. What motivated Tucker to situate a protest in a library and to seek civil rights redress through a staged sit-in demonstration? What was the role of public libraries in the formation of White and Black Alexandrian social and cultural communities? Why is the protest an important symbol for Black and White Alexandrians, their library communities and patrons, and the nation's social, southern, and civil rights historians?

While this is the first full-length scholarly treatment of the topic, the history of the Alexandria Library is recorded in varying degrees of detail in several other publications. In her admirable biography of Samuel Tucker, written for a young-adult audience, Nancy Noyes Silcox includes a summary chapter about the library demonstration. Beverly Seehorn Brandt's master's thesis and Jeanne G. Plitt and Marjorie D. Tallichet's brief journal article both chronicle the library's history but omit essential details. Brandt, for example, provides only cursory coverage of the years 1938–58, so she does not mention the sit-in, its outcome, or its ramifications. William Seale's history of the library, published under the auspices of the Alexandria Library Company, contends that the sit-in resulted in its immediate integration—an egregious error. In *The Desegregation of Public Libraries in the Jim Crow South*, Wayne A. Wiegand and Shirley A. Wiegand outline the demonstration, presenting it as one of several grassroots initiatives that married civil rights with local activism in southern communities. To date, the most thorough treatment of the library protest is J. Douglas Smith's *Managing White Supremacy*, which recounts Tucker's desegregation effort within the racialized contexts of politics, citizenship, and managed White supremacy in Jim Crow Virginia. By merging the Commonwealth's policy of hegemonic tradition with so-called radical Black activism, Smith situates Tucker and the sit-in as elements of a changing social, civil, and political landscape.[32]

Samuel Wilbert Tucker was a change agent motivated by personal and professional experiences with discrimination to improve the lives of Alexandria's Black citizens. Though only twenty-six years of age, he was determined to confront the inequities of systemic racism and paternalistic managed race relations imposed by de facto and de jure White supremacy because he understood the significance of access to public libraries not only for educative purposes but also for recreational pursuits. In his communication with city manager Carl Budwesky, he expressed his displeasure with the city's Jim Crow response to the court ruling on George Wilson's writ of mandamus, stating "Our position [opposing segregated facilities] is well fortified by those fundamental rights of the citizen which exist as the basis and foundation of government. Any attempt at segregation contravenes the basic and underlying principle of the common law."[33]

CHAPTER ONE

# Black Access to Public Libraries

*The Infrastructures of Black Literary and Print Culture*

During the Jim Crow era, Blacks in the southern states were routinely denied access to local Whites-only public libraries. That service denial did not change until after the U.S. Supreme Court's landmark 1954 decision in *Brown v. Board of Education*, passage of the Civil Rights Act of 1964 and the Voting Rights Act of 1965, and, especially, the definitive 1966 decision in *Brown v. Louisiana*, in which the Court ruled that "regulation of libraries and other public facilities" must be "reasonable and nondiscriminatory." Although Blacks in the North did not generally face the overt segregation that southern Blacks endured, they, too, sometimes experienced discrimination in library access, and segregated residential housing meant that library branches were often segregated by default. If southern Blacks had any access at all, it was most often through Black library branches, which were often inferior to White libraries in their construction and collections, or through philanthropic initiatives, county library demonstrations, federal programs, itinerate libraries, or association-based facilities such as the Mississippi Freedom Libraries. Makeshift arrangements also existed, in which readers had the use of a box or two of books that were periodically exchanged. However, even when southern libraries were supposedly integrated or desegregated, those terms were interpreted along a continuum of access conditions. For example, many White libraries imposed service or collection restrictions, such as excluding Blacks from public meetings or special events; imposing constraints on the use of certain components of the collection; or limiting African Americans to specific, often undesirable, areas of the library—such as near the janitor's closet, the bathrooms, or the delivery and trash doors.

Nevertheless, Blacks were unwavering in their pursuit of library access, even when it was substandard or discriminatory and even when they were forced to fund and stock their own improvised libraries.[1]

In May 1961, the *Wilson Library Bulletin* published an article in which Black librarians shared their perspectives about racial segregation in southern public libraries, a report that exposed the subtleties of the terms *segregated* and *desegregated* in various communities. In the article, Virginia Lacy Jones, the dean of the School of Library Service at Atlanta University, noted that while some so-called desegregated libraries allowed Blacks to use the card catalog and withdraw books, they did not permit them "to browse, use the reference or periodical collection, or to sit in the library and read," except, occasionally, in designated, segregated areas. Other White libraries permitted only Black adults, not young people, to use the facilities, or they made special arrangements for authorized Black professionals to use noncirculating materials in designated areas. In other instances, Blacks were allowed to use all library service areas but were not allowed to attend special programs, meetings, or events. Jones said that some Black library staff members were prohibited from attending staff meetings but were given copies of the minutes afterward. Certain desegregated libraries assigned segregated entrances, exits, and bathrooms to Black and White patrons. In the same article, Milton S. Byam, the Brooklyn Public Library's superintendent of branches, noted that books in segregated Black libraries were neither as good nor as plentiful as those in White libraries, which was a particular disservice to African American patrons when the White facility was a central library. He contended that all central libraries should be immediately integrated, even if the branches remain segregated. The quality of the books in Alexandria's Robert H. Robinson Library was proof of Byam's claim. Its collection during the mid-twentieth century consisted primarily of castoffs from the Alexandria Library—used and out-of-date materials that White patrons saw as unusable and donated books that reflected the needs and interests of White donors, not those of the readers at the Black branch. The few new books in the Robinson Library's collection were considered a luxury.[2]

For Whites, denying Blacks access to libraries was a logical, reasonable extension of the dictates of White supremacy. Libraries were components of information infrastructures, bastions of knowledge and culture that Whites wanted to reserve for themselves. Recent scholarship in the fields of book history, library history, information studies, and ethnic and women's studies has addressed this assumption of privilege and its intersections with race, ethnicity, gender, and class. These researchers have often taken an interdisciplinary approach: for example, Black journalists, editors, writers, and academics have examined Black literary and print culture as a way to preserve and publicize African American concerns, ideas, opinions, and perspectives on contemporary issues. In doing so, they have engaged not only in discourse on racialized literary and print culture but have also incorporated discourse on attendant implications and entitlements of racial, social, political, gender, class, and institutional infrastructures.[3] Their arguments and discoveries have been crucial to my research into the Black literary and print cultures of Alexandria, Virginia.

During the eighteenth century, some enslaved Blacks were taught to read, primarily so that they would have access to the gospel. At this time, southern Whites saw reading as a benign skill that was compatible with Black enslavement. By 1820, however, as abolitionist movements were evolving and expanding, those views about reading had shifted. Now southern Whites viewed Blacks who could read and write as dangerous and potentially subversive because they had the ability to create travel and manumission papers for the enslaved. Whites' response was to prohibit Blacks from reading, writing, or possessing books. Yet enslaved and free Blacks were undaunted: they valued reading and writing and literacy's links to power and liberation, and many continued to surreptitiously and proactively acquire those skills.[4]

According to the scholar E. J. Josey, libraries have played an essential role in the liberation movement of Blacks because their function in information infrastructures enables self-empowerment. Beginning in the early nineteenth century, free Blacks in the Northeast and the Midwest established literary societies and social libraries as successors to the mutual aid and improvement societies they had founded in the 1770s. Marya Annette McQuirter reports that, as early as 1814, Black churches in Washington, D.C., operated and supported schools and literary and historical societies that promoted reading, writing, critical thinking, oratory skills, and social justice. Although some Black churches sponsored literacy classes and book clubs for children and adults, that was not always the case. Neither Lillian S. Patterson nor Lovell A. Lee, whom I interviewed for this book, recalled that their Alexandria churches had offered such services. But in the secular sphere, literacy projects often flourished. In the late nineteenth and early twentieth centuries, some Black literary societies converted their association meetings into community events, in which readers would read chosen works aloud so that illiterate listeners could participate in discussions. By the late nineteenth century, meetings of Black literary societies such as the Bethel Historical and Literary Association in Washington, D.C., and the Boston Literary and Historical Association in Massachusetts drew hundreds of attendees to their meetings. These educative spaces offered Blacks alternatives to similar Whites-only facilities, opening opportunities not only for literacy but also for discussions of social and political activism, self-determination, racial uplift, and freedom. They were especially appealing to Black women, who were uniquely empowered by library texts. According to Caitlin M. J. Pollack and Shelley P. Haley, some of these women later became librarians and racial activists. But not all Black literary societies were so egalitarian. Some, like White literary societies, were restricted by gender, class, or religious affiliation.[5]

With the establishment of Parker-Gray High School in 1932, Alexandria's Black students were finally able to acquire a local secondary-school education. Although Parker-Gray High School had a library, its use was reserved for its students, not for the general public. Black adults' source for materials was the Frederick Douglass Literary and

Industrial Association in Washington, D.C., a Black library and reading room established in 1890 by Magnus L. Robinson, a prominent Black citizen and a native of Alexandria.[6] Samuel Tucker and other Black Alexandrians routinely traveled to Washington to use the Literary and Industrial Association Library as well as the District of Columbia Public Library (founded in 1903 and integrated from its inception, despite widespread segregation elsewhere in the city) and the integrated Library of Congress.[7]

During the dedication ceremony for the District of Columbia Public Library, the city's commissioner, H. B. F. MacFarland, proudly declared:

> The library will not only be central to all sections of the District, but near to some of the most important institutions of the public school system, with which we desire to integrate it. The Central High School, the [B]usiness High School, the McKinley Manual Training School for white pupils, the General Armstrong Manual Training School for colored pupils, will all be its neighbors.[8]

Andrew Carnegie, who funded the library's construction, also addressed the attendees: "To hear that there are promptly to be close to this library two manual training schools, one of these for colored people, and also a business high school, making this an educational center with the library serving all, enables me to assure myself that here beyond doubt is a wise use of surplus wealth, and this is reward enough." Carnegie routinely funded segregated Black branch libraries, but relatively few communities sought funding for integrated libraries. Thus, these words from him were atypical: usually he bowed to the mores of southern communities, but now he was aligning himself with the desires of the city's library trustees, who wanted the institution to be integrated.[9]

The three integrated libraries in Washington, D.C., provided resources for self-education, research, personal and professional enrichment, literary and cultural pursuits, entertainment and recreational pursuits, and preparation for participation in civic life. However, for most Blacks who lived outside of the city, the time and expense involved in traveling to these facilities posed an unreasonable burden. In addition, service hours did not accommodate many people's schedules, though the Literary and Industrial Association did try to adjust to workers' needs. Its reading room was open Monday to Saturday from 10:00 a.m. to 4:00 p.m.; Sunday hours were 2:00 p.m. to 7:00 p.m. Speaking at the 1890 opening of the Literary and Industrial Association, Robinson called it the second "colored" library in the nation, founded with "the sole purpose of [providing] literary culture" to the area's Black residents. He praised the new reading room as "a place dedicated to literature of a sound and wholesome character and the pursuit of industry" and promised that "a series of free lectures on cleanliness, industry, etc., would be given from time to time."[10]

According to Robinson, the country's first dedicated library for Blacks had been established in the Hillsdale (Anacostia) neighborhood of Washington, D.C. But he had to know that this assertion was false because he himself had just established a Black library and reading room in Alexandria in 1889 that he had named the Frederick Douglass Library Association. The facility's years of operation are unclear, but for a while it gave Black Alexandrians a center for social, intellectual, and cultural pursuits. That library, however, was not the first either. In 1936, Dorothy B. Porter, a renowned Black librarian, historian, and bibliophile, published an article that listed forty-five African American educational and cultural societies, most located in the Northeast, that had been established in the first half of the nineteenth century to serve free Blacks:

> These organizations were known not only as literary societies, but also as debating and reading-room societies. . . . Some of the expressed reasons for the organization of these institutions were the stimulation of reading and the spreading of useful knowledge by providing libraries and reading rooms, the encouragement of expressed literary efforts by providing audiences as critics and channels of publication for their literary productions[,] and the training of future orators and leaders by means of debates.[11]

Black literary societies abounded during this period. The earliest, the Reading Room Society, was founded in 1828 in Philadelphia. Debating societies were popular because they helped to hone critical-thinking and oratory skills. Seven were established before 1837. Three Black literary societies were founded in the District of Columbia: the Washington Conventional Society was formed in 1834 and the Debating Society and the Literary Society were founded at some point before 1837. According to Porter's research, Maryland had two Black literary societies, both established before 1835: the Phoenix Society and the Young Men's Mental Improvement Society for the Discussion of Moral and Philosophical Questions. However, her article lists no Black libraries, literary societies, or reading rooms in Virginia or elsewhere in the South during this period. Her compilation is noteworthy for including numerous organizations established by and for Black women, the majority of which supported literary pursuits. The Female Literary Society, established in Philadelphia in 1831, and the Afric-American [sic] Female Intelligence Society, formed in 1832 in Boston, were among the earliest educational societies of any type. The New York Garrison Literary Association (also known as the New York Garrison Literary and Benevolent Society), established in 1834 in New York City, was unique because it served Black youths ages four to twenty. The society was extremely active and became well known as a major center for the acquisition of useful knowledge. Its facility stocked titles relating to "religion, virtue, literature, the downfall of prejudice, and slavery and oppression."[12]

During the 1830s, David Ruggles, a Black printer, journalist, and bibliophile in New York City, was an ardent and fearless abolitionist whose home was a stop on the Underground Railroad. He collected Black books, periodicals, and newspapers and established a circulating library for Blacks funded by selling books, particularly antislavery titles; collecting fees for "rented" books; and collecting library members' dues. To support Black literary and print culture, he published pamphlets and lists of books for Black readers in various newspapers that publicized the works of Black authors; prioritized Black lives, perspectives, voices, and experiences; and promoted race consciousness. The production of such compilations, first by Ruggles and later by twentieth-century luminaries such as Ralph Ellison and Richard Wright, served as antiracist strategies to counter the myth of Black intellectual inferiority.

In 1834, Ruggles was a member of the New York Garrison Literary Association's executive committee, and that same year he opened the first documented Black bookstore in the country. The store specialized in anti-slavery titles and operated successfully until 1839, when it was destroyed by a White mob. In the June 16, 1838, issue of the Black newspaper the *Colored American* (which itself maintained a reading room), Ruggles announced, "I have opened a READING ROOM, where those who wish to avail themselves of the opportunity, can have access to the principal daily and leading anti-slavery papers, and other popular periodicals of the day." His shop was typical of the many Black bookstores that functioned as sites of African American sociopolitical resistance; and like them, Ruggles and his sociopolitical activities were subjected to unwanted attention and frequent physical attacks from Whites who opposed them. He was also jailed on multiple occasions for his activist endeavors.

Though early Black educational societies differed in certain respects from later library reading rooms, all of these organizations were founded to enable free Blacks to engage in literary, cultural, oratorical, scientific, religious, and moral pursuits. Porter notes that many of the early institutions served as both antislavery and literary societies until 1857, when most shifted their focus to literary pursuits. Arguably, their most important role was to serve as sites for educational enrichment, literary and cultural pursuits, social interaction, and racial uplift where Blacks were not subjected to the racial discrimination, hostility, and rejection they faced in similar White organizations. According to Porter, most Black literary societies and reading rooms were short-lived, and the associations that succeeded them also existed only briefly. In this regard, the Frederick Douglass Literary and Industrial Association was exceptional because it was still operating into the 1930s, more than a decade after Magnus Robinson's death in 1918.[13]

In 1890, Magnus's brother, the Reverend Robert B. Robinson, and Grant Hawkins, an associate, purchased two lots in Alexandria, where they constructed a new headquarters for what had been Magnus's first library venture, the Frederick Douglass Library Association. Their decision attests to the success of the Washington, D.C., reading room, though the exact relationship between the two institutions remains unclear. Magnus

Robinson had worked as a journalist or editor for the *Baltimore Sun*, the *Baltimore American*, and the *Lynchburg Daily News*, and he was the first Black journalist employed by the *Baltimore Daily Bee*. Sometime after 1876 he and his brother established the *Virginia Post* in Harrisonburg, which operated successfully for three years. In 1888, he founded the *National Leader*, a Black newspaper in Washington, D.C., which he relocated to Alexandria in 1890 as the *Weekly Leader*. The Library Association's years of operation are unknown, but records do show that Robert B. Robinson established another reading room in Alexandria in 1919 "in memory of the colored soldiers who died in France."[14]

Between the 1920s and the mid-1930s—the period known as the Harlem Renaissance—Black creativity flourished, particularly in culturally rich Black urban communities in the Northeast and the Midwest. Much of this creativity was inspired by civil rights, social rights, and political activism; the new militancy of returning Black veterans; the Great Migration; and the legal successes of the NAACP. The writing, art, music, dance, theater, politics, and philosophy of this New Negro Movement were dominant forces during the period, and not just in the North. The historian Ebony Vanessa Bowen has traced the activities and patrons of Georgia Douglass Johnson's Saturday-night literary salon in Washington, D.C., which operated from 1921 to 1928 and became an intellectual, cultural, and artistic hub comparable to Harlem. However, the Great Depression reduced the popularity of African American literary societies and salons, and "[Black] pundits in the 1930s and '40s tended to depreciate the achievements of the New Negro Movement, calling instead for a more politically engaged, socially critical realism in literature."[15]

Many in the Black community found books too expensive to purchase and turned to cheaper options such as newspapers and periodicals. Some, however, were able to acquire affordable in-home libraries through special advertising offers or from catalogue sources such as Sears, Roebuck & Co., though their book choices were always limited. Book advertisements often touted the credentials of their selection committees, and catalogue offerings sometimes hawked incentives such as "bookcase included." Companies such as the Book-of-the-Month-Club, founded in 1926, were popular with readers, though they were criticized for

standardizing reading habits. Yet while some literary critics bemoaned
the limitations on personal selection created by market-driven reading
options, everyday readers were grateful for the opportunity to acquire
their own libraries. This attitude became an element of public library
offerings as well. As Thomas Augst notes, "while private philanthropists
borrowed from European models of connoisseurship, antiquarianism,
and scholarship in amassing their collections, public libraries in the
twentieth century would develop standards of literary taste that were
shaped by the commercial marketplace."[16]

According to Eliza Atkins Gleason, there were 774 public libraries
in the thirteen southern states in 1939, and only ninety-nine of them
admitted Blacks. Virginia had sixty-five public libraries, but only fourteen admitted Blacks. Blacks thus had access to 21.54 percent of the
state's libraries, though they made up 26.85 percent of Virginia's total
population (see table 1).[17] Blacks were able to use the Virginia State
Library (now known as the Library of Virginia) only if they sat at a
specific, segregated table in the main reading room.

Although Virginia's 1926 Public Assemblages Act mandated segregation in all public meeting spaces, including public libraries, the
Fourteenth Amendment to the U.S. Constitution guaranteed all American citizens the same rights, privileges, and protections under the law,
which meant that Blacks could not legally be denied access to tax-supported municipal institutions. Segregation was legally mandated, but
total exclusion was not. Prior to court-mandated desegregation, however, exclusion was the rule rather than the exception when it came to
Black admission to Whites-only public libraries.[18] A few municipalities
bowed to Black pressure for library access by voluntarily integrating
or accepting legally mandated desegregation, but Whites typically
appeased African American demands for library access by establishing
separate-and-unequal Black branch libraries. Some accommodating
Blacks accepted and used these inferior Jim Crow facilities in lieu of no

## TABLE 1. PUBLIC LIBRARY SERVICE TO NEGROES IN 1939
## FROM LOCAL PUBLIC LIBRARIES

| STATE | Total Libraries in State† | Number of Libraries in State Serving Negroes‡ | Percent of Libraries in State Serving Negroes‡ | Negro Percentage of Total Population | Negro Population | Total Number of Negroes with Service | Percentage of Negro Population with Service |
|---|---|---|---|---|---|---|---|
| Alabama | 20 | 4 | 20 | 35.7 | 944,834 | 138,565 | 14.67 |
| Arkansas | 42 | 2 | 4.76 | 25.8 | 478,463 | 56,814 | 11.87 |
| Florida | 56 | 8 | 14.29 | 29.41 | 431,828 | 117,612 | 27.24 |
| Georgia | 93 | 4 | 4.3 | 36.83 | 1,071,125 | 169,515 | 15.83 |
| Kentucky | 70 | 10 | 14.29 | 8.65 | 226,040 | 87,870 | 38.87 |
| Louisiana | 29 | 3 | 10.34 | 36.94 | 776,326 | 169,941 | 21.89 |
| Mississippi | 37 | 3 | 8.11 | 50.24 | 1,009,718 | 66,633 | 6.6 |
| North Carolina | 80 | 16 | 20 | 28.98 | 918,647 | 244,320 | 26.6 |
| Oklahoma | 79 | 8 | 10.13 | 7.19 | 172,198 | 44,809 | 26.02 |
| South Carolina | 32 | 4 | 12.5 | 45.65 | 793,681 | 122,117 | 15.4 |
| Tennessee | 57 | 4 | 7.02 | 18.25 | 477,646 | 225,513 | 47.21 |
| Texas | 114 | 19 | 16.67 | 14.68 | 854,964 | 249,626 | 29.2 |
| Virginia | 65 | 14 | 21.54 | 26.85 | 650,165 | 189,790 | 29.19 |
| **TOTAL** | **774** | **99** | **12.79** | **26.07** | **8,805,635** | **1,883,125** | **21.39** |

*Source*: Eliza Atkins Gleason, "Table 7: Public Library Service to Negroes in 1939 from Local Public Libraries," in *The Southern Negro and the Public Library: A Study of the Government and Administration of Public Library Service to Negroes in the South* (Chicago: University of Chicago Press, 1941), 90. © 1941 by The University of Chicago Press. Reprinted with permission of The University of Chicago Press.

Note: In the text explicating her table, Gleason notes that numbers of libraries providing service could be misleading because they may not reveal that some service provided to Blacks at main libraries was restricted or that Blacks in the area did not know service was available because that information was intentionally withheld from them. Such could not be evaluated as equal to service in main libraries that had no restrictions. Gleason cites Kentucky as an example of a state with misleading information. All total population figures are from U.S. Bureau of the Census, *Fifteenth Census of the United States: 1930*, https://www.census.gov. All other data are from Gleason's questionnaires and personal visits.

†Based on the *American Library Directory* (New York: Bowker, 1939).

‡According to Gleason, "these figures represent *libraries* as governmental units, not separate *agencies* of service, such as branches or stations."

library access at all. Others, however, refused to be appeased, and they refused to patronize substandard Black branches. They would accept nothing less than full integration of White public libraries because both Whites and Blacks viewed libraries as self- and community-empowering institutions. As Alexandra Zukas writes, access to libraries constitutes a form of noncompulsory civic participation. Library patronage signals a commitment to personal and community intellectual development and acknowledges that library service is worthy of patrons' time and taxation. Borrowing library resources is an indicator of the collection's value and of a particular item's significance. To be denied access is to be denied the rights of citizenship in a democratic system.[19]

Between 1889 and 1923, Andrew Carnegie and the Carnegie Corporation funded the construction of about 1,680 public library buildings in 1,412 American communities, which received a total of $41,033,850 in Carnegie funds. To receive funding, many communities submitted grant proposals, some of which the Carnegie Corporation denied. In other cases, the corporation directly offered funds to communities, and some of them rejected these grants. Money was refused for various reasons, but one was linked to White fear that Carnegie would mandate integrated facilities. In other cases, city officials refused to comply with the corporation's requirement to allocate municipal funds for the annual support of the library. Richmond, Virginia, for example, which was viewed as the cultural center of the Commonwealth, refused to accept a Carnegie grant, and the Richmond Public Library Board established the Whites-only Dooley Library in 1924 without corporation money. They also resisted integration and in 1925 opened the Rosa D. Bowser Branch Library at the Phillis Wheatley Branch of the Young Women's Christian Association, establishing it as a segregated facility for Blacks. In 1936, in an attempt to compel the desegregation of the Dooley Library, a member of the local chapter of the NAACP filed a writ of mandamus with the city. Although unsuccessful, that civil rights effort was an early step in the process of the library's integration. But it was not until 1947 that the board, urged to action by Richmond's Black communities and the Business and Professional Men's Council, an activist arm of the NAACP-linked Leigh Street YMCA (the Black offshoot of Greater Richmond's White YMCA), voted to voluntarily integrate the Dooley Library. Legal mandates to desegregate were not required, though the library chose to admit only Blacks over the age of sixteen. Thus, a policy of de facto segregation continued at the library into the 1960s because Black children were excluded until that time. Paradoxically, when the board announced the 1947 plan to integrate the Dooley Library, it simultaneously announced that two new Black branches would be constructed in African American neighborhoods. Board members hoped that this maneuver would limit the number of Black visitors to the main library.[20]

Several municipalities in Virginia—among them Bedford, Brookneal, Chatham, Culpepper, Halifax, Marion, Orange, Richmond, and Waynesboro—offered integrated services in their main libraries by 1947. Some had been integrated from their inception, and some integrated peacefully, but others involved controversy and resistance and required legal challenges to implement desegregation. In the 1960s, following the *Brown v. Board of Education* ruling, efforts intensified to integrate or, if necessary, desegregate southern libraries (see table 2).

Efforts in 1960 to integrate the Petersburg, Virginia, public library drew considerable negative media attention. As late as 1959, five years after the *Brown v. Board of Education* decision, African Americans remained relegated to the Blacks-only basement of the city's McKenney Public Library. In June of that year, the Reverend Wyatt Tee Walker, a Black patron, unsuccessfully attempted to borrow a book from the library's first-floor Whites-only section and was refused service, a decision based solely on his race. A minister at the Gillfield Baptist Church in the 1950s, Walker at various times served as president of the Virginia chapters of the NAACP and the Congress of Racial Equality and was the executive director of the Southern Christian Leadership Conference. In the early 1960s, he became a top assistant to the Reverend Dr. Martin Luther King, Jr., organizing civil rights marches, boycotts, and sit-ins and becoming a leading voice for civil rights in Virginia.

On February 27, 1960, Walker, along with the Reverend R. B. Williams; Jim Gunther, the president of the local NAACP chapter; and a group of high school and college students, took part in a peaceful sit-in

## TABLE 2. THE LIBRARY INTEGRATION PROCESS IN VIRGINIA CITIES, BY YEAR

| | | | | |
|---|---|---|---|---|
| Alexandria | [1959; 1962]‡ | | Montross | Nd |
| Arlington | X | | Newport News | — |
| Bedford | X1944 | | Norfolk | — |
| Brookneal | X1939 | | Orange | 1946 |
| Chatham | 1940 | | Petersburg | 1960 |
| Courtland | X1958 | | Portsmouth | 1960 |
| Culpepper | 1946 | | Pulaski | X |
| Danville | 1960‡ | | Purcellville | 1957 |
| Fairfax | X | | Richmond | *1947 |
| Falls Church | X | | Roanoke | Nd |
| Fredericksburg | — | | South Norfolk | X1952 |
| Front Royal | 1953 | | Suffolk | 1959 |
| Halifax | X1938 | | Urbanna | Ns |
| Harrisonburg | — | | Waynesboro | 1945 |
| Hopewell | 1950 | | Williamsburg | Nd |
| Leesburg | X | | Winchester | 1953 |
| Marion | 1946 | | | |

*Data from:* Bernice Lloyd Bell, "Table 6: Pertinent Data Concerning the Integration Process in Thirteen Southern States," in "Integration in Public Library Service in Thirteen Southern States, 1954–1962" (master's thesis, Atlanta University, 1963), 113–15.

‡   These dates were not included in Bell's data but were corroborated by my research. The Alexandria Library was desegregated for Black adults and high school students in 1959. The library was not desegregated for Black elementary school students until 1962.

X   Used alone or with a date indicates that the library has always been open to all races

Nd   No definite date

Ns   Not sure

—   Information unavailable

*   The Richmond Public Library began to admit Black patrons age 16 or older in 1947, but it continued to exclude Black elementary school and middle school children until the 1960s.

demonstration at the McKenney Public Library. Walker and some of the students were arrested and convicted of disorderly conduct. Robert H. Cooley, Jr., an attorney for the protesters, asked Samuel Wilbert Tucker to take on their case, which he won on appeal. The confrontation that developed during the sit-in led the city manager to close the library for a few days, and the city council quickly and unanimously passed an anti-trespass ordinance. The library reopened a few days later, though still on a segregated basis. The NAACP attorneys who represented the arrested protesters filed a federal lawsuit requiring Petersburg to desegregate its public library. Additional demonstrations in March 1960 led to the arrest and jailing of more protesters, and the library was closed again, this time, indefinitely, pending a ruling on the case. On October 6, Judge Albert V. Bryan decided not to rule on the case, arguing that the indefinite library closure meant that the problems enumerated in the complaint were no longer issues. The situation became racially charged. On November 4, a city councilman offered a resolution intended to diffuse tensions and reopen the library. His resolution was supported by the city manager and approved unanimously by the city council; and on November 7, the library reopened on a desegregated basis.[21]

Efforts to desegregate the Danville Confederate Memorial Library drew even more negative attention, both nationally and internationally. On April 2, 1960, inspired by the Petersburg demonstration as well as by restaurant sit-ins in Greensboro, North Carolina, and, perhaps by the one at the Alexandria Library, sixteen Black high school students, led by Robert A. Williams, attempted to withdraw books from Danville, Virginia's Whites-only library. As in Petersburg, the students were turned away solely because of their race. Williams's father, Jerry Williams, was an NAACP attorney, and he had counseled his son on what could be accomplished through use of the law. The next day, the city council passed an ordinance restricting library use to existing library card holders, but protesters continued to work to desegregate the facility. Many of the protesters were arrested and jailed. In response, the NAACP took the city of Danville to court and won an injunction mandating desegregation. The city, however, refused to comply with the order; it held a referendum, and residents voted to close the library rather than admit Blacks. Not all of Danville's citizens, however, were pleased with the referendum outcome. Some citizens wanted to keep the library and bookmobile closed with a private library opened for the exclusive use of Whites; others wanted the library to be reopened and desegregated. A subsequent statement from a hearing before a subcommittee of the Department of Education regarding the 1963 Library Services Act notes the following:

> In Danville and elsewhere, the fairly incredible view is being expounded that it would be better to close the libraries than to admit negroes to them. Such a position is simply absurd ... [for] a library is something special. The treasures a good library can make available do not belong to a community except in a narrow and legalistic sense; the accumulated inheritance of the mind belongs to mankind. To deny negro citizens free and equal access to books is an indefensible act of discrimination.[22]

Protracted legal, municipal, and citizen battles ensued, and during those months the library and the city received increasingly negative publicity. On September 13, 1960, the city council voted to reopen the library under a ninety-day trial policy of "vertical integration." To keep patrons from lingering in the building, all of the library furniture was removed. As the historian Stephen Cresswell writes, patrons were encouraged to comply with a "get-your-book-and-get-out plan." On December 10, the day before the trial policy was due to end, a few pieces of furniture were returned to the library, and desegregation became permanent. However, at that point, all prospective patrons were required to pay a $2.50 fee for public library use in addition to the taxes already mandated for citizens by the city, and they were also required to complete an onerous, four-page application designed specifically to disincentivize Blacks' use of the library. According to the 1963 subcommittee statement, "Six months later the Danville library service was 'gradually returning to normalcy' but with only about two-thirds of its former patronage. Membership at the White and Negro branches in early June 1961 was about 6,000 compared with the earlier combined enrollment of 10,000. Only a small number of Negroes [twenty-five] have applied for cards at the formerly all-white main library."[23]

According to Martha Claire Catlin, historian for the Alexandria Monthly Meeting of the Religious Society of Friends (AMM), from the inception of the Woodlawn Meeting, an antislavery colony located nine miles south of Alexandria that was nurtured by the AMM, the Friends "interacted with, welcomed, sold land to, helped educate, and extended legal assistance and political support to African Americans."[24] They also supported libraries and print culture as sources of knowledge acquisition in "the service of Truth," a Friends' principle or testimony. Blacks were always welcome at the AMM's meetings and in their library.

During the 1930s, the economic crises brought about by the Great Depression heightened the Friends' concerns about social issues such as education and libraries. Though the Friends, for the nominal sum of $1, had granted the city a ninety-nine-year lease on their burial grounds for use as a construction site for the new public library, the library board refused to consider integrating the library and they refused to permit AMM members to worship at the library while renovations were underway on the Woodlawn meetinghouse. According to Catlin, some AMM Friends concluded that the library board saw their aid as a backdoor attempt to break the color barrier.

As Dorothy G. Harris has shown, the Friends have played a role in the American library movement by making their large and valuable holdings available to the public, thereby contributing to the literary and print cultures of communities. Catlin stated that, "from the 1930s until the 1970s, when the [Woodlawn] addition was built[,] . . . AMM's office and its library holdings" were in Washington, D.C., though Black Alexandrians were always welcome to use them. Travel to this destination, however, was an issue. Lovell A. Lee, an area resident, said that he was not aware of any other District of Columbia library options and "did not hear of anyone speak of [them]." In addition, "travel to the Woodlawn location in a rural neighborhood several miles from Alexandria would . . . have made it an unlikely alternative for city residents."[25]

In addition to their work reinforcing moral behavior and supplying spiritual and social support, YMCAs functioned as education centers for adults and youths by providing libraries and literary and print-culture infrastructures for their patrons. Lectures, programs, and resources on biblical and business topics were primary focuses, but other fields of study were also addressed. As community institutions with a broad reach, they would have been a plausible alternative for Black access to print culture. Unfortunately, in Alexandria, they were not.

According to Cephas Brainerd—historian, lawyer, and chairman of the YMCA International Committee—as of 1876 the YMCA had 478 nationwide associations, 319 of which had libraries, and 201 of which had reading rooms. The largest YMCA library was in Washington, D.C., and the city was also home to the Anthony Bowen YMCA, established in 1853 as the first Black association in the world. The YMCA in Richmond, Virginia, one of the principal associations in the country, had been established in 1855 and by the 1870s housed 3,600 volumes. Although Brainerd reports that "the reading rooms of the associations [were] always free to the general public," in Alexandria that did not include Blacks because the city, like many local communities, had a separate Black YMCA. Lovell A. Lee, who spent time at Alexandria's Black YMCA, told me it did not have a library.

Though routinely underfunded and marginalized, Black associations had the autonomy to implement programs of racial uplift and self-determination and during the civil rights era, they served as meeting places for activists. Even in the absence of a library or reading room, such sociopolitical activities spurred critical thinking and oratory skills. Beginning in 1931, efforts to desegregate the YMCAs were implemented though many local White associations, including Alexandria's, ignored the initiative. Another desegregation attempt was made by the National Council in 1946 with similar results. Racial discrimination was finally banned in all YMCAs in 1967, but it is unclear exactly when Alexandria's YMCA was integrated.[26]

Given the lack of local access to libraries, alternative book sources for Blacks were even more important. When I asked Lovell A. Lee and Lillian S. Patterson if there were any Black bookstores or reading rooms in Alexandria before, during, or after the construction of the Robinson Library, both said that they remembered no other facilities. This suggests that the Frederick Douglass Library Association and Robert B. Robinson's reading room had ceased to exist by the late 1930s. Lee recalled White bookstores in Alexandria but said that his parents didn't patronize them. Patterson told me that her father used the public library in Washington, D.C., but she did not know if he also patronized the Frederick Douglass Literary and Industrial Association or the Library of Congress. Lee's family didn't patronize the District of Columbia's public library, but he began going there on his own once he was old enough. However, neither he nor his family members patronized any Black bookstores in Washington, D.C. Gladys Howard Davis told me that her family acquired books from the White people for whom her mother worked and that her mother also scoured rummage sales for reading materials so that the family always had access to books. In fact, her family accumulated so many books that her father, a bricklayer, built an addition to their house to accommodate them. Asked if she patronized the Alexandria Library after 1959 when it began to admit Black adults and high school students, Shirley M. Lee, Lovell Lee's wife, said yes and added that when the facility began to admit youngsters, "I took my children [there] so they could get library cards." Her husband "patronized the [Alexandria Library] during [his] years in high school and was pleased [to do so] because it represented access." When I asked how the librarians treated him, he responded, "They were courteous," a comment echoed by Gladys Davis.[27]

# CHAPTER TWO

# Bold Beginnings

*The NAACP, Samuel Wilbert Tucker,*
*and the Quest for Educational Equity*

Decades after the conclusion of the Civil War and the demise of Radical Reconstruction, racial antagonisms continued to pose problems in southern bastions such as Virginia. Some White southerners acknowledged the moral imperatives of Reconstruction, but many others believed that its social and political initiatives imposed northern perspectives about race, interracial relations, and Black civil rights on the region. Historian Raymond Arsenault writes that the dominant image of the 1870s South "was that of a 'tragic era' sullied by corruption and opportunism." This image persisted in the decades that followed Reconstruction. J. Douglas Smith remarks that, in Virginia, divergences in the interpretation of social equality fomented the most heated debates. White elites associated social equality with an irrevocable loss of prestige and supremacy as well as with fears of racial amalgamation and miscegenation. But Earl Lewis contends that the definition of social equality as "interracial social mingling" was completely "foreign" to many Blacks. Instead, they associated social equality with opportunities for "equal pay, equal access to education and public facilities, and an equal chance at earning a living regardless of race."[1]

As long as Whites remained in control of racial issues, they could manipulate the contradictions inherent in these disparate interpretations to their advantage. Yet increasing demands to extend full citizenship to Blacks and a growing number of direct civil rights actions by African American citizens challenged established social norms and White control of race relations. Whites could no longer rely on genteel paternalism to mollify Blacks, and Blacks would no longer accept pacification to maintain racial harmony. Alarmed at the increasing rate and assertiveness of Black demands, even progressive Whites such as Virginius Dabney, the editor of the *Richmond Times-Dispatch* and a supporter of the Commission on Interracial Cooperation, viewed Black activism as radicalism. As Smith writes, after years of frustration with the pace of momentum toward social equality, not to mention the omnipresence of Jim Crow policies, "Blacks understood that separate had never been, nor would it ever be, equal. Whites acknowledged no other alternative." He situates what Blacks interpreted as activism and Whites interpreted as radicalism in the context of "managed race relations":

> As the United States plunged into World War II, white elites labeled African Americans who demanded their rights as citizens and the most rabid white southerners as equal threats to racial harmony and social order. The inability of self-proclaimed whites of goodwill to distinguish morally or intellectually between the two underscored the emptiness of paternalism and the limits of managed race relations.[2]

Black dissatisfaction with social and civic inequities and discrimination began to mount in the early 1930s, among workers in a diverse array of professions—barbers, seamstresses, garbage collectors, New Deal employees, teachers, and applicants to graduate and professional schools. All sought nondiscriminatory civil rights and equal opportunities in employment and education. The NAACP strove to secure equitable compensation for Black elementary and secondary teachers and in 1937 joined forces with the Virginia Teachers Association on behalf of a Norfolk, Virginia, plaintiff. Earlier in the decade, the NAACP had pursued legal cases challenging the exclusion of Black students from graduate and professional schools based solely on their race. The organization sponsored a national study, conducted in 1929–31, that documented the growing tide of racial dissatisfaction.

The study's findings were compiled and analyzed by Nathan Ross Margold, a White, Harvard-educated attorney with expertise in constitutional law, who was a former assistant U.S. attorney for the Southern District of New York. The creation of the study's report was funded by

Charles Garland, a White philanthropist and founder of the American Fund for Public Service, which was committed to anti-capitalist interests and radical social and economic causes, including the welfare of Black Americans. Margold's analysis focused on racial discrimination in public schools and the inequitable distribution of public funds, and it concluded that the NAACP's priority should be "the total abolition of racial segregation in tax-supported educational institutions."[3]

The NAACP was founded in 1909 with the purpose of seeking justice and full civil, social, and political rights for African Americans. Led by W. E. B. Du Bois, Ida B. Wells, Mary White Ovington, Henry Moskowitz, William English Walling, Archibald Grimké, Lillian Wald, and Oswald Garrison Villard, the association welcomed White participants who supported NAACP causes and helped fund its agenda. The NAACP reached a major milestone in its goals with the success of *Pearson, et al. v. Murray* (1936), a test case argued by its litigation director, Charles Hamilton Houston, and his protégé, Thurgood Marshall. The objective of the case was to ensure the admission of Donald Gaines Murray to the University of Maryland School of Law, which had rejected his initial application solely on the basis of his race. Houston and Marshall based their arguments on a legal strategy devised by Margold to challenge the separate-but-equal doctrine using the equal protection clause of the Fourteenth Amendment to the U.S. Constitution. Margold had drawn his strategy from the Supreme Court ruling in *Yick Wo v. Hopkins* (1886), which had reversed earlier decisions from the Supreme Court of California and the Circuit Court for the District of California because "racially discriminatory application of a racially neutral statute violates the Equal Protection Clause of the Fourteenth Amendment." In his ruling on *Pearson, et al. v. Murray*, Carroll J. Bond, chief judge of the Maryland Court of Appeals, wrote: "The case, as we find it, then, is that the state has undertaken the function of education in the law, but has omitted students of one race from the only adequate provision made for it, and omitted them solely because of their color. If those students are to be offered equal treatment in the performance of the function, they must, at present, be admitted to the one school provided."[4]

In 1939, during its thirtieth annual national conference, which was held in Richmond, Virginia, the NAACP not only incorporated Margold's institutional recommendation into its resolutions but also added statements on civil rights and education to refine its organizational focus. Resolution V, Civil Rights, states, "We urge state legislation with adequate penalties to prevent discrimination against persons because of race, creed or color, by persons or places operated for the public and maintained with public as well as private funds." Resolution VI, Education, asserts, "The NAACP favors universal education, equality in school terms, teachers' salaries, and school facilities. Where separate schools are maintained the standards should be the same." *The Crisis*, the NAACP's journal, founded and for many years edited by Du Bois, reprinted these resolutions and the keynote address of Judge William Henry Hastie, Jr., in its September 1939 coverage of the association's conference. Although Hastie supported the association's resolutions, he looked forward to the ultimate goal of desegregated schools: "Now we must stand at a point where the South must take a fresh look at education . . . and determine whether it will move toward the abolition of discriminations all along the line, whether it will soberly take stock and realize that sooner or later, the cost of separate education will become prohibitive."[5]

The NAACP's new resolutions incentivized affiliated Virginia lawyers to document legal cases in which the separate-but-equal clause that appeared in the 1896 ruling in *Plessy v. Ferguson* was not being implemented.[6] With the full support of the NAACP, these attorneys then initiated legal cases on behalf of citizens who had been denied equal protection under the law. Samuel Wilbert Tucker, who was probably a member of the NAACP and likely attended the 1939 conference, was aware of Margold's recommendation and the organization's new resolutions. He was among the talented young Howard University alumni who embraced opportunities to force Virginia courts to mandate equal protection. However, he also differed from many of them. Whereas other attorneys worked to bankrupt state and municipal governments that preferred to maintain segregated public facilities, Tucker, like Hastie,

would settle for nothing less than full desegregation. Combining public protest, nonviolent civil disobedience, and municipal litigation,
his grassroots civil rights strategy endeavored to dismantle the social,
political, legal, institutional, and racial barriers that barred Blacks from
Alexandria's tax-supported Whites-only public library.

Historians Charles M. Payne and Adam Green maintain that while
the "Master Narrative" posits that Blacks "did little to challenge their
oppression," this assumption does not "take seriously 'ordinary' people
whose years of persistent struggle often made the big events possible."[7]
Countless similar microhistories exist, documenting lesser-known early
community activities conceived and implemented by local citizens, who
used municipal legal systems and individual and group agency to change
the terms and conditions of Black lives. These local efforts often became
models for subsequent regional and national endeavors. An examination
of the link between the initiatives of national organizations such as the
NAACP and the microlevel activities of local leaders and community
members reveals how direct-action public protest, nonviolent civil
disobedience, and challenges to municipal judicial systems were used
first as local strategies for self-determination before being embraced by
the Civil Rights Movement.

The story of A. Philip Randolph offers an example of this progres-
sion. Randolph was a civil rights leader as well as an important voice
in the American labor movement and the American Socialist Party, and
he served as president of both the Brotherhood of Sleeping Car Porters
and the National Negro Congress. In 1941, he planned a march on
Washington that became a model for the famous 1963 march, "particularly its use of large-scale direct-action protest in a powerfully symbolic
setting, its focus on influencing the federal government, and its careful
orchestration of national news coverage to multiply the impact of the
planned demonstration."[8]

Randolph had been inspired by Gandhi's nonviolent civil disobedience tactics, which by 1939 had already influenced Tucker. To
accomplish his microcosmic public-protest goals, Tucker, like Gandhi,

had chosen an iconic setting for his demonstration with a focus on influencing the city's municipal government, and he prearranged local and national media coverage to maximize its impact—strategies that reappeared in the large-scale actions of subsequent decades, such as students' restaurant sit-ins in Chicago in 1942, conducted under the auspices of the Congress of Racial Equality; those in Washington, D.C., initiated by Howard University students in 1943 and 1944; as well as the widely publicized Greensboro, North Carolina, restaurant sit-ins of the 1960s. Tucker's civil rights protest did not succeed in its stated mission of desegregating the city's White public library. Nevertheless, the demonstration was a watershed moment not only in the microhistory of the city of Alexandria but also in American public library history, American social and southern histories, and civil rights history.

Samuel Wilbert Tucker was born on June 18, 1913. He was the second of four children in an educated, middle-class family with long-standing roots in Alexandria. The Tucker home was on Queen Street in the city's Uptown section, a predominantly Black neighborhood. At the time, Queen Street was the primary commercial district for Black Alexandrians, while King Street, located two blocks further south, was the central commercial district for Whites and it remains a vital and popular commercial area today.[9]

The Tucker family viewed education and activism as a means to personal and communal agency, and the parents encouraged and empowered their children to achieve their full potential. At a time when few southern Blacks had had opportunities to receive a secondary education, Tucker's mother, Fannie Williams Tucker, had graduated from Virginia Normal and Industrial Institute, a historically Black college in Petersburg and the nation's first fully state-supported four-year college for African Americans. Before her marriage, Fannie Tucker had been a teacher; and afterward she continued to emphasize the importance of education for success. She taught Samuel to read before he entered kindergarten, and he remained a voracious reader throughout his life. Tucker's father, Samuel Appleton Tucker, Jr., was an industrious and enterprising businessman who at various times had worked as an insurance agent and a bartender and had operated a grocery store and a restaurant. In 1924, he purchased an office building, where he worked as a realtor while he studied law. Unfortunately, though he sat for the bar exam several times, he never passed it. Nonetheless, he was a committed community activist and a founding member of the Alexandria chapter of the NAACP. In 1939, he and his colleagues helped to establish Hopkins House, a local Black community and social service center that remains in operation today.[10]

The Tucker parents refused to capitulate to the bigotry and oppression of Jim Crow, and their example had a significant influence on the lives and perspectives of their four children. Still, the family dealt with struggle and humiliation. At the age of three, Tucker watched as Alexandria policemen dragged his pregnant mother from the family's home. She had committed no crime; she had simply been a bystander during a neighborhood incident. Tucker's wife, Julia Spaulding Tucker, later spoke of the event's emotional and psychological impact on her husband. Two years later the child had another experience that profoundly affected his life: for the first time he heard his father sing "We Fought Every Race's Battle but Our Own." In a 1985 interview Tucker remarked that that moment had a powerful influence on his subsequent life, career, and activism. Julia Tucker recalled a third important event in her husband's young life. When he was eight or ten years old, "He got a little job in the home of somebody his father knew, a white family, and . . . at lunch time . . . they put Tucker on the porch and the others ate inside. And when he told his mother . . . she said, 'You don't go back there anymore.'"[11]

At the age of fourteen, Tucker had his first clash with Alexandria's legal system. On June 21, 1927, the police arrested him, along with his older brother George and his younger brother Otto, following a confrontation with Lottie May Jernigan over trolley-car seating. Jernigan, a White woman, had filed a criminal warrant of disorderly conduct against the boys, charging them with "assault and abusive language" because the children had refused to relinquish their seats. Jernigan did not need the seats the boys were occupying; there were available seats in the car's Whites-only section. She apparently objected to the fact that the children had turned their reversible seats to face each other in order to converse. The police court filed no charges against eleven-year-old Otto but did levy a fine for disorderly conduct against the older boys: $5 plus court costs for Samuel, $50 plus court costs for George. After the attorney Tom Watson, a Black Alexandrian and a business associate of the boys' father, appealed their convictions, an all-White, all-male jury decided that the two boys had committed no crime, and all charges were dropped. Tucker's memory of the incident strengthened his resolve to continue to oppose racial discrimination by legal means.[12]

Tucker attended Parker-Gray Elementary School, which had been established in 1920 to serve Alexandria's Black students in grades 1–7. In 1921, rather than concede to community demands for a Black high school, the city added an eighth grade. According to the local historian Stephen J. Ackerman, in 1923, Tucker skipped from the fourth to the sixth grade. Clearly he was a capable student, but the closest northern Virginia high school for African Americans was in Manassas, a city located thirty-five miles west of Alexandria. In part to shorten their children's commute but primarily to ensure that their children received a premier education, many Black Alexandrian parents borrowed District of Columbia addresses so their children could commute to Washington for high school. When Tucker registered to attend the city's Armstrong Technical High School, he gave the address of a friend of his father as his residence. This renowned school for Black students, originally known as Armstrong Manual Training School, had been founded in 1902 on accommodationist principles espoused by Booker T. Washington. Tucker graduated in 1929 at the age of sixteen.[13]

At the age of sixteen Tucker began his undergraduate studies at Howard University, arriving at the institution at a critical juncture in its history. The scholar Zachery R. Williams refers to the period between the 1930s and the 1960s as Howard's golden years, a time when many of its scholar activists earned world renown in their fields and the university became known as the preeminent Black academy. During Tucker's enrollment at the school, Charles Hamilton Houston established the nation's first program in civil rights law, oversaw the university's full accreditation, and converted the school from evening-only programs into a full-time institution. During this same period, Howard Thurman, Howard's chaplain from 1932 to 1944 and an outspoken proponent of Gandhi's nonviolent civil-disobedience protest strategies, was actively encouraging students to pair faith with social justice. Tucker learned about Gandhi's nonviolent civil disobedience from Thurman and used it as a key element in his own desegregation tactics. Thurman's interest in nonviolent activism was likely also influenced by his relationship with Rufus Jones, the Quaker philosopher and mystic with whom he studied at Haverford College in 1929. Both men were also associated with the Fellowship of Reconciliation, an interfaith, pacifistic organization founded in 1915 to address "human and civil rights issues through advocacy, activism, and educational programs." It remains "the oldest and largest organization of its kind, promoting peace and active nonviolence with a diverse membership spanning many religious, spiritual, and cultural traditions."[14]

Both Houston and Thurman served as mentors to Tucker, influencing his legal career and his social activism, but his interest in the law was also nurtured by the attorney Tom Watson, who had long shared office space with his father. Thanks to Watson, Tucker was able to self-educate himself in the law. By the age of ten, he was reading Watson's law books, and as a teenager he began to prepare court documents for Watson's legal cases and to do legal research at the Library of Congress. By the time he graduated from Howard in July 1933, he was firmly committed to his future career. For his first job after graduation, he served as a substitute teacher at the Parker-Gray School. That same year, Tucker established a night-school program for Black adults. Then, in 1934, just a year after receiving his baccalaureate degree and only seven years after his confrontation with Jernigan, he passed the bar exam on his first sitting. Tucker took the oath of office as a member of the Virginia Bar Association that same year in the same courtroom in which he had previously faced Jernigan, his first legal opponent. However, at the age of twenty, he was too young to qualify for a law license, so he deferred his legal career until later that year, after his twenty-first birthday (see fig. 1).[15]

Figure 1. Anonymous photographer, "Samuel Wilbert Tucker in white suit, circa 1940." In the collection of the Alexandria Black History Museum and reprinted with its permission.

From the onset of his professional legal career, Tucker was committed to serving the social- and civil-justice needs and interests of the Black community. He began his legal practice in Alexandria in the same Queen Street neighborhood in which he had been raised. For two years he focused on community law, providing legal education and services for small businesses and residents of the city's Black, modest-income communities. Every day, en route to his office, he passed the Alexandria Library, and every day he was reminded that its policies barred Blacks from entry, despite the fact that their taxes contributed to its municipal funding. Though such policies were common during this era, they infuriated Tucker, and he became increasingly motivated to take proactive legal recourse (see figs. 2 and 3).[16]

Tucker's frustration with the legacies of inequity, his refusal to endure racial bigotry, and his admiration for the effective legal strategies of Houston, Margold, and Marshall inspired his orchestration of the 1939 sit-in demonstration to desegregate Alexandria's public library. His insistence on legal and interpersonal respect later motivated him to extend the commitment to social justice initially waged against the library system of Alexandria to include the desegregation of the public-school systems that served Black students throughout Virginia.

A local case in 1935 attested to the usefulness of litigation as a strategy to compel social change. Thurgood Marshall, representing the NAACP, accepted the assignment of arguing a discrimination charge against the Commonwealth of Virginia on behalf of a teacher named Alice Carlotta Jackson. Jackson had responded to Marshall's plea for volunteers willing to participate in legal suits to force Virginia to accept Black graduate students in its public institutions or to subsidize their education at equitable institutions elsewhere. Although she was highly qualified, her application to the Graduate School of the University of Virginia had been rejected solely on the basis of her race. The university rector had written:

> The education of white and colored persons in the same schools is
> contrary to the long established and fixed policy of the Common-
> wealth of Virginia. Therefore, for this and other good and suffi-
> cient reasons not necessary to be herein enumerated, the Rector

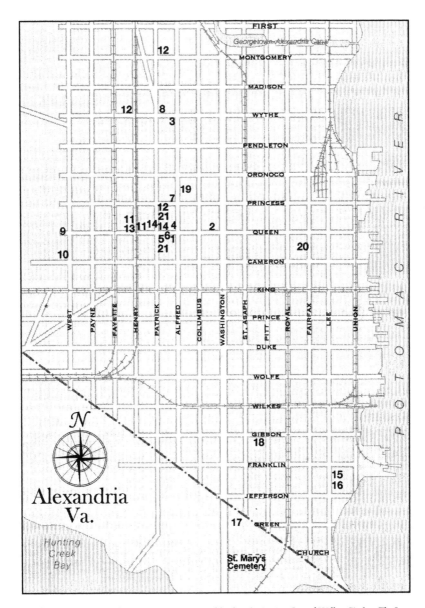

Figure 2. Nancy Noyes Silcox, "Queen Street Neighborhood Map," in *Samuel Wilbert Tucker: The Story of a Civil Rights Trailblazer and the 1939 Alexandria Library Sit-In* (Arlington, VA: Noysil, 2014), 24. © 2014 by Nancy Noyes Silcox. Reproduced with the permission of the author.

## Queen Street Neighborhood Map Key

1. Tucker house, 916 Queen Street.
2. Alexandria Library, 717 Queen Street.
3. Robert Robinson Library, 638 North Alfred Street.
4. Ebenezer Baptist Church, 909 Queen Street.
5. Northwest Pharmacy, 924 Queen Street.
6. Duncan house, 922 Queen Street.
7. Samuel A. Tucker, Jr.'s real estate office, Thomas Watson's law office, and S.W. Tucker's law office, 901 Princess Street.
8. Parker-Gray School, 901 Wythe Street.
9. Jefferson High School, 300 North West Street.
10. Alexandria High School, Cameron and North West streets.
11. Grocery stores (white-owned) 1007, 1023, and 1101 Queen Street.
12. Grocery stores (black-owned) 712 North Henry Street, and 313 and 901 North Patrick Street. Tucker's father and his friends ran the grocery at 313 North Patrick in 1920.
13. 1101 Queen Street. Site of a white-owned grocery store in 1915. By 1924, was the location of the Lincoln Theater. By 1934, replaced with the Capitol Theater.
14. Royal Meat Market (white-owned), 300 North Patrick Street, relocated to 301 North Patrick Street in 1941.
15. Tucker's father's family home, 702 South Lee Street.
16. Zion Baptist Church, 714 South Lee Street.
17. School where Tucker went for first grade. It was in the 900 block of South Washington Street across from St. Mary Catholic Church Cemetery.
18. Snowden School for Boys, 600 South Pitt Street.
19. Hallowell School for Girls, 413 North Alfred Street.
20. Alexandria Police and Corporation Courts, 126 and 132 North Fairfax Street.
21. Funeral homes (black-owned): John T. Rhines & Co. 221 North Patrick Street; W.C. Arnold, 311 North Patrick Street.

Figure 3. Nancy Noyes Silcox, "Queen Street Neighborhood Map Key," in *Samuel Wilbert Tucker: The Story of a Civil Rights Trailblazer and the 1939 Alexandria Library Sit-In* (Arlington, VA: Noysil, 2014), 25. © 2014 by Nancy Noyes Silcox. Reproduced with the permission of the author.

and Board of Visitors of the University of Virginia direct the Dean
of the Department of Graduate Studies to refuse respectfully the
pending application of a colored student.

In her reply to the rector's letter, Jackson inquired about the "other
good and sufficient reasons" for her rejection, but "the University's
Rector declined to elaborate on the Board's decision." The NAACP case
drew considerable negative national media attention to the discriminatory situation, and in response Virginia established a separate-but-
equal graduate school for Black students at Virginia State University
in Petersburg in 1935. Then, in February 1936, the general assembly
passed House Bill 470, also known as the Dovell Act, which awarded
travel and tuition grants to qualified Black students to attend graduate
school at equitable institutions outside of Virginia that offered similar
programs of study. Employing the terms of the Dovell Act, Marshall
forced the general assembly to pay for Jackson's graduate studies at
Columbia University in New York City. In the meantime, the NAACP's
suit against the University of Virginia on behalf of Jackson was settled
out of court.[17]

Inspired by Marshall's success with the Jackson suit and the *Pearson,
et al. v. Murray* case, Tucker decided to extend these arguments to the
arena of public library discrimination. He understood that municipal
libraries were also sites of education access and intellectual development. His own research at the integrated Library of Congress had
provided him with the opportunity for a legal education, and he knew
that opportunities for self-education, cultural enrichment, and professional advancement in a public library should be available to all citizens,
regardless of race. Tucker recognized that Black Alexandrians had a
particular need for the self-directed educational opportunities provided
by public libraries because the city had not given them a chance to earn
a secondary education until 1932 or had even had a night-school option
until 1933, when Tucker himself had created one.

In addition, Tucker knew that public libraries fueled community
growth and development, enabled patrons to establish a useful knowledge base, and provided resources for recreational reading. During Jim

Crow, many of the available Black sites for communal social and cultural interaction in the city were limited to church settings; in contrast, the Alexandria Library gave Whites a nonsectarian site for personal and professional reading, reference research, community activities, meetings, book clubs, and social and cultural events. It offered story hours and homework assistance for children and gave adults access to local and national newspapers, which enabled them to keep abreast of local and national news, conduct job searches, seek housing options, and buy or sell goods and services. Tucker believed the same opportunities should be available to the city's Black residents. In his opinion, desegregation of the Alexandria Library would not only benefit the city's Black residents but would also provide a precedent for desegregating White public library systems in other Virginia municipalities.

But Tucker would not settle for the objectives in the *Pearson, et al. v. Murray* and Jackson cases. He wanted nothing less than full integration at least or desegregation of the Alexandria Library. Tucker knew that the Jim Crow mandates dictating the normative standards of Black life in the microcosm of Alexandria mirrored those of the macrocosm of the South. He also knew that separate facilities neither would nor could ever be equal. Officials in the city of Alexandria had taken 143 years to establish a free public library for White citizens. Clearly, they would feel no urgency to provide a library for Blacks, which in any case would certainly be inferior to the Alexandria Library in both construction and resources.

As I discussed in the introduction, Tucker conceived a two-pronged legal assault to force Alexandria to desegregate its only public library. First, he would implement a test case to determine whether the library would issue a reader's card to a Black resident without the force of a legal mandate. If that action was unsuccessful, he would follow up with a writ of mandamus to compel compliance. While he awaited a ruling on the writ, he would bring the city to court to compel the library to comply with the equal protection clause of the Fourteenth Amendment to the U.S. Constitution. He would strengthen his legal argument with a public library sit-in demonstration predicated on the nonviolent civil-disobedience tactics he had learned from Howard Thurman.

Tucker was not the first person to use the sit-in tactic. During the mid-1930s, the newly formed United Automobile Workers union organized numerous sit-down strikes at various General Motors plants and affiliated industries. In 1936, auto workers demonstrated in two strikes in Flint, Michigan; a Bendix strike took place in South Bend, Indiana; and there were strikes at plants in Atlanta, Kansas City, and Cleveland. That same year, rubber workers conducted successful sit-down strikes against General Tire and Rubber in Akron. In 1937, about 200,000 auto workers conducted a sit-down strike at the Chrysler plants in Detroit.[18]

Clearly, Tucker was a determined and persistent man; and while his family, Tom Watson, and his mentors at Howard helped him build those strengths, and others were honed by his impressive military career. In 1933, while at Howard, Tucker participated in the Reserve Officers Training Corps, and in 1934 he became a second lieutenant in the infantry reserve. In 1936, he was assigned to the Civilian Conservation Corps camp at Gettysburg, Pennsylvania—the only such camp to have Black officers. In 1941, he began active military duty as a first lieutenant in the all-Black 366th infantry regiment. In 1945, he was promoted to major and, in 1946, he was honorably discharged. Meanwhile, he continued his law practice and his activism. In 1945, he testified before congressional committees on behalf of the NAACP and refuted Virginia's denial of racial discrimination in voter registration. In 1946, he moved his law practice from Alexandria to Emporia and served as a cooperating attorney for the NAACP's legal defense fund. In that capacity, Tucker unsuccessfully appealed the death sentences of the Martinsville Seven, a group of Black men convicted of raping a White woman, arguing that the death sentence was inequitably imposed on African American defendants.[19]

In 1947, Tucker married Julia E. Spaulding. Julia had grown up in Newport News, Virginia, and had earned a teaching degree at West Virginia State College. Before her marriage, she had taught school in Maryland. Like her husband, Julia Tucker was an education and civil rights activist, and in Emporia she helped register Black citizens to vote. Although the couple never had children of their own, both served as mentors to the young people around them.[20]

In 1961, Tucker and Henry L. Marsh III formed the legal partnership of Tucker and Marsh; and, in 1962, Tucker began serving as
chair of the legal staff of the NAACP's Virginia state conference. He
later represented Virginia, Maryland, and the District of Columbia on
the organization's national board of directors. In 1966, Oliver White
Hill, a fellow Howard alumnus, joined his law firm, which relocated to
Richmond under the name Hill, Tucker, and Marsh. The firm became
Virginia's legal leader in matters related to school desegregation. As a
cooperating NAACP attorney, Tucker successfully argued several cases
before the U.S. Supreme Court. His most notable Supreme Court argument was *Charles C. Green, et al. v. County School Board of New Kent County,
et al.* (1968), in which he challenged legislation enacted by the county
to implement school desegregation on a strictly voluntary basis. The
Court held that "New Kent County's freedom-of-choice desegregation
plan did not comply with the dictates of *Brown v. Board of Education of
Topeka* (1954) and was therefore unconstitutional." According to *The
Encyclopedia of Civil Rights in America*, the case "did more to advance
school desegregation than any other Supreme Court decision since
*Brown v. Board of Education*." In 1976, the NAACP awarded Tucker the
prestigious William Robert Ming Advocacy Award in recognition of
his work on behalf of the organization.[21]

Tucker's niece, the Reverend Deborah Thomas-McSwain, described
her Uncle Wilbert as a kind, generous, and thoughtful man who always
made time to spend with her. His home, she said, was filled with music.
During his service in Italy, he had learned to love opera, and in Emporia
the sound of operas on his stereo reverberated across his fifty-acre property. He played the piano and showed his niece how to waltz; and when
Thomas-McSwain began studying to become an opera singer, Tucker
taught her Italian so she would understand the words she was singing.
He had a photographic memory, which helped him in his law practice,
and was gifted at math which enabled him to teach his niece mathemat-
ical concepts she had not learned in school. Thomas-McSwain recalled
visiting her uncle in Emporia during the summer and at Christmas. One
year she bought him an autoharp as a gift, and even without lessons he
instinctively knew how to string and play it.[22]

Samuel Wilbert Tucker died on October 19, 1990. He is buried at Arlington National Cemetery next to his brother George. Following his death, the Virginia State Bar Association, which had previously attempted to strip him of his law license as punishment for his activism on behalf of school desegregation, established the Oliver W. Hill and Samuel W. Tucker Scholarship. In 1998, the city of Emporia erected a monument to commemorate his life and work; and in 1999, Alexandria's school board voted to name a school in his honor. The Samuel W. Tucker Elementary School was the city's first new school building in thirty years.

# CHAPTER THREE

# Prelude to the Sit-In, Part One

## *History of the City of Alexandria*

The city of Alexandria is a vital and historic port community, situated on the Potomac River in northern Virginia, about eight miles south of downtown Washington, D.C., and forty-seven miles south of Baltimore. As of 2020, the city had a population of nearly 160,000.[1] Alexandria's geographical location, rich history, and diverse demographics have all combined to create its vibrant character, and its proximity to the nation's capital has had a strong influence on its political and social history.

Artifacts found in the region suggest that Indigenous people began visiting the area around present-day Alexandria more than 13,000 years ago. These people of the Woodland Period established trading villages along the Potomac, and those of the Paleo-Indian Period (c. 11000 BCE–7500 BCE) and the Archaic Period (c. 7500 BCE–1000 BCE) visited or inhabited the area. Archaeologists have speculated that the Woodland people visited the marshes in early spring to harvest tubers, a time when other foodstuffs were scarce, and later in the season may have temporarily settled along the river to exploit the bountiful fish runs. During the early centuries of the period, Indigenous people created and used pottery, and eventually they began to build permanent settlements and to harvest agricultural products such as maize, squash, and beans. At Jones Point, in the far southern reaches of modern-day Alexandria, artifacts and dark soil stains are probably remnants of the wooden homes built during the Woodland Period—the site's first permanent structures.[2]

Europeans arrived at the beginning of the seventeenth century, and their early interactions with the Woodland Indians are known as the Contact Period. John Smith mapped the Potomac River in 1608 and encountered the Indigenous Tauxenents and Nacotchtanks, both affiliated with the Conoy Chiefdom, as well as Dogue and Algonquin speakers and the people in the trading villages of Nameranghequend, Assaomeck, and Namassingakent. In 1654, Dame Margaret Brent acquired seven hundred acres of local land, and in 1669, John Alexander purchased sixty acres that Sir William Berkeley, the governor of Virginia, had originally deeded to the English ship captain Robert Howson. European settlers intended to use this land for tobacco cultivation, and they established plantations during the late seventeenth and early eighteenth centuries. Trade in tobacco began in the 1730s, and Alexandria's commercial character was bolstered by an influx of British merchants and their imported goods. The proximity of an easily traversable natural waterway made the town ideal for port traffic, especially since it was already serving as an inspection site for exported tobacco crops. Great Britain used the growing metropolis as a shipping center for its flourishing colonial tobacco industry, and those ships also carried wheat, flour, and fish to England, Europe, and the Caribbean. Return voyages brought enslaved Africans and finished goods into Virginia.[3]

The success of this sea-based mercantile trade prompted investors to create inland routes into western markets. With other Potomac River towns, Alexandria began to develop the Chesapeake and Ohio Canal, colloquially known as the C & O Canal, a significant infrastructure investment that improved water transportation locally and into the frontier. In 1747, commercial planters formed the Ohio Company to support new land speculation into northwestern territory.

Alexandria was not the young town's first name. In 1732, residents, merchants, and businessmen began to refer to the area as Hunting Creek Warehouse. Yet as historian Diane Riker notes, "For the first dozen years of its history, Alexandria, Virginia, was a town with two names" because some of the town's most prominent citizens referred to it as Belhaven. Others, including mapmakers, accepted and used both names.[4] In 1748, a coalition of Virginian businessmen and British merchants asked the colonial government for permission to formally found a town named Alexandria, as a tribute to John Alexander, whose seventeenth-century holdings formed the majority of the town's land area. Later that year, the colony's general assembly authorized the founding, and a board

of trustees was formed in 1749 to serve as Alexandria's local govern-
ing body. Soon thereafter the British government granted the Ohio
Company 800,000 acres of land for commercial speculation, including
the land in Alexandria. All of the town was offered for sale at public
auction, in half-acre lots. A small parcel of land identified as Market
Square was reserved specifically for a business district. (Today that
section remains a vital commercial center and is the longest continually
operated market in the United States.) Throughout town, landowners
divided and subdivided their lots, renting them to artisans, grocers, merchants, tavern operators, and tradesmen. The new community prospered
during the next few decades. In the mid-1750s, Alexandria served as an
assembly area for British troops during the French and Indian War, and
Major General Edward Braddock used the city as his command post as
he planned his campaign against the French in 1755. In 1779, after the
American Revolution, Alexandria was incorporated as a town in the
Commonwealth of Virginia, the first one established on the outskirts
of what would become the District of Columbia. By the end of the
eighteenth century, Alexandria was an official port of entry for foreign
ships, a major export center, and one of the busiest ports in the country.[5]


The selection of a site for the nation's capital was a hotly contested issue,
and it was entangled with other disputed matters that were dividing
northern and southern interests. Treasury Secretary Alexander Hamilton
had proposed economic reforms—among them, allowing the federal government to assume the young nation's $80 million Revolutionary War
debt—that would vest significant power with the federal government
rather than with the individual states. This was anathema to southerners,
who also did not want the new capital to be located in a northern state.
James Madison, a Virginia congressman and an advocate for southern
interests, argued that it should be situated in an area "friendly to slaveholding agricultural interests." In a bold tactical gambit, Secretary of
State Thomas Jefferson agreed to persuade Madison and other powerful
southern owners of enslaved people to accept Hamilton's proposed
economic reforms, including assumption of the war debt, if the capital

were located in the South. Jefferson's proposal was self-serving. As the owner of a sizable population of enslaved labor, his compromise ensured that the nation's capital would remain a community of enslavers and that the territory's trade in Black men, women, and children would be strongly influenced by southern interests.[6]

In 1789, the Commonwealth of Virginia signed a preliminary agreement allowing Alexandria to shift to the jurisdiction of the federal government and thus become part of the capital site. Congress renamed the town Alexandria County, and it was ceded to the District of Columbia by congressional action on July 16, 1790, the official date of the district's founding. On February 27, 1801, Alexandria County was annexed by the District of Columbia. Likewise, nearby George, Maryland, first established in 1751 and incorporated as George Town in 1789 (later to be known as Georgetown), was ceded to the District of Columbia. Together the municipalities of Alexandria County and George Town provided additional land for the federal government along the Potomac and Anacostia rivers. Both annexations were overseen by President George Washington, a long-time Alexandria resident with a vested interest in the city's business affairs.[7]

Between 1801 and 1815, banking and shipping ventures fueled growth and prosperity in Alexandria, particularly during the War of 1812, even though the city was briefly captured and looted by the British in 1814.[8] These war years accentuated the paradox of enslavement and freedom that the Revolutionary War had brought to the fore a few decades earlier. In Virginia, enslaved Blacks who had escaped from bondage and Blacks acquired through British conquests were promised their freedom if they served in the British military. Their familiarity with the countryside and its waterways gave Britain a distinct strategic advantage. Virginians, whose freedom and wealth were predicated on the labor of enslaved people, refused to recognize that Blacks' struggle for liberty paralleled their own struggle for independence. In the first decades of the nineteenth century, as planters faced economic decline and their labor needs decreased, enslavement became a double-edged sword. According to historian Alan Taylor, racial tensions heightened during the War of 1812 because southern Whites perceived the formerly enslaved combatants as an "internal enemy" to be feared and restrained. As Whites perpetuated enslaved labor, they were increasingly snared by intensified vigilance, suspicion, and hostility.[9] On February 18, 1815, the U.S. Senate ratified the Treaty of Ghent, which ended the War of 1812 and, according to the *Alexandria Gazette*, saved the city from certain destruction. With the war over, Americans began to spend money, often in independent investment ventures.[10] But trouble lay ahead. Triggered by European monetary crises, the Panic of 1819 was exacerbated by lax American banking regulations and excessive speculation in western expansion. The nation's monetary system collapsed, and the ensuing depression lasted through 1821. Alexandria's building, banking, and business interests, many of which were entangled in western specu-lation, were deeply affected. Some enterprises, however, weathered the storm and became extremely profitable. In the 1830s, for example, the Alexandria Canal Company began work on the Alexandria Canal, which was completed in 1843. The new waterway, along with the C & O Canal's link to Cumberland, Maryland, made Alexandria a hub for coal, wheat, corn, whiskey, cornmeal, and flour shipments from the West. Items shipped from Alexandria included fish, salt, plaster, and lumber. At the same time, various railroad schemes were underway. In 1847, the Orange and Alexandria Railroad was founded and became the start of a major railway system. In 1851, the city had cemented its position as a railway and industrial center with the establishment of the Virginia Locomotive and Car Works, and its dependence on the canals for water transport began to deteriorate.[11]

During the years when it was part of the federal government, Alex-andria functioned under the control of Congress and the District of Columbia (see fig. 4). Though Alexandrians were denied a voice in presidential and congressional elections, they had welcomed annex-ation because they assumed that the government would implement infrastructure improvements, new construction, and enhanced com-munity development. They were disappointed. More often than not, Georgetown reaped the benefit of these projects while Alexandria languished. In addition, because White Alexandrians relied on the availability of enslaved labor both in the city and its outlying agricultural areas, they began to worry that the District of Columbia was leaning toward abolishing the enslavement of Blacks within its boundaries. Already Virginia's strictures on the trade in enslaved Blacks were laxer than Washington's. Given these resentments, many Alexandrian businessmen and entrepreneurs began to lobby for change, and on July 9, 1846, Congress voted to allow Alexandria's retrocession to Virginia. In a referendum on September 2, 1846, White male Alexandrians voted 763 to 222 to end their annexation to the District of Columbia and return to the Commonwealth of Virginia; and on March 20, 1847, Virginia officially took over jurisdiction.[12]

Alexandria under congressional and District control was far more hospitable to its growing population of free Blacks than it was under the jurisdiction of Virginia. During the city's association with the District of Columbia, they were still constrained by race-based politics and policies, but both elite and poor free Blacks were able to build and nurture communities and institutions such as churches, businesses, social organizations, mutual aid societies, and schools. They were also able to engage in discretionary pursuits. The few elite free Blacks who had acquired property, financial security, and a modest measure of accommodation from Whites concentrated primarily on maintaining their freedom and economic stability. But the vast majority of the free Black population were relatively poor and worked as domestics, skilled and unskilled laborers, factory and dock workers, tenant farmers and farmhands, and peddlers. Ira Berlin maintains that Whites tended to be more suspicious of free Blacks than of enslaved Blacks. They distrusted their enhanced personal agency and the fact that they occasionally reinforced race loyalties by hiring the enslaved, forging passes for them, loaning them money, hiding them, or standing in for their owners in situations of need. When they could, the enslaved reciprocated by patronizing Black cookshops and boardinghouses, warning free Blacks about slave patrols, and supporting them with stolen food and clothing.[13]

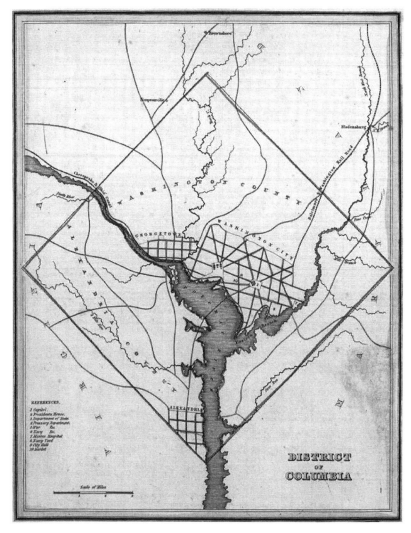

Figure 4. "Map of the District of Columbia" [1835], in *Comprehensive Atlas* (Boston: Bradford, 1836), n.p. Archived in the Geography and Maps Division, Library of Congress, http://www.loc.gov.

In 1790, when Alexandria was still under Virginia's jurisdiction, fifty-two free Blacks lived in the town. In 1810, when data from the first decennial census were compiled after the city's annexation to the District of Columbia, its free Black population had increased to 836—a leap of more than 1,500 percent. Exact population figures for the District's various sections—Washington, D.C., George Town, D.C., and Alexandria, D.C.—are not available, but the census lists its total free Black population at 1,572. Thus, we can extrapolate that the combined free Black population of George Town and Washington was 736—almost 12 percent less than Alexandria's. By 1850, three years after Alexandria had been retroceded to Virginia, the free Black population had increased by nearly 430 percent to 4,427 (2,090 males, 2,337 females). The city's White population totaled 7,218 (3,388 males, 3,830 females), and its population of enslaved people totaled 1,445 (586 males, 859 females).[14]

Free Blacks were a familiar, albeit segregated, minority presence in Alexandria. The first free Black community, known as the Bottoms, was formed at the town's southwestern edge; and by 1810, another, community known as Hayti, had been established in the city's southeastern corner. By the middle of the nineteenth century, Uptown (in the northwestern corridor) and Petersburg (better known as the Berg or Fishtown) were established near the northern waterfront. After the Civil War, these communities expanded to include the Hill, Cross Canal, the Hump, and Colored Rosemont. In 1910, Black communities included neighborhoods around the city's center and along its far edges.[15]

The formation of separate, race-specific institutions such as churches and schools by Blacks in Alexandria and elsewhere was born of necessity. Philip S. Foner comments that "the history of the establishment of the first independent African church clearly illustrates how white racism stimulated black separatism." Historian Foner further maintains that Black denominations seceded from their White counterparts because of racial restrictions, not doctrinal differences. He notes that, before 1811, "black and white Baptists in Virginia worshipped together and there appears to have been no segregated arrangements within the sanctuaries." In 1811, however, Alexandria's First Baptist Church began to confine Black parishioners into a racially restricted section of the meetinghouse. In response, African Americans chose to establish independent Black churches where they could freely worship without racial discrimination or racist stigmas.[16] The history of Black schools followed a similar pattern. In Virginia, as in other southern states, Whites believed that

Blacks lacked the aptitude for learning so there was no need to educate them. As a result, African Americans established separate schools for their children, many of whom were educated in the District of Columbia or in socially conscious institutions such as those operated by the Society of Friends. When Alexandria was under the District's jurisdiction, all Black children were legally entitled to a public education; but after retrocession, the Commonwealth closed its few available public schools for African American children. Blacks who sought an education had to attend private academies in the District of Columbia or Alexandria, or use Friends' schools, or underground classes taught by local Black women.[17]

Enslaved Black Alexandrians endured far worse fates. In 1808, the U.S. government outlawed the importation of Black Africans for enslavement, so trading in domestic enslaved Blacks became the only way to maintain the "peculiar institution" that was now endemic to the South's agricultural economy, particularly in the lower states, where cotton was king. Black individuals and families held in bondage had always been subject to sale or separation, but after 1808 the trade in free Blacks and captured bondspeople escalated. In Virginia, tobacco plantation fortunes declined, creating a surplus of enslaved Blacks available for purchase. Meanwhile, plantation owners in the lower South were eager for more enslaved labor to plant, cultivate, and harvest the ever-expanding cotton fields, so large numbers of enslaved men and women from Virginia were sent southward. Until 1806, enslaved children were routinely sold with or without their mothers, but in that year Louisiana, a prime market for the sale of enslaved laborers, changed its laws, declaring, "Every person is expressly prohibited from selling separately from their mothers children slaves under ten years of age." This meant that Virginia-based traders in enslaved Blacks were obliged to keep mothers and young children together.[18]

By the 1830s, the Washington area was the center of southern trading in domestic enslaved Blacks. The largest of those companies was the highly profitable Alexandria-based firm of Franklin and Armfield, sometimes referred to as Franklin, Armfield and Company. Although Franklin and Armfield was Alexandria's most active trading operation, the city was also home to a number of smaller yet robust trading firms.

Franklin and Armfield revolutionized the trade's business model by eliminating middlemen and their attendant costs, owning rather than leasing the ships that transported enslaved Blacks, and operating as an interstate trading complex.[19] The firm was established in 1828 by Isaac Franklin, a Tennessee planter and trader, and John Armfield, a North Carolina trader. It became the nation's most profitable interstate domestic trading company and is reputed to have sold up to 1,200 enslaved men, women, and children annually. The firm controlled almost half of the coastal trade from Virginia and Maryland to Louisiana. Armfield would acquire enslaved Blacks at low prices, warehouse them in the firm's Alexandria pens—known as *slave jails* or *slave prisons*—and deliver them by ship or on foot first to New Orleans and then to Natchez, Mississippi, where Franklin would sell them for higher prices. The two men were close friends as well as savvy business partners who thoroughly enjoyed their work. They were also known to be unusually cruel, especially toward enslaved females, whom they frequently raped and abused and then mocked.

In 1831, Rice Carter Ballard joined Franklin and Armfield in forming a second, separate business known as Franklin, Ballard, and Company, which also traded in enslaved Blacks. Like his partners, Ballard was famously abusive to enslaved females.[20] It was Ballard's responsibility to amass enslaved Blacks in the Richmond area, who would then be delivered to Franklin for sale in New Orleans and Natchez. The partners hired a number of company agents to gather together Blacks in other areas of Virginia and Maryland.[21] In 1835, Franklin retired to his Tennessee plantation, and Ballard relocated to Natchez to handle the firms' sales transactions. Armfield continued to manage operations in Alexandria and New Orleans. Franklin died in 1946 and, as executor of his will, Armfield helped to oversee his former partner's Louisiana plantations. By 1836, Ballard was no longer directly involved with Franklin and Armfield but there was business correspondence as late as January 1856 as the former partners endeavored to resolve their complicated financial affairs.[22] Beginning in 1836 or 1837, the facility owned by the firm of Franklin and Armfield was sold to a succession of traders, beginning with one of its former agents, George Kephart, who ran it as Kephart and Company until 1845. It later became Bruin and Hill (until 1852), Millan and Grigsby (until 1858), and Price, Birch, and Company (until 1861).[23] In 1861, the Union forces who were occupying Alexandria converted the premises into a jail for Union soldiers and captured Confederate soldiers. The building occupied by Franklin and Armfield was purchased by the city in the spring of 2020 from the Northern Virginia Urban League, which still maintains offices in the structure. While under its ownership, the Urban League, paradoxically, renamed the building Freedom House Museum. It currently operates under the auspices of the Office of Historic Alexandria and educates visitors about the city's history in the trade of enslaved Blacks and the operation of Franklin and Armfield.[24] The museum was granted National Landmark Status in 1978 and Virginia Landmarks Registry approval in 1979. Approval for a Historical Highway Marker was granted by the Virginia Department of Historic Resources in 2005.

Enslaved Blacks were omnipresent in Alexandria and Washington, D.C., and the spectacle of coffled bondspeople marching through the streets underscored the paradox of "slavery in the shadow of liberty." While the Compromise of 1850, which overturned the 1820 Missouri Compromise, led to the demise of the trade in the District of Columbia, it merely postponed the national debate on Black enslavement and did not end enslavement itself. Historian Ernest B. Furgurson explains: "The Compromise of 1850 was actually a series of bills passed mainly to address issues related to slavery. The bills provided for slavery to be decided by popular sovereignty in the admission of new states, prohibited the slave trade in the District of Columbia, settled a Texas boundary dispute, and established a stricter fugitive slave act."[25] After its enactment, the city's major trading enterprises simply moved from the District of Columbia to Virginia, and the trade in enslaved Blacks continued to prosper in Alexandria, now under Virginia's jurisdiction. In 1860, Washington had a population of 75,080: 55,764 Whites (nearly 80 percent of the total); 11,131 free Blacks (nearly 16 percent); and 3,185 enslaved men, women, and children (nearly 5 percent). That figure for free Blacks included many who left Alexandria after retrocession to reside in the District's more secure and less restricted environment, where, among other benefits, Black children were legally entitled to an education. In April 1862, in the wake of Union losses at the Battle of Shiloh and under pressure from abolitionists, President Abraham Lincoln signed congressional legislation that freed all enslaved residents in the District of Columbia.[26]

Meanwhile, on April 17, 1861, Virginia's general assembly voted to secede from the Union "with the proviso that secession be confirmed by public referendum." Historian William Seale maintains that Alexandrians demonstrated unionist sympathies before the Civil War; but by the time they held their public referendum on May 24, popular sentiment had changed. Michael Lee Pope reports that "Four out of five precincts voted in favor of secession, and the final tally showed that nine out of 10 voters wanted to formally leave the United States of America." However, Alexandria's proximity to the nation's capital, combined with its strategic waterways and railways and its thriving commercial and industrial centers, made the city too important to relinquish, so the Union army took over. Following this move, Alexandria's loyalist faction attempted to seize control of city hall and cement Union power in the city. Such divided allegiances were typical of communities in the upper South. As James M. McPherson contends, "the balance of military manpower from these states favored the South. . . . Nevertheless, the ability of the North to mobilize [so] much manpower from slave states gave an important impetus to the Union war effort."[27]

On the day Virginia voted to secede, 13,000 Union troops crossed the Potomac River to occupy strategic points in the region, including the city of Alexandria, which was immediately transformed into a military camp. Local Confederate troops were ill equipped to mount a defense and left Alexandria to join their comrades elsewhere. More than half of the city's residents fled to other locales in the South or to join the Confederate army. Those who remained lived under martial law and were subject to curfews, supply shortages, and personal property confiscation for use by Union troops. More than thirty buildings in the city were converted into hospitals. To protect the waterways and railways, workers constructed forts around the city, which became a port, supply, and hospital hub for the entire Union army and the headquarters of its military railway system.

Although Union forces controlled Alexandria throughout the war, public sentiment continued to favor the Confederacy. Wartime activities brought money and visitors into the city and led to civic and infrastructure improvements, but individual Alexandrians endured considerable emotional and economic hardship, and they resented the presence of the Union troops. When the war ended, the troops left; and with their facilities demolished or plundered, the city struggled to cope. Gradually, however, industrial development returned. In 1869, Robert Portner established Tivoli Brewery, which became one of the most successful businesses in the city; and in the following year, the Alexandria Marine Railway and Ship Building Company was established. The link between the railways and the port became a key to Alexandria's long-term recovery.

Slowly, Alexandrians agreed to sign amnesty pledges, though romanticized ideations of antebellum life lingered in the collective memories of White residents for generations. Countless Confederate memorials were built throughout the South, including Alexandria's iconic image of a lone Confederate soldier, arms crossed, positioned with his back to the North as an intentional affront to the Union. In 1889, twenty-four years after the end of the Civil War, the Robert E. Lee Camp of Confederate Veterans erected a bronze statue in Alexandria, at a prominent intersection in Old Town. Titled *Appomattox*, it was "based on a figure in [the] painting 'Appomattox' by John Elder [and] sculpted by M. Casper Buberl . . . [and] commemorates [the] spot from which local troops left town to join [the] Confederate army [in] 1861." The monument was unusual in that it was privately owned but situated on public land. Like many statues erected throughout the South during Jim Crow, it was a clear testament to the prioritization of sectional rather than national interests.[28]

During the Civil War, more than 7,000 formerly enslaved men, women, and children arrived in Alexandria. As Bruce Levine writes, "southern masters had bolted from the Union precisely to strengthen their grip on . . . black workers. Instead, however, secession and the war that it initiated were now enabling thousands of slaves to bolt toward freedom."[29] Some of these newcomers fled north while still in bondage; others arrived after the enactment of the Emancipation Proclamation on

January 1, 1863. Most of the escapees were destitute, and many died of malnutrition, illness, or disease. They all sought protection from the Union troops, who derisively referred to them as "contraband," a term originally coined by General Benjamin Butler in May 1861 to describe three Black fugitives from a Confederate labor battalion who had sought refuge in his Union camp. The escapees referred to themselves as "freed-men." Many were housed in cramped military barracks; but despite their meager living conditions, they quickly assumed agency over their situation. Establishing makeshift communities, they supported them-selves by working for the Union forces, finding positions in domestic service, construction, and port, railway, supply, and hospital occupa-tions. For many, this was the first time they were paid for their labor.[30] The religious communities of free Blacks welcomed the freedmen and women, and both young and old learned to read and write from free Blacks or other freedmen. The sick were treated at L'Ouverture Hospital, a segregated facility originally constructed by the federal government to treat Black soldiers in the U.S. Colored Troops; and the dead were buried at Freedmen's Cemetery. In 1864, L'Ouverture Hospital became the site of Alexandria's first recorded civil rights demonstration, when 443 convalescing members of the Colored Troops protested the burial of enlistees in Freedmen's Cemetery rather than in Soldiers' Cemetery (now known as Alexandria National Cemetery) with their White com-patriots. The protest was successful, and the Black soldiers were disin-terred from Freedmen's Cemetery and moved to Soldiers' Cemetery in 1865. Shortly after the Civil War, during the creation of new, southern, state constitutions, Black Alexandrians initiated further civil rights activism when they organized a Negro convention in the city.[31]

There was enormous disagreement about how the Union should be socially and politically reconstructed after the war. Some stakeholders wanted to punish the South, a stance that engendered southern animos-ity and resentment. Others argued for conciliation and the preservation of states' rights, which antagonized northerners, who had just won a war predicated on the federalization of the government. Bruce Levine writes that many White southerners, "hope[d] that even if slavery were abolished, white landowners would be permitted through state and

local laws to impose tight controls over the lives and labors of the freed-
people." This hope was realized through systematic implementation of
state and local laws known as Black Codes. To ensure compliance with
the codes, hate groups such as the Ku Klux Klan emerged to terrorize
Blacks into submitting to White supremacist imperatives. Historian
W. E. B. Du Bois explains:

> [An] understanding between the planters and poor whites . . .
> was accompanied by deference to [the planters'] social status,
> by eagerness . . . of the poor whites to check the demands of the
> Negroes by any means, and by willingness to do the dirty work
> of the revolution . . . with its blood and crass cruelties, its bitter
> words, upheaval and turmoil. This was the birth and being of
> the Ku Klux Klan.[32]

The most contentious postwar issues involved the distribution of
southern land previously dominated by large-scale planters and the
destiny of thousands of newly freed, homeless, jobless, and primarily
illiterate Blacks. Eric Foner contends that in the postwar South, as in
other nineteenth-century societies that abolished policies of enslavement, access to land and the establishment of a new, disciplined labor
system were dominant concerns. Many Blacks who had been enslaved
had previously farmed for plantation owners, and they now strove to
obtain small parcels of farmland they could cultivate for self-sufficiency
and autonomy. Within a few years, for example, freedmen were culti-
vating former plantation land throughout Virginia, including Robert
E. Lee's property in Arlington, a mere eight miles from Alexandria.
Foner further argues that the legacy of enslavement, social and economic
changes, and Reconstruction's ultimate failure made the South the
country's most problematic economy well into the twentieth century.[33]

Far less controversial was the Bureau of Refugees, Freedmen, and
Abandoned Lands, better known as the Freedmen's Bureau. The bureau
was a program of the American Freedmen's Inquiry Commission, created
by the War Department and officially established by congressional vote
in 1865. Its mission was to assist emancipated Blacks, destitute Whites,

and Black veterans with food, shelter, and medical assistance. The bureau also provided freedmen and women with educational opportunities and helped them with labor and legal matters, such as employment contracts. The bureau founded more than 3,000 schools serving more than 150,000 students and offered financial assistance so that Black students could attend colleges and normal schools. Although most of the bureau's programs were discontinued after 1869, aid for education continued until 1870 and for Black veterans until 1872. Independently, freedmen and women contributed to communal self-sufficiency by creating a variety of fraternal and sororal, benevolent, and mutual aid societies.[34]

Alexandria's protracted recovery from the war was affected not only by Union occupation and withdrawal but also by the success of the ports in Baltimore and Richmond. Though its rivals drew commercial trade away from the city, Alexandria's port area remained active, and its expanding rail systems eventually made it the rail gateway to the South. The Alexandria Canal was reopened in 1867 and operated, with diminishing traffic, until 1886. The 1880s also brought electricity and telephone service throughout the city. Recovery slowed the economic panics of 1893 and 1907. Yet at the cusp of the twentieth century, Alexandria's railways continued to spur growth, employment, and development, drawing more people to the region and stimulating the emergence of suburban neighborhoods beginning in the 1890s. The Washington, Alexandria, and Mount Vernon Electric Railway installed streetcars in 1892, just four years after Frank Julian Sprague had introduced the technology in Richmond, and they, too, facilitated development of the city's outlying areas.[35] The success of Old Town breweries spurred economic growth and employment opportunities. In addition, Old Dominion glass works, Pioneer Mills, Thomas W. Smith's steam engine company, and James Green's furniture factory also brought new industries and employment opportunities to town.

Following the construction of the Potomac Yard Railroad in 1905, Alexandria continued to shift from a seaport economy to a dynamic hub for rail transport. During World War I, the shipbuilding and munitions industries created strong growth and jobs as did evolving economic ties with Washington, D.C. In the early 1930s, the Ford Motor Company built a plant on the Potomac River to service automobiles and distribute parts. The company's ten-year history in Alexandria reflects the ebb and flow of the city's economic and industrial fortunes.[36] While growth was good in some sectors, overall it was limited. Certain neighborhoods fell into disrepair, and until World War II Alexandria remained a moderate-sized city.

The Great Depression had an enormous impact on Black and White communities both nationally and locally. Reductions in producer and consumer durable goods affected the operation and expansion of railway lines and canals, and many Alexandrians lost their jobs. Blacks, however, were more profoundly affected than Whites, thanks to the hierarchical nature of White-Black relations in the South. New Deal programs enacted in 1933–36 drew thousands of new federal employees to the Capital region, many of them Black, though overall these programs benefited Whites far more than Blacks. Still, Alexandria was an affordable residential option for many of these new employees, and its population steadily increased. By the end of the 1930s, 5,281 of the city's 33,523 citizens (almost 16 percent) were Black, 28,219 (slightly more than 84 percent) were White, and 23 individuals (0.07 percent) were listed as "other races."[37] Despite these demographic changes, social changes occurred slowly. Since 1890, the repressive Jim Crow laws that had succeeded the Black Codes continued to control Black lives.[38] Yet a few Black citizens implemented social initiatives and spoke up for their civil rights.[39] In the microenvironment of 1930s-era Alexandria, limited areas of the city were integrated, and Black and White citizens comingled in those neighborhoods. For the most part, however, prevailing social mores and de jure policies upheld the South's institutionalized racism. Most of Alexandria's residents adhered unequivocally to the strict, behavioral norms of Jim Crow's White supremacist politics and practices, which reinforced the separation of the races in housing, transportation, and public facilities and services. Acknowledged by all, endorsed by Whites, and resented by Blacks, this race-based public management was the city's daily environment when Samuel Tucker conceived and implemented the 1939 sit-in demonstration for African American access to the Whites-only public library.

# CHAPTER FOUR

# History as Context

## *The Era of Jim Crow*

The term *Jim Crow* derives from a song and dance with origins in Africa and later performed by enslaved Blacks in America. In the early nineteenth century, the White performer Thomas Dartmouth "Daddy" Rice appropriated the term, using it as the name of an antebellum-era character in his minstrel shows. Rice even billed himself as the "Original Jim Crow" to distinguish himself from other White minstrels.[1] Historian Leon F. Litwack writes that by the 1890s, the term *Jim Crow* as used by Whites gradually moved out of its minstrel context and came to connote the codified subordination and oppression of southern Blacks.

With the end of Radical Reconstruction in 1877, southern legislatures, dominated by White Democrats, began to gradually enact repressive state and local Jim Crow laws and reinforce racially discriminatory customs. Many of these laws and customs were offshoots of the Black Codes implemented in 1865–66 to control African Americans after the Civil War. Their objective was to impose a system of inequitable and discriminatory treatment of Blacks while reinforcing and perpetuating White supremacy.

In the 1870s, as Confederate veterans seized local political power, the southern wing of the Democratic party, known as Redeemers, gained seats in Congress and began to implement their political, economic, and racially discriminatory policies. During this same period, northerners began to acquiesce to southern racial mores. By the late 1880s, conditions for Blacks had badly deteriorated. Lynchings and anti-Black rhetoric flourished, and a White coalition of Black Belt planters, which included elite city dwellers and agrarian radicals, began to disenfranchise Blacks and segregate virtually every aspect of their lives. This disempowerment was forcefully implemented because these Whites believed that segregation was the only way to prevent "social equality," by which they meant both integration and miscegenation. At this time, however, Blacks still possessed the rights associated with the Thirteenth, Fourteenth, and Fifteenth amendments as well as those related to the Civil Rights Act of 1875, which prohibited discrimination in trains, hotels, and other public spaces. For them, it was a period of great optimism, and they looked forward to the future and a better life than most Blacks had ever known. For the first time, they shared the rights and privileges that Whites had always possessed but they had always been denied: freedom, citizenship, equal rights under the law, and, for Black men, enfranchisement.

However, in 1883, the Supreme Court overturned the Civil Rights Act of 1875, ruling it unconstitutional because it had not been authorized by the Fourteenth Amendment. Then, in the late 1890s, a confluence of forces strengthened the reemergence of White supremacy. Central to the rise of Jim Crow was the U.S. Supreme Court's 1896 decision in *Plessy v. Ferguson* that separate-but-equal accommodations on Louisiana's railroad cars were constitutional. Legislation was passed throughout the country, but especially in the South, to mandate racial discrimination and racial segregation or, in some instances, total exclusion of Blacks in housing (which typically was de facto segregated or segregated by personal preference); employment; schools and libraries; medical and mental-health facilities; institutions for the visually, hearing, and language impaired; restrooms; drinking fountains; restaurants and bars; hotels; public conveyances; theaters and other places of entertainment; recreational facilities; poorhouses; the military; cemeteries; prisons; churches; jails; and phone booths. In Atlanta, courtrooms reserved separate Bibles for Whites and Blacks. Labor rights were eliminated, and crackdowns on "vagrancy" and numerous minor offenses resulted in harsh penalties that disproportionately affected Blacks.[2]

Jim Crow legislation focused on completely disenfranchising and, by extension, disempowering Blacks. Literacy tests, poll taxes, administrative loopholes, and trick questions—such as guessing how many bubbles were in a bar of soap or how many jelly beans were in a jar—were imposed as ways to impede Blacks from registering to vote or casting votes. As justification for their actions, Whites invoked "the mythology of Reconstruction," arguing that carpetbaggers from the North and scalawags from the South had unduly influenced unsophisticated Black voters. So-called scientific theories such as eugenics lent credence to the myth of African American inferiority. Racism was further perpetuated with biased and sensational news coverage and popular-culture stereotypes about Blacks, which spurred White violence, lynchings, and riots and incited domestic terror groups such as the Ku Klux Klan. Brutal lynchings became a form of mass entertainment, especially for rural southern Whites, and they often involved the mutilation or burning of Black bodies or the riddling of victims' bodies with bullets. In 1899, the *Washington Post* reported on the near lynching of William Dodson, a Black man from Alexandria: "Nearly two hundred persons went across the Aqueduct Bridge from Washington, some on wheels, others in carriages, and many afoot, all curious ones, who wanted to see the fun."[3] Though Dodson survived the ordeal, lynchings did occur in Alexandria in 1897 and 1899, and White mobs in Virginia killed two Black men in 1917 and another in 1918.

The Commonwealth's new constitution of 1902 mandated political disenfranchisement of Blacks and poor Whites, codified segregation, and officially ushered in the era of Jim Crow. By 1910, Black voting rights were fully eradicated in the southern states, and segregation in public spaces was strictly enforced.[4] In 1902, Virginia passed an ordinance requiring the segregation of streetcars in specific localities, including City of Alexandria and Fairfax County; and in 1904, Virginia authorized, but did not mandate, streetcar segregation in every city. In 1906, Virginia passed a statewide statute that required segregated Jim Crow streetcars in every municipality in the Commonwealth. Blacks responded by implementing streetcar boycotts in Richmond in 1904–5. In 1906, there were streetcar boycotts in Danville, Lynchburg, Portsmouth, Norfolk, and Newport News. The response to an article in the April 17, 1904, issue of the *Richmond Times-Dispatch* announcing the Virginia Passenger and Power Company's plans to segregate the races on city streetcars was swift and decisive. Blacks' boycott of the transit line began on April 19, and front-page coverage appeared in the *Richmond Planet*, the *Richmond Times-Dispatch*, and the *Richmond News Leader*.[5]

The era of Jim Crow was marked by strict, interpersonal racial etiquette as well as legislated racial discrimination. Blacks of all ages were expected to be deferential to Whites in all daily matters; and social transgressions such as failing to address Whites as "sir" or "ma'am" or speaking up for civil and human rights could result in punishments as harsh as lynching. Personal slights, humiliation, dehumanization, subjugation, and disrespect were a way of life for Black Americans, an illustration of the strategic public dynamics at work between the powerful and the powerless. Blacks were expected to move off the sidewalk into the street whenever they encountered a White person. Whites called Black women and men "girl" or "boy" regardless of their age. African Americans were expected to relinquish their seats on public conveyances when Whites told them to do so, even when those instructions were arbitrary or capricious. Black customers in stores had to wait to be served—if they were served at all—until all of the White customers had been served, even if they had arrived after the African Americans did or were in the store simply to chat. As a physical display of their power and authority, Whites might intentionally drop items to force Blacks to bend down subserviently to retrieve and return them. Many homeowners would refuse to sell or rent property to Blacks or would knowingly and purposefully sell or rent them only dilapidated properties, which they would not repair.

Yet hegemonic imperatives of Black oppression were neither ignored nor unopposed by African Americans. Just as the enslaved employed what James C. Scott terms the "hidden transcripts" of subtle resistance to domination in the antebellum South, Robin D. G. Kelley writes that urban Blacks during the era of Jim Crow employed "seemingly innocuous, individualistic acts of survival and opposition [that] shaped southern urban politics, workplace struggles, and the social order generally." Such acts illustrate the ways in which the oppressed may publicly appear to be acquiescent when they are, in fact, undermining the authority of their dominators. Scott reminds us not to assume that all hidden transcripts are true and spoken in freedom any more than all public transcripts are false and issued out of necessity. Rather, he advises assessment of the discrepancies between hidden and public transcripts to gauge "the impact of domination on public discourse."[6]

Overall, however, White attempts to undermine Reconstruction were predicated on the need to demonstrate Black inferiority in order to justify their own claims of superiority. As Leon F. Litwack writes,

> The language whites employed to describe Reconstruction, the methods used to subvert the Radical governments and black voting, and the determination to indoctrinate future generations with the idea of Reconstruction as a "tragic era," betrayed white fears that this experiment might actually succeed in restructuring the South and racial relationships. Whites employed terror, intimidation, and violence to doom Reconstruction, not because blacks had demonstrated incompetence but because they were rapidly learning the uses of political power, not because of evidence of black failure but the far more alarming evidence of black success. This was clearly unacceptable to a people who deemed themselves racially superior and who resisted any evidence to the contrary.[7]

Blacks exercised their own agency in their responses to institutionalized segregation, economic exploitation, disenfranchisement, and escalating racial tensions. Some emigrated to Africa, as urged by Henry M. Turner of Georgia, a bishop of the Black African Methodist Episcopal Church. Others separated themselves from White communities. As early as 1879, Benjamin "Pap" Singleton, a Black realtor from Nashville, had espoused the idea of internal colonization as a reflection of Black pride and nationalism. In response to this notion, all-Black communities were established in Kansas, Oklahoma, Mississippi, and elsewhere, though their reliance on White county governments for public services limited their autonomy. Other Blacks were determined to stay where they were and fight to change the system of their oppression. The Knights of Labor and the National Negro Congress recruited tens of thousands of Blacks, and many more became active in the Populist movement, and a number became committed activists, joining or founding local chapters of national organizations such as the NAACP. Most, however, joined the Great Migration, as waves of southern rural Blacks moved to northern industrial cities such as New York, Chicago, Detroit, and Philadelphia. Though their wages were low and their living conditions often abysmal, the move allowed them to escape the South's de jure segregation, terror, and violence. There was less discrimination in the North, Blacks could vote, and they had better employment opportunities. Between 1916 and 1940, about 1.5 million Black people left the South for northern urban centers. A second wave, between 1940 and 1970, drew about 5 million southern Blacks, many of them skilled workers, into northern and western industrial cities. Nicholas Lemann writes, "The black migration from the South was one of the largest and most rapid mass internal movements of people in history—perhaps *the* greatest not caused by the immediate threat of execution or starvation. In sheer numbers it outranks the migration of any other ethnic group—Italians or Irish or Jews or Poles—to this country."[8]

In 1944, Gunnar Myrdal published his two-volume study, *An American Dilemma: The Negro Problem and Modern Democracy*, with the support of the Carnegie Foundation. Myrdal's findings generated deep national and international embarrassment; and by the late 1940s, Jim Crow was beginning to crumble. In 1950, a pair of landmark legal decisions—*Sweatt v. Painter* and *McLaurin v. Oklahoma*, both spearheaded by the NAACP—marked the end of the separate-but-equal doctrine in graduate and professional education. The association's lawyers laid a path for the 1954 Supreme Court ruling in *Brown v. Board of Education*, which overturned *Plessy v. Ferguson* and outlawed the concept of separate but equal. Many White southerners, however, openly defied the rulings. Senator Harry F. Byrd, Sr., the leader of Virginia's political machine, promulgated what he called the Southern Manifesto, which was signed by more than a hundred southern politicians. In 1956, responding to the passage of *Brown v. Board of Education*, Byrd called for "Massive Resistance" in Virginia laws and policies opposing public school desegregation. Enacted in 1958, they withheld state funding from any school that desegregated. Many Virginia schools opted to close rather than accept federally mandated desegregation, and White students shifted into private schools supported by state and county tuition grants and tax credits. The state made no arrangements to educate Virginia's Black students, so many received instruction in makeshift classrooms or churches or were taught in schools operated by the Society of Friends and other socially conscious organizations. Some Black students lost as many as five years of formal education. In January 1959, when the Commonwealth's school-closing law was ruled unconstitutional, the general assembly repealed Virginia's compulsory school attendance law and made the operation of public schools a local option for counties and cities. Schools in a few Virginia communities chose to desegregate rather than remain closed; but in May 1959, Prince Edward County closed its entire school system rather than desegregate. Most Virginia schools remained segregated into the 1960s. Only after years of civil rights marches, demonstrations, sit-ins, embarrassing national and international news coverage, and the passage of the Civil Rights Act of 1964, the Voting Rights Act of 1965, and the Fair Housing Act of 1968 was Jim Crow officially defeated, though vestiges of resistance remained.[9]

Alexandria's public schools began the process of desegregation in February 1959, when U.S. District Judge Albert Bryan ordered the city's school board to admit nine Black students to three all-White schools. The process of desegregation was not completed until 1965, when John Albohm, the school system's new superintendent, closed Parker-Gray High School just as T. C. Williams High School was open-ing. In 1971, he transferred all students from the city's two predomi-nately White high schools, Hammond and George Washington, to T. C. Williams, which then became Alexandria's only public high school.[10]

For Blacks, the era of Jim Crow was rife with disappointment, disillusionment, and frustration, yet its miseries were tempered by the wonders of Black success. Both individuals and groups displayed remarkable endurance and resilience in the face of daily debasement and dehumanization and achieved numerous small victories over Jim Crow and the White status quo. Blacks created families, nurtured their aspirations, built communities and businesses, attended schools and churches, and established organizations for practical and social support. The twentieth-century's first generation of Blacks was, on the whole, less willing than the older generations to accept paternalism and accom-modation and more willing to agitate for change. Though they did not achieve all of their objectives, they paved the way for future generations to force change, particularly through legal means.

During Jim Crow, Alexandria's Black residents dealt with discrimination in nearly every facet of their public lives. In addition to segregated schools, churches, restrooms, water fountains, public accommodations, and seating on public transit, there were segregated lunchrooms, hairdressers, barbershops, and funeral homes as well as Black grocers and a Black bakery. John Wesley Jackson, the bakery's proprietor, also opened his home to Black travelers, because there were no other available Black lodgings in the city. Thinking back to that era, Lillian S. Patterson recalled, "Blacks could shop in large White clothing stores such as Montgomery Ward, J. C. Penney, and Lerner Clothing Store, as well as other small stores, but Whites were always served first." She continued: "Blacks were employed in White stores, but their jobs were restricted to the back of the store and in the kitchen. They only worked out front if they were cleaning."[11]

Lovell A. Lee remarked:

> Alexandria was a typical, segregated southern town, and for the most part Blacks lived in pockets of the city. As Blacks would move into predominantly White neighborhoods, Whites would move out, though some stayed. I remember when they were recently debating a name change to T. C. Williams High School because of the school's namesake's segregationist attitudes. [But] T. C. Williams wasn't a segregationist. He was a racist. Segregationist is too generous a term to use for him. White schools always received new books. We were always given the well-used books from the White schools. Only about 10 percent of the books we received were new. When the George Washington High School was opened in 1935, there was a large auditorium, a huge athletic field with stands, and a separate building for shop classes. When the [new] Parker-Gray High School was built for Blacks in 1950, it had none of those things. Black students had to take a truck ride to access the athletic fields at Potomac Yards. Alexandria's superintendent of schools always attended George Washington graduations. He never attended Parker-Gray graduations. Instead, he always sent

a representative. I remember sitting in the Jim Crow seats at the rear of the bus behind the back door, though Whites sometimes occupied those seats, thereby depriving African Americans of their only seating options. I also remember ordering food at the end of the counter at soda fountains and going to the back door to order food from White restaurants. We had to place our orders, then leave the premises, because Blacks could not consume food with Whites. When you shopped for clothes, you couldn't try them on "because you might contaminate them." You had to hold them up, measure them against your body, and hope they fit. But in spite of segregation, my grandfather owned a barbershop from 1900 to 1908 in the 200 block of King Street and he cut hair for Whites as well as Blacks.

Shirley M. Lee recalled that Black and White adults "got along" whereas children "played together like brothers and sisters." Lovell A. Lee remembered playing with White children of his age but said that White and Black adults adapted to segregation by "staying in their own lane."[12]

Restrictions on voting, housing, jobs, and education were implemented to control the lives and activities of Blacks. Asked about restrictions on Black voting in Alexandria, Lillian Patterson did not remember her parents having problems voting but said they did have to pay a poll tax: "However, I remember on one occasion during my youth when I went with my grandmother to vote, the poll worker looked at my grandmother's ballot, which he wasn't supposed to do." She added, "When I turned twenty-one and registered to vote, I didn't have to pay a poll tax. . . . I don't know if my parents had to own property to register to vote or to cast a ballot, but when I registered to vote I didn't own any property and I had no problems registering or voting." Lovell Lee said, "I had to pay a poll tax of $1, but otherwise I had no problems registering or voting. I was eager to vote and registered as soon as I was old enough." He also strongly encouraged his wife to register to vote.[13]

Like other places in the South, Alexandria was residentially segregated, and the Federal Housing Administration was complicit in enforcing such policies around the nation. In Alexandria, Blacks were routinely blocked from obtaining home mortgages, which forced them to live in segregated housing, to rent inferior White-owned properties, or to relocate to Washington, D.C., where housing was more readily available. In her study of Black housing in Alexandria between the 1930s and the 1960s, Krystyn R. Moon reports an incident involving the Reverend Dr. John C. Davis and his wife, who had $30,000 to purchase a home but were refused housing in in Alexandria simply because they were Black. Shirley Lee told me that, after her marriage in 1958, she and her husband were forced to move to Washington, D.C., where they lived from 1960 to 1965 "because we couldn't find housing in Alexandria." Restrictive covenants against Blacks, in place by the early 1900s, disregarded the equal-access dictates of the Fourteenth Amendment until 1948, when the Supreme Court ruled them unconstitutional in *Shelley v. Kraemer*.

To acquire land for industrial construction, Alexandria implemented eminent domain in Black neighborhoods. This overlapping of industrial properties and Black neighborhoods conflicted with city mandates, which prohibited the construction of industrial facilities within a half mile of residential neighborhoods. In 1939, Alexandria began building public housing, but severe inequities continued until passage of the Civil Rights Act of 1964, the Voluntary Open Housing Ordinance of 1967, and the Fair Housing Act of 1968. Even today, residents of Black neighborhoods in the city often experience displacement as city housing is demolished and expensive condominiums are constructed.[14]

Black children and adults had fewer social and recreational options than Whites did, but they made the most of their available choices. Denied access to Alexandria's Whites-only municipal swimming pool, they swam in the Potomac River until 1951, when the brothers Morris Leroy Johnson, age eleven, and Lonnie Richard Johnson, age nine, drowned while swimming. In 1952, in response to those tragic accidents and to the deaths of other youths who similarly drowned, the city built the segregated Johnson Pool, where Shirley Lee worked as a lifeguard and a swimming instructor. When I asked her what she did for fun during her youth, she said, "My friends and I played jacks, board games, cards, and hopscotch. I also enjoyed playing with dolls and going to the movies. . . . I went to Washington, D.C., to learn how to swim because I enjoyed the water. . . . I also went to Fort Belvoir [an Army base in Fairfax, Virginia, about eight miles from Alexandria] to swim in their pool because it was integrated." In addition, two Black elementary schools—Parker-Gray and Lyles-Crouch—had playgrounds.

Adults also had entertainment options. The Elks Home (now known as Elks Lodge Alexandria 48), a Black social club modeled after the Whites-only Benevolent and Protective Order of Elks, hosted nationally known performers. The Daughters of Zion, a Black sororal benevolent association, and two Black fraternal service organizations—Odd Fellows Hall and Rising Star—also offered entertainment for Black adults. Other African American fraternal and sororal associations provided mutual aid, neighborhood social support, and racial consciousness and uplift. The Departmental Progressive Club was organized in 1927 by seven African American men, all federal employees, to provide "wholesome recreation" for the Black community. Alexandria's seven Black churches were primary outlets not only for the practice of faith but also for social engagement, racial pride, community identity, and leadership opportunities. Some churches sponsored literacy classes for children and adults, book clubs, social activities, and outreach programs. The local Black YMCA, founded during Reconstruction by George Lewis Seaton, a free Black man, master carpenter, builder, and state legislator, offered social engagement and racial uplift in a sectarian environment. At Jimmy Webster's Home and Store, African American Alexandrians could periodically gather, drink beer, and dance to jukebox music.

As early as 1908, movie theaters attracted children and adults in Alexandria. In Old Town, White Alexandrians had access to the Metropolitan Moving Picture Company and the Alexandria Amusement Company. If Black Alexandrians had access to these venues, they were undoubtedly relegated to inferior, segregated sections. The Capitol Theater, built in the 1930s specifically for Black Alexandrians, operated from the 1930s until 1948. After it closed, Blacks were limited to watching films at the segregated Carver Movie Theater.[15]

Employment opportunities in Alexandria were also segregated, and African American men, whether skilled or unskilled, were frequently offered only the most difficult, undesirable, and dangerous jobs. Many worked at the Bryant Fertilizer Plant, on the wharfs, at the Old Dominion Glass Factory, and for the railway companies. Some worked at a bakery operated by the federal government. Black men held jobs as carpenters, bricklayers, coopers, masons, joiners, blacksmiths, and laborers. Professional offices and commercial establishments offered Blacks jobs as clerks and messengers. Black women were employed as teachers in African American schools and as domestic servants and service workers. Some Black Alexandrians traveled to Washington, D.C., to work on federal construction projects, in civil service jobs, for government contractors, or in small businesses. Many worked in enterprises owned and operated by Blacks, in both Alexandria and the District of Columbia.[16]

Black residents of Alexandria took advantage of their proximity to Washington, D.C. The capital was home to one of the wealthiest Black communities in the country, Howard University was the nation's most prestigious Black college, and the Washington bureau of the NAACP offered legal-defense options in local Blacks' fight for civil equality. Taking advantage of the easy commute from Alexandria, both students and adults traveled into Washington for jobs, education, libraries, culture, entertainment, and social outlets. They also read the African American newspapers and magazines that were published and sold in the District, preferring them over their hometown newspaper, the *Alexandria Gazette*, whose coverage privileged the racial, social, political, economic, and legal status quo.[17]

In the early twentieth century, most Alexandrians traveled into Washington, D.C., using the growing network of electric railcars. Alexandria's electric railway system offered particular benefits to the residents of Del Ray, a thriving commuter community located outside the city limits until 1930, when it was annexed to Alexandria.[18] On the evening of June 13, 1902, Mary Custis Lee, a daughter of Confederate General Robert E. Lee and Mary Anna Custis Lee, was arrested for sitting in the segregated Jim Crow section of a Washington, Alexandria, and Mount Vernon Electric Railway car. She had boarded the conveyance in Washington, heading for Alexandria with her Black maid; apparently, the two women regularly traveled in this fashion.

Newspaper accounts reported that Lee was laden with baggage and simply wanted to sit close to the exit. Though the conductor repeatedly asked her to move to the White section of the streetcar, which had plenty of available seating, she refused. When asked to relinquish her seat in the Black section for an African American passenger, she refused again, even though the Black section of the car was now standing room only, and Lee was occupying a seat that could have been used by a Black traveler.

When Lee finally disembarked in Alexandria, two police officers arrested her. Given her prominent social status and her father's renown, they released her on condition that she appear for a court hearing the following day. When she failed to appear, George R. Simpson, the mayor of Alexandria, who was officiating at the city's police court, continued without her. She had claimed ignorance of the 1902 city ordinance mandating railway car segregation, though all of the cars had clearly posted placards announcing the new law and the conductor had repeatedly informed her about it. The police and the conductor testified against her, and Lee was found guilty and fined the minimum penalty—forfeiture of her $5 bond. Historians differ in whether or not they believe Lee's claim of ignorance. Scott E. Casper contends that she knowingly violated the segregation ordinance, while her biographer, Mary P. Coulling, maintains that she rode in the car's Black section purely as a convenience. "But in spite of her action, [Lee] was no reformer and like her parents regarded blacks as inherently inferior. Rather, her response appears to have been a purely personal reaction to an irritating regulation that interfered with her traditional travel arrangements." Soon after the incident, the *Colored American* reported, "We understand that [Lee], by reason of her culture and aristocratic antecedents, is liberal upon matters relating to the rights of man and has no patience with . . . petty racial animosities."[19]


As previously mentioned, two documented lynchings took place in Alexandria during the Jim Crow era. In the early morning hours of April 23, 1897, Joseph H. McCoy, a nineteen-year-old Black Alexandrian teenager, was lynched from a lamppost at the corner of Cameron and Lee streets in Old Town. He had been accused of sexually assaulting his White employer's daughters. Such accusations were often lodged against Black males to justify lynchings and perpetuate White domination and racial terror. Initially, McCoy denied the charge, but he later confessed, possibly under coercion. He was arrested without a warrant and denied the right to a fair trial. White mobs made two attempts to remove him from the police station where he was being held. The first attempt was unsuccessful; but during the second, police officers were overpowered by the mob, and McCoy was forcibly taken from his cell, lynched, shot multiple times, and bludgeoned with an ax. The coroner's jury determined that he had died by "strangulation at the hands of parties unknown." No Whites were ever held responsible for McCoy's murder, but in the wake of his death rumors of Black retaliation led to the arrest of several African American men. McCoy was interred at Alexandria's Penny Hill Cemetery, the burial site for indigents. William Gaines, the pastor of Roberts Chapel (now known as Roberts Memorial United Methodist Church), officiated at the funeral service. On April 23, 1897, the *Washington Post* reported that "several colored people" attended the funeral.[20]

On August 8, 1899, Benjamin Thomas, a sixteen-year-old Black Alexandrian, was lynched from a lamppost at the corner of South Fairfax Street near King Street in Old Town. He had been accused of attempting to sexually assault Lillian Kloch, an eight-year-old White girl, though the child, who was the only witness, repeatedly gave conflicting testimony about the purported crime. Thomas was jailed and was not allowed to testify in his own defense. A mob overpowered the jail guards, retrieved the keys to his cell, bound his neck and arms with rope, and dragged him half a mile through Old Town, initially on his back and then face down on the cobblestone streets. His body was brutalized, and he was shot two hundred times by members of the mob. The coroner's jury determined that he had died from a gunshot wound to the heart. Although no members of the White mob were ever held responsible for Thomas's extralegal murder, the Black male community leaders who had advocated for his protection were arrested. Between 500 and 2,000 people were participants in or observers of this racial-terror crime. Benjamin Thomas was buried at Penny Hill Cemetery without the benefit of a church funeral. Later, a memorial service was held for him at Shiloh Baptist Church.[21]

At least four other Black men were threatened with lynching while jailed in Alexandria: William Dodson on July 14, 1899, just three weeks before Thomas's lynching; Edward Jenkins on May 12, 1904; Robert Proctor on October 28, 1904; and William Turner in May 1920. During Turner's incarceration, there were reports of a threatened race riot by Blacks from Washington, D.C. However, the executive council of the Interracial Congress called those rumors "pernicious, false and misleading."[22]

Between 1880 and 1930, close to seventy Blacks were lynched by White mobs in Virginia. In the 1920s, when states in the lower South were experiencing decreases in mob violence, Virginia was experiencing increases. In response, Louis Isaac Jaffé, the editor of the *Norfolk Virginian-Pilot*, a White newspaper, published a series of excoriating editorials condemning the racial-terror violence. Thanks largely to Jaffé's efforts, Virginia's governor, Harry F. Byrd, Sr., signed legislation on March 14, 1928, that recognized lynching as a state crime. Although this was the nation's first and strictest antilynching statute, no White perpetrator was ever convicted of the racial-terror lynching of a Black citizen under the law. Rather, the law was used to penalize White men for committing crimes against other Whites.[23]

In the 1920s and 1930s, racially segregated resorts were established on Alexandria's Potomac River shoreline. Restrictive covenants excluded Blacks from some neighborhoods in Alexandria and from the Whites-only town of Potomac, which was annexed to Alexandria in 1930. Then, in 1935, the city built the Whites-only George Washington High School in the Del Ray neighborhood. All of these acts exemplify the continuing environmental, social, temporal, and spatial segregation in Alexandria in the years before the library sit-in. They also explain why events and circumstances concerning the desegregation of the city's library system moved so slowly.

# CHAPTER FIVE

# Prelude to the Sit-In, Part Two

## The Genesis of the Alexandria Library

America's earliest subscription-based libraries (often referred to as *pro-prietary, social, parochial, circulating,* or even *public* libraries) opened in the 1740s and became increasingly popular between 1790 and 1850. Interest in the idea began as early as 1731, and the first library, the Philadelphia Library Company, was incorporated in 1742. Though they were city institutions, these operations were not subsidized by public taxation and were never intended to serve the public broadly. Instead, library partic-ipation was limited to individuals—primarily men—who shared similar racial and ethnic backgrounds, social standing, and financial means.[1]

Those limited parameters were expanded in 1835, when New York State enacted a law requiring free, tax-supported library services in school-district facilities. Although they were located in schools, these libraries were supposed to be available to the general public. Some were referred to as "public libraries," though they did not correspond with the contemporary concept of a public library.[2] In 1837, Massachusetts and Michigan enacted similar laws; and by 1873, nineteen states, includ-ing Virginia (in 1870), had school-district library provisions (see table 3).[3] However, these school-district libraries also had their limitations. According to a U.S. Bureau of Education assessment, the districts were "too small; . . . the amount of money annually raised in each district was insufficient; [and] the number of volumes in each was too small to secure anything like public interest in the care, preservation, or circulation of the books."[4] Though school-district libraries did not succeed in their mission to provide the public with free access to libraries, their creation and operation established three basic principles for the future founding of true public libraries: free library service subsidized with taxation, state aid to libraries, and acknowledgment of libraries as educational entities.[5]

**TABLE 3. ENACTMENT OF SCHOOL DISTRICT LIBRARY LAWS, BY STATE AND YEAR**

| | | | | | | | |
|---|---|---|---|---|---|---|---|
| New York | 1835 | | Maine | 1844 | | California | 1866 |
| Massachusetts | 1837 | | Ohio | 1847 | | Kansas | 1870 |
| Michigan | 1837 | | Wisconsin | 1848 | | Virginia | 1870 |
| Connecticut | 1839 | | Missouri | 1853 | | New Jersey | 1871 |
| Rhode Island | 1840 | | Oregon | 1854** | | Kentucky | 1873 |
| Iowa | 1840 | | Illinois | 1855 | | Minnesota | 1873 |
| Indiana | 1841 | | Pennsylvania | 1864 | | Colorado | 1876 |

*Source:* U.S. Department of the Interior, Bureau of Education, *Public Libraries in the United States of America: Their History, Condition, and Management* (Washington, DC: Government Printing Office, 1876), 38–57; U.S. Bureau of Education, *Statistics of Libraries and Library Legislation in the United States* (Washington, DC: Government Printing Office, 1897), 524.

** In Oregon, the school law of 1854 provided for the appointment of a school librarian. The state constitution of 1857 provided for the purchase of school libraries and supplies. The general school law of 1870 provided for the provision of school libraries.

Several political, economic, social, and intellectual factors contributed to the emergence of tax-subsidized public libraries. One was a belief in individual and community progress based on the right to knowledge and humans' unlimited potential for rational thought and self-improvement. Another was an increase in opportunities for free public education, including the adult education provided by lyceums and subscription libraries, which later propelled the momentum for public library creation. Other factors included advancements in science and technology, which mandated continuing education; evolutions in American literature and publishing; the demand for an enlightened citizenry; a perceived need for moral grounding to offset the mounting problems of urbanization; and growing national prosperity, which increased individuals' discretionary time and financial resources.[6]

A facility established in Peterborough, New Hampshire, in 1833 is regarded as "one of the first, if not the first," municipally supported, free public libraries.[7] In 1848, Massachusetts became the first state to enact a law that enabled Boston to establish and maintain a library with tax revenue. In 1851, that act was broadened to apply the state provisions for library subsidies to all of the communities in the state. The genesis of the free public library movement began with the implementation of similar laws in twenty-eight other states and the District of Columbia between 1848 and 1896. Of those states, only two—Texas (in 1874) and Mississippi (in 1892)—were in the South (see tab. 4). Virginia did not enact state provisions for public library services until 1942. Mary Edna Anders writes that more than 70 percent of southeastern public libraries were established after 1919. In 1946, the *Richmond Times-Dispatch* published a feature article noting that Virginia lagged in the development of public libraries and that bookmobiles were the only library access for many rural citizens.[8]

**TABLE 4. ENACTMENT OF ENABLING LAWS FOR PUBLIC LIBRARIES, BY STATE AND YEAR**

| | | | | | | | |
|---|---|---|---|---|---|---|---|
| Massachusetts | 1848† | | Texas | 1874 | | Kansas | 1886 |
| | 1851‡ | | Connecticut | 1875 | | Wyoming | 1886 |
| New Hampshire | 1849 | | Rhode Island | 1875 | | North Dakota | 1887 |
| Maine | 1854 | | Michigan | 1876 | | Pennsylvania | 1887 |
| Vermont | 1865 | | Nebraska | 1877 | | South Dakota | 1887 |
| Ohio | 1867 | | California | 1879 | | Washington | 1890 |
| Colorado | 1872 | | Minnesota | 1879 | | Mississippi | 1892 |
| Illinois | 1872 | | New Jersey | 1879 | | Utah | 1896 |
| Wisconsin | 1872 | | | | | | |
| New York | 1872 | | Montana | 1883 | | District of Columbia | 1896 |
| Indiana | 1873 | | New Mexico | 1884 | | | |
| Iowa | 1873 | | Missouri | 1885 | | | |

Source: U.S. Bureau of Education, *Statistics of Libraries and Library Legislation in the United States* (Washington, DC: Government Printing Office, 1897), 524–26.

†Boston only

‡All cities and towns in Massachusetts

The Library Company of Alexandria, founded on July 24, 1794, at John Wise's home, began as the successor to the short-lived Society for the Promotion of Useful Knowledge, an organization started in 1789 as a social club for prominent White Alexandrian men, where they could share their interests in literature and science and engage in critical thinking and oratory. Although the majority of the Library Company's 119 original members were merchants, the august body also included ministers, doctors, and other professionals. Initial members included, among others, the Reverend John Muir, Dr. Elisha Cullen Dick, John Wise—whose Lloyd House residence later served as a home for the library—Charles Lee, Samuel Craig, and Edward Stabler, proprietor of the Stabler Apothecary. A few women used their husbands' member-ships to borrow books, and gradually a few others purchased member-ships of their own. They included Eliza Summers, Eleanor Davis, and Mary Lee Fitzhugh Custis, who joined the Library Company in 1798, 1801, and 1817. The Library Company of Alexandria was chartered by Virginia's general assembly on January 9, 1799.[9]

The Library Company was referred to as a circulating library, and subscribers were required to pay an initiation fee and annual dues of $12. Nonsubscribers could "'hire a book [for] one shilling per week for a folio, nine pence for a quatro, and six pence for octavos and duodec-imos.'" Rural subscribers were permitted to borrow books for "double the time of town residents, except in the case of new publications."[10]

The library had nine directors as well as elected officers, who included a president, a treasurer, a secretary, and a librarian. The Rev-erend John Muir was elected as the first president, Samuel Craig the first treasurer, and Edward Stabler the first secretary and librarian. The first orator to speak at a Library Company meeting was Ludwell Lee, the president of Virginia's senate. Stabler's apothecary shop served as the library's first home. The first collection included titles approved by the directors. Most were purchased from the bookseller James Kennedy, who succeeded Stabler as librarian and gave the library its next home, but some were purchased from John Lockwood and John V. Thomas. To increase the collection's size, additional purchases were made, and book donations were accepted in lieu of the annual dues. The organization's first acquisition was probably *The American Encyclopedia*, which was presented to Dr. James Craik by General George Washington. The first library catalog, published in 1801, listed 452 books. The Library Company made a concerted effort to acquire rare books; and in 1822, Philip Miller's *The Gardener's Dictionary* became its first such acquisition. Over the years, the rare-books collection was expanded to include volumes on law, government, history, politics, geography, science, philosophy, religion, morals, biography, travel, and fiction. The library also circulated magazines, newspapers, and pamphlets, all of which were very popular. By 1856, the catalog listed 4,841 books.[11]

Over time, the library underwent significant changes. The first took place in 1818, when Kennedy, who had served as librarian for twenty-four years, resigned after being ordered to extend the library's limited hours of operation. He was succeeded by William G. Cranch, Jr., who was elected librarian and treasurer and tasked with increasing memberships, and the library moved its collections to the New Market House, adjacent to City Hall. Library members resolved to form a committee of books that would be responsible for future purchases. They agreed to expand history and science materials when funds permitted, and the treasurer was instructed to return all funds to the chairman after current expenses were paid. Members were invited to suggest titles for purchase consideration. William Seale remarks that space constraints required periodic purges of materials, but it is not clear who had the authority to make those decisions or to stipulate removal protocols.[12] The changes made indicate an increased concern for the needs and interests of users and for the fiscal responsibilities of the library's administration.

Further operational changes took place amid the Panic of 1819, when numerous businesses and financial institutions closed and many Alexandrians moved West. Although the city suffered financially, the Library Company continued to thrive, and plans were underway to construct a new building. To accommodate patrons' dwindling finances, annual dues were reduced from $12 to $3. Clearly, however, the library was seen as a municipal asset, and local newspaper coverage of its events and activities highlighted its importance in the community.[13]

In 1824, Benjamin Hallowell, a highly regarded Quaker educator and orator, established Alexandria Academy, a school for boys; and in 1827, his wife, Margaret, opened a school for girls at the same site. By 1830, a hundred coeducational students were enrolled in day and evening programs at the Alexandria Academy. While the Library Company's directors dreamed of a new home for their increasing collections, Hallowell dreamed of expanding his school's facilities with a library, reading room, lecture hall, and meeting space. Hallowell was also the founder, with other local civic leaders, of the Lyceum Company, and his school hosted its lectures. He envisioned a space that would be suitable for featuring presentations by local and nationally known luminaries and debates would address literary, scientific, and historical subjects. Thus, the prospect of a union between the Library Company and the Lyceum Company initially seemed to be mutually beneficial.[14]

After negotiating the complicated terms of a merger, the two institutions agreed to unite but to retain separate officers and boards of directors to maintain their independence. The Library Company began selling subscriptions at $25 per share to raise funds for the construction of the new Lyceum. The building was completed in 1839, and the new library reading room opened in October 1840, with memberships "available to all, upon application to the secretary."[15] Nonetheless, the application process, an annual membership fee of $5, and limited hours of operation largely restricted its use to a specific clientele. Under the contractual terms negotiated, the Library Company paid rent to the Lyceum Company, moved its collections into the building, and surrendered its annual patron dues to the Lyceum Company for five years. In addition, the library came under the supervision of a board of curators (see fig. 5).[16]

Although the reading room and library were popular venues and the lectures were unqualified successes, both the Library Company and the Lyceum Company had money problems. Disagreeing about administrative authority and fiscal management, they dissolved their formal merger. The Library Company, in particular, struggled with the loss of its autonomy. Though its collection remained in the Lyceum, and

Figure 5. Andrew J. Russell, photographer. "Alexandria's Lyceum, probably in fall or winter c. 1862–1863, when the building was used as a ward of the Baptist Church General Hospital (across the street) during the Civil War. Some of the medical staff are posing on the front steps." Courtesy of the Office of Historic Alexandria, City of Alexandria, Virginia/The Lyceum Collection. Reprinted with permission.

library staff made valiant efforts to serve the reading public, the uneasy alliance continued only because each organization paid for its privileges and its space.[17] In 1852, however, the Library Company took on new life, when members of the Young Men's Society stepped in to revitalize it. The number of stockholding members increased, a detailed catalog of books was published, and the library planned a series of fundraising lectures with both local and national speakers.

The Civil War affected that momentum. When Union forces occupied Alexandria in 1861, the Lyceum was commandeered as a barracks and later as a federal hospital. Some of the collection was dispersed to the homes of members for safekeeping; other books remained on the hospital shelves and were temporarily or permanently "borrowed" by Union soldiers as a source of entertainment. After the war, the city and the library struggled to recover. Eventually, in 1870, the directors devised strict new rules for book borrowing and raised funds to support library operations. The library briefly moved to the Alexandria Christian Association before leasing new space on King Street in Old Town. Committees were established to sort the remaining books and furnish the library, and the membership recruited a new director. Subscribers' wives held a fundraising event that was so successful that it became an annual event. In 1872, Emma J. Young was hired as the first female librarian, and the library's lecture program resumed. When Young retired in 1873, Emily English replaced her. But, as always, money continued to be a problem. Following the Panic of 1873, library patronage waned, and in 1879 the Library Company ceased operations.

Almost twenty years later, in 1897, a group of Alexandria women led by Virginia Corse, Mrs. William B. Smoot, and Virginia Burke established the Alexandria Library Association, which functioned for the next forty years. The association supplemented existing titles from the Library Company with new acquisitions, implemented new rules, and resumed fundraising events. In 1899, Andrew Carnegie, who had been an Alexandria resident during the Civil War, donated $500 to the organization. He was disappointed, however, when the city council refused to allocate funds to support the library, so he never again contributed, in spite of numerous solicitations.[18] Alice Green, who will reappear as a library assistant during the 1939 sit-in, served as the association's librarian; and committees or volunteers performed routine library functions, such as cleaning and repairing books.

In May 1903, following brief negotiations, the Alexandria Library Association moved to Lee Camp Hall in Old Town, a site commonly known as Confederate Hall. The venue served as the library's home for thirty-four years, until a formal, standalone library building was constructed in 1937. Lee Camp Hall had originally been purchased to house Confederate veterans, and it was now overseen by the Mary Custis Lee Chapter of the United Daughters of the Confederacy. Corse and Smoot, along with Mary Powell, served as principals in what the group now considered to be "Alexandria's public library."[19] In fact, however, the Alexandria Library Association remained a private entity.

A library endowment fund was established in 1904, and donors occasionally made small deposits. In 1906, staff members produced a book catalog, and a 1912 supplement shows that 7,915 books were being circulated among patrons. Seale writes, "No mention is made in the records of use of the library by African Americans, and while their patronage is doubtful, it is not impossible but undocumented either way."[20] In 1914, in an effort to enhance the library's appeal to children, staff created special exhibits, organized book fairs, and purchased additional children's titles. That same year, they also expanded the magazine collection, which was a popular feature among adults. The board considered enlarging the fiction collection; but Alice Green reported that reference books and nonfiction were the most popular materials, so the library made additional purchases in those areas instead. In a grand civic gesture, the library expanded evening hours during World War I and arranged special loan terms to accommodate soldiers.[21]

In spite of limited personnel and funds, the Library Association worked hard to cater to its constituencies, and it made repeated, unsuccessful attempts to establish an alliance with the city's school system. The library's appeal was clear, but it remained a subscription service, though residents increasingly sought the creation of a true public library. The association's existing space was too small to accommodate either an expanded patron base or substantial collection additions; so in 1930, after considerable research, its board decided to try to convince the city council to establish a true public library. The following year, the council appropriated $1,000 for a municipal facility, and the library board attempted to stimulate community interest in the project. Nonetheless, no further action was taken.[22]

Prospects for a public library improved in 1936, when Dr. and Mrs. Robert South Barrett proposed to donate funds to construct a public library building, to be named in memory of Dr. Barrett's mother, Kate Waller Barrett, a physician, humanitarian, social crusader, and political reformer who had occasionally advised the Library Association. The terms of the donation included use of the association's endowment for library furnishings and a commitment from the city for operating expenses. The proposal was officially presented to the association's board in January 1937, and later that month the Alexandria Library Association, the Barretts, city officials, and representatives of the Alexandria Monthly Meeting of the Religious Society of Friends signed a contract. The association agreed to form and manage the public library, the Barretts agreed to donate funds to construct a building, the city council agreed to pay $5,000 per year for operation expenses, and the Alexandria Monthly Meeting agreed to a ninety-nine-year lease on the Quaker burial ground where the library would be sited, for the nominal sum of $1. Construction funds also came from the federal Public Works Administration, and the Works Progress Administration provided the labor. Stakeholders established a library board comprised of three members of the association, two mayoral appointees, and two members of the city council. Beatrice Workman was appointed temporary librarian.[23]

The Alexandria Library opened as a free, tax-supported public library on August 20, 1937, though, as I will discuss, it exists thanks to a public-private partnership and decades of financial negotiations, not because of altruism or concerns about the well-being of the community. The new library was popularly known as the Free Library or the Queen Street Library. When the public library project was first discussed, the Library Association had considered the question of Black access to the new facility but chose to make no changes to its racially discriminatory policies. The subject was broached again in March and April 1939, when board members acknowledged that Black citizens needed library services. Nevertheless, they again took no action. According to Seale, "in a context of segregation, it was a thorny subject." He adds that "a 'colored branch' was anticipated," but "a peaceful demonstration . . . threw the library open to all." In fact, however, neither the August 1939 library sit-in nor the subsequent court hearings led to the library's integration. Instead, the board referred that decision to the city council, which chose to maintain the library's racially discriminatory policy and construct a separate-and-unequal Black branch. The Robert H. Robinson Library opened for Black Alexandrians in April 1940. The central public library was not fully integrated until 1962—twenty-three years after the sit-in and eight years after the Supreme Court's *Brown v. Board of Education* ruling.[24]

At the meeting in June 1940, the chair of the library board shared a letter from the Virginia Library Association inviting the Alexandria Library Association to become an affiliate. Board members unanimously accepted the invitation. At a February 1941 board meeting, the members discussed a similar invitation from the Alexandria Council of Social Agencies. This invitation, too, was unanimously accepted.[25] The Alexandria Library Association briefly became the Alexandria Library Society, but in 1947 the organization was restructured and renamed the Alexandria Library Company. Memberships were capped at thirty; the city would continue to provide funding from municipal taxes, the Library Company would be "answerable only in financial matters," and the board would meet once a year or "on call." In addition, the Library Company would elect three members to serve on the board and the city council would appoint three.[26] Thus, technically, the library is a public facility because most of its operational funding is derived from municipal taxes. But the Library Company, a private entity, is still a major player in the system's management and it continues to provide a portion of its funding.

Ellen Coolidge Burke, a long-time Alexandria Library employee, was appointed director of the Alexandria Library System in 1948 and served in that capacity until her retirement in 1969. Under her leadership, bookmobile services were implemented in 1962, and the building was enlarged with a 14,600-square-foot addition in 1964. The library system opened two new branch libraries during Burke's tenure: the Ellen Coolidge Burke Branch in April 1968 and the James M. Duncan, Jr., Branch in December 1969. Library services greatly expanded in the 1980s and 1990s. In 1982, the system automated its catalog services, and it added young adult services in 1986. The Alexandria Library was closed for renovations between 1993 and 1995, and four free Internet-capable computers were installed at that time. On March 14, 1996, the library's website went live.[27]

On January 31, 2000, the city's Charles E. Beatley, Jr., Central Library opened on Duke Street in the West End of the city, and the Alexandria Library became the Kate Waller Barrett Branch, which is home to the library system's local history and special collections divisions and a talking-books division for visually impaired patrons. In 2005, the online catalog began offering downloadable audiobooks, and all branches began to provide Internet access. Rose T. Dawson was appointed executive director of the library system in 2008, the first African American to hold that position. In 2015, the city asked the library system to manage the Alexandria Law Library, which brought the total number of branches in the system to four. The Law Library is housed in the courthouse on King Street in Old Town.[28]

Today, the Alexandria Library Company continues the work it began more than 225 years ago. In addition to preserving books (more than 3,000 titles from the original Alexandria Library Company collection are housed at the Barrett Branch), it participates in the administrative operation of Alexandria's public library system and sponsors an annual lecture at a gala event every winter. In 1985, the Lyceum, which in the interim had served as a private residence and then an office building, became the city's history museum under the auspices of the Office of Historic Alexandria. As of 2021, Kristin B. Lloyd is its curator and acting director. The Lyceum houses permanent exhibits of texts, archival prints, photographs, maps, ceramics, silver, furniture, Civil War memorabilia, and local artifacts; and its changing exhibits explore specific aspects of the city's history. The lecture hall that Benjamin Hallowell envisioned as a community cultural and educational center continues to host lectures, documentary film screenings, concerts, meetings, receptions, and other public activities.

# CHAPTER SIX

# Prelude to the Sit-In, Part Three

*Premises and Rationales*

As historian Robert Jones Shafer writes, "[when dealing] with an individual's actions . . . it is relevant to probe his motives."[1] In the microhistorical context of the Alexandria Library sit-in Samuel Tucker was a change agent. Thus, studying his rationales and motivations for action is fundamental to understand why and when he chose to use that form of civil disobedience to achieve his goal. While some southern Blacks resisted Jim Crow imperatives, most did not because they saw accommodation as key to their safety and survival in the hostile, hegemonic environment of White supremacy. Bold young attorney Tucker, however, was willing to challenge the social and cultural status quo as well as local and state laws and to agitate for change to systemic racial oppression in the pursuit of Black self-interest that he viewed as a legal entitlement. In this chapter, I examine why he did so.

The 1937 construction of Alexandria's first public library was a momentous event for the city's White residents. Prior to that date, the Alexandria Library Association's subscription-based format had limited access to services and resources by class as well as by race; only residents with ample income and time could afford the fees and accommodate the library's restricted hours of operation. A broad constituency of the city's White citizens who had waited for years to access free public library services were now loath to relinquish the privilege of racial exclusivity to Blacks, particularly in an era when Black access to a range of services was strictly limited by law and custom. In an *Alexandria Gazette* article published shortly after the library sit-in, Mrs. Albert A. Smoot, the president of the Alexandria Library Board, wrote that White citizens had waited for 143 years to obtain the free library services that Blacks had sought only since 1937. She did not acknowledge the fact that Black Alexandrians had also waited during those 143 years for access to tax-subsidized public library services.[2]

By 1940, other southern cities—including three in Virginia—were offering their Black citizens access to their main public libraries, and the Alexandria Library could have drawn on those local precedents. The library in Halifax, which opened in 1938, immediately offered integrated service to all patrons, as did the library in Brookneal when it opened in 1939. Chatham's library began as a Whites-only facility but was integrated in 1940, the year that Alexandria built its segregated Black branch.

Samuel Tucker's options, however, were severely limited. Both he and his brother Otto were turned away when they applied for library cards in 1938, as was his friend George Wilson in March 1939. So Tucker realized that more direct action would be required, so he filed a writ of mandamus to compel the librarian to accept Wilson's application. Tucker might have chosen instead to make a direct plea to the library board, but its members were part of Alexandria's old southern guard, and Tucker knew they were intransigent on the subject of integration. As discussed in the previous chapter, the board had considered allowing Blacks to use the new library but ultimately took no action, reasoning that Black access was not an entitlement so they were not required to provide library services to the city's African American residents. Tucker might also have submitted a petition to the library board and the city council, but again he would have needed the support and approval of the old guard, who had little incentive to act. In addition, Black Alexandrians formed a relatively small number of the city's population (4,912 Black men, women, and children out of a total population of 24,149), and Tucker would have struggled to secure sufficient signatures to support a petition. Some Blacks would have been fearful of White reprisals, and others might have been reluctant to make a public commitment to the cause. Political action was pointless because both the city council and the city's political machinery were controlled by establishment stalwarts. Moreover, Alexandria's Black voting bloc was

far too small and too socially and politically divided to have a significant impact on a citywide vote, even if African Americans could have
convinced a sufficient number of city council members to support their
quest for a policy change, which was unlikely.

Many older Black Alexandrians who adopted accommodationist
attitudes were reconciled to Jim Crow and White paternalism, even
though they were routinely subjected to de facto and de jure discrimination and were routinely disrespected, humiliated, and dehumanized.
They could not be persuaded to challenge the social or political status
quo. Tucker knew that most of his support for library desegregation
would come from younger Blacks like himself, who rejected White
paternalism and Black accommodation and were willing to mount a
direct confrontation in opposition to Jim Crow and Virginia's Public
Assemblages Act. Although that act required strict segregation in
all public meeting spaces, including public libraries, the Fourteenth
Amendment to the U.S. Constitution guaranteed all American citizens the same rights, privileges, and protections under the law, which
meant that Blacks could not legally be denied access to a tax-supported
municipal institution. Enforcement of the amendment, however, would
require a protracted legal battle because White supremacy was systemic
and Virginia was exploiting the *Plessy v. Ferguson* decision to uphold
and perpetuate racism as well as the 1902 state constitution, with its
overt segregationist platforms.

Yet Tucker was also aware that there were not enough younger Black
Alexandrians to effectively confront the status quo and that some would
eventually bow to family fears for their safety. He may have hoped to
persuade Whites to share public library access with Blacks but given
that option's dubious potential for success, he devised a strategy that
might have a more positive outcome. Personal and professional experiences convinced him that a legal approach would be the most viable
way to desegregate the Alexandria Library, and he saw a municipal
court confrontation as an ideal opportunity to challenge the local and
state segregation laws that were being used to exclude Blacks from the
Whites-only library.[3]

Tucker was among the first generation of Black lawyers born after
passage of the Commonwealth's racialized 1902 constitution and the

implementation of de jure segregation. They had always lived under Jim Crow conditions, and they found the nature and manner of their oppression unacceptable. Tucker, like many graduates of Howard University's elite law school, was eager to contest Jim Crow's authority by curtailing, if not eliminating, discriminatory legislation and customs.

However, the NAACP did not sanction Tucker's proposed gambit for the library protest. At the time, its attorneys were more focused on helping Black students gain admission to graduate and professional schools than on desegregating public libraries, which they did not yet perceive as educational institutions in their own right. We can assume, however, that Tucker was certainly aware of the civil rights and education resolutions that the NAACP adopted on July 1, 1939, and that he anticipated applying Margold's legal tactics to address discrimination in a public library subsidized with municipal taxes (see chapter 2). Although Charles Hamilton Houston, Tucker's mentor at Howard, attempted to dissuade him from his plan to pursue a civil rights trial for Black admission to the Alexandria Library, he nonetheless agreed to serve as Tucker's legal counselor should he decide to follow that course of action.

Tucker was familiar with the ongoing civil rights activism of the "Don't-Buy-Where-You-Can't-Work" boycott campaign, which took place in at least thirty-six cities in the North, Midwest, and South, including Washington, D.C., between the late 1920s and the late 1940s. The boycotts were the culmination of years of frustration over the failure of White-owned businesses in Black neighborhoods to hire African American sales clerks. To make matters worse, during the Great Depression the few Blacks employed by such businesses were routinely fired to open positions for White sales clerks. The boycotts sought to achieve equity in hiring practices, but they also manifested the Black community's collective economic power. They were a nonconfrontational way to protest discrimination and were thus a popular tool among conservative Black business and professional men and Black clergy. August Meier and Elliott Rudwick write: "As the least aggressive kind of protest, the least militant variety of what today is called nonviolent direct action, [boycotts] fitted the conservativism of Negro leaders in southern cities during a period of accommodation."[4]

Although White businesses in Chicago, Cleveland, Baltimore, Newark, New York City, and Washington, D.C., initially succeeded in obtaining injunctions to halt the boycotts, the U.S. Supreme Court reversed lower-court rulings in 1938, thereby confirming the right of protesters to picket companies with discriminatory hiring policies.[5] Tucker, however, recognized that the boycott strategy was not the best choice for his library action. Boycotts require a measure of leverage in inequitable situations, whereas sit-ins, while remaining nonviolent, are a more direct and less accommodating approach to public protest. They are also ideally suited for demonstrations in spaces where sitting and reading are already primary activities.

In tracking the dominant narrative of the civil rights struggle, the historian Jacquelyn Dowd Hall considers Bayard Rustin's conception of the classical phase of protests, which he marks as beginning with the 1954 *Brown v. Board of Education* ruling and concluding with the passage of the Civil Rights Act of 1964 and the Voting Rights Act of 1965. I would extend that timeline to the 1966 Supreme Court ruling in *Brown v. Louisiana*, which stipulates that the operation of libraries and other public facilities must be "reasonable and nondiscriminatory." Hall, too, argues for moving beyond Rustin's frame into a broader, more historically inclusive narrative that situates southern civil rights struggles within the national contexts of race, class, gender, civil and social rights, and labor rights. In her view, a "'long civil rights movement' took root in the . . . late 1930s." Theodore Carter DeLaney also underscores the links between early civil rights protests and those of later decades, noting that we have much to learn about how the efforts of protesters in the 1920s and 1930s assisted later activists. Clearly, Tucker's 1939 demonstration is one of those early protests that had repercussions in subsequent decades.[6]

Among the earliest actions in this "long civil rights movement" were the protests against university policies that students and alumni conducted at historically Black colleges and universities (HBCUs). Beginning in 1919, with their response to Shaw University's closure of its medical, law, and pharmacy schools, activists launched protests at HBCUs throughout the 1920s and 1930s, opposing institutional prohibitions against challenges to Jim Crow segregation and supporting the right to engage in activism and demand improved educational standards. In 1924–25, Fisk University students protested the shutdown of the student newspaper and magazine. In 1925, Howard University students participated in a week-long protest demanding increased student involvement in administrative decisions and a prohibition against mandatory chapel services and Army Reserve Officer Training Corps enlistment. All Howard presidents to that date had been White, but in 1925 students and alumni demanded a Black president; and the following year Mordecai Wyatt Johnson, a Black Baptist minister, was hired to lead the institution. In 1927, students at Hampton University protested the administration's opposition to the screening of the documentary film *Chang*, which traced the life of a Laotian tribesman who had moved from his secure village home and was struggling to adapt to new surroundings. Campus chapters of national organizations such as the NAACP were frequently involved in litigation on behalf of protesting students.[7]

On December 11, 1934, four Black civil rights leaders were arrested in Washington, D.C., after forming a picket line to call attention to the national issue of lynching and with the goal of convincing Attorney General Homer S. Cummings to discuss antilynching legislation during his upcoming National Crime Conference. For months, the NAACP had been attempting to persuade Cummings to add the subject of lynching to the conference agenda, to no avail. W. E. B. Du Bois favored agitation against such racial-terror violence; and during Jim Crow, *The Crisis*, under his editorship, regularly featured political discourse on lynching. Now, after Cummings refused to consider the subject, the picketing protesters went further. On December 13, seventy people, most of them Howard University students, stood silently in a park carrying small signs and wearing nooses around their necks. In a gesture intended to placate the protesters, Cummings's office released an official statement: "the [National Crime Conference] condemns the use of methods of dealing with industrial conflicts and racial antagonisms which are not in accord with orderly and lawful procedures and urges the administration of all phases of public safety by legally constituted law enforcement agencies only."[8]

Howard students were particularly active in civil rights protests. On April 12, 1935, 250 of them were among the 3,000 students from elite Black institutions who conducted antiwar and antifascism strikes. In addition, more than six hundred Howard students refused to attend classes. As a voracious reader of Black and White local and national newspapers, Tucker was undoubtedly aware of the students' fervor. He was also aware of the numerous sit-down strikes, particularly among auto workers, that took place during the 1930s (see chapter 2) and with the labor-rights activities of organizations such as the Howard University–linked National Negro Congress, a cross-class coalition of 585 organizations representing laborers, business owners, clerics, elected officials, and civil rights associations, which held its first conference in Richmond in 1936. The congress worked to oppose Jim Crow and demand economic and social justice, advancement, and industrial and political democracy for Black workers.[9]

For Richmond, 1936 was an important year in the fight against Jim Crow. In an effort to compel the integration of the Richmond Public Library, a member of the local chapter of the NAACP filed a writ of mandamus with the city. The legal challenge was unsuccessful, but it was a step in the process of Richmond's library integration and surely influenced Tucker. Not until 1947, after eleven more years of protests, was the Richmond Public Library quietly integrated without the force of a legal mandate. Even then, however, integration was incomplete because only Blacks age sixteen or more could use the facility.[10]

Also in 1936, the ALA also held its annual conference in Richmond. The conference drew more than 3,000 attendees, and the city anticipated visitor expenditures of approximately $200,000, making it the local media's top news story between May 11 and May 16. It was extensively covered in leading White newspapers such as the *Richmond News Leader* and the *Richmond Times-Dispatch* as well as in the Black *Richmond Planet*, a staunch champion of African American civil rights. Undoubtedly, Tucker followed the coverage in all of them, particularly the news of ALA's self-imposed racial dilemma and its implications for the organization. As Virginia's capital and cultural center, the city was steeped in racism and segregation. Black conference attendees, for example, were excluded from meetings in segregated hotels, private clubs, and other venues and from meetings and special events during which food was served because interracial dining was prohibited. After its experience in Richmond, the ALA did not hold another conference in the Deep South for twenty years.[11]

Tucker made use of his media savvy as he planned his protest. To ensure wide coverage of the sit-in, he asked local and national Black and White newspapers to record and photograph the events as they happened. Though he anticipated that some White newspapers would present the sit-in as an affront to the status quo, he knew he could count on Black newspapers to document it as a challenge to Jim Crow and a demand for social change. As Thomas J. Sugrue explains, "the black press served as an indispensable resource for civil rights activists around the country. Widely circulating . . . black newspapers informed their readers of racial injustices around the country and reported extensively on those who challenged racial inequality."[12]

In 1939, Tucker and other Black activists were also influenced by ominous global political events. Black soldiers who had fought in World War I had returned to find their wartime heroics erased by the realities of segregation on the home front. Now, with unrest growing in Europe, they were determined not to be disappointed again. Historian Glenda Elizabeth Gilmore explains, "In the summer of 1939, as white Americans anxiously debated being drawn into war, black Americans attacked Jim Crow with renewed vigor. Their campaign to link the Nazis and Dixie had begun to pay off. Support for dismantling white supremacy was stronger than ever before, some of it coming from white Southerners themselves." The New Deal's assault on the South's economic structure, for example, exposed the price of Jim Crow and provided incentives for national efforts to eliminate both poll taxes and sharecropping.[13]

Tucker's younger sister, Elsie Tucker Thomas, later recalled that the idea for the library sit-in demonstration had originated with her brother Otto, who was familiar with the 1934 sit-ins conducted by Howard University students in opposition to university policies. In a 1985 interview, Samuel stated that he and his brother had planned the library sit-in together, coming up with the idea while driving from

Richmond to Alexandria. In the same interview, Otto mentioned that, while attending Howard's law school, he had taken a course in constitutional law from Charles Houston that had assured him of his legal right to use the library.[14]

Whatever the plan's origins, given the protest options available to him and his familiarity with the NAACP's legal tactics and precedents and the potential of nonviolent civil disobedience to effect change, Tucker recognized the efficacy of a sit-in demonstration to force Alexandria to desegregate its only public library. He correctly anticipated that the protesters would be arrested, and he planned to serve as their legal counsel.[15] Tucker's professional and community standing, his knowledge of the law and the Constitution, and his personal and economic autonomy vis-à-vis the White community afforded him the independence to undertake a sit-in as a protest strategy. Of all the possible alternatives available, he believed it would have the greatest chance of success and would be the ideal way to pair ideologically based, nonviolent public protest with federal civil rights law to effect change. The scholar Christopher W. Schmidt remarks: "Although the linkages are often complex, formal legal developments—including the proclamations of the Supreme Court—can play a role in shaping the course of social protest activity, just as these protest activities can set in motion legal claims that shape the course of formal legal developments."[16]

# CHAPTER SEVEN

# A Seat at the Reading Table

*The 1939 Alexandria Library Sit-In Demonstration*

In 1937, the board of the new Alexandria Library decided that only the city's White residents and taxpayers should have free access to the new facility. Though Black residents and taxpayers were denied access, nonresident Whites were permitted use the library for the nominal fee of $1.50 per year.[1] The Alexandria Library Company and the city council had studied the feasibility of creating a separate branch for Black Alexandrians, but they took no action on the matter before the new library opened. During a meeting in June 1937, one board member, a Miss Stephens, expressed her belief that "the colored library should be started as soon as possible," but there is no record of further discussion of the matter.[2] "Miss Thomson, chairman of the committee appointed by Mrs. Scott to discuss [the] problem [of Black access to library services] with the Library Committee of the City Council, said she had been unable to accomplish much but that there would be a meeting with the council committee that afternoon." There is no subsequent report on this scheduled meeting in the library board meeting minutes.

Individually, Samuel Tucker and his younger brother Otto tried to submit user card applications at the Alexandria Library in 1938. Their requests, however, were denied and they were told that the library operated exclusively for Whites. Nevertheless, their efforts are evidence of early, peaceful attempts to secure library privileges.

A year later, on April 10, 1939, Mrs. Albert A. Smoot introduced the subject of a "colored library" during a board meeting. A Mr. Williams suggested that "some arrangement be made with a colored school library, and that books be contributed from Alexandria Library friends" while Dr. Ernest A. DeBordenave "advised making a survey of facilities for reading among the colored people."[3] After discussing the possibility of establishing a branch or an annex, the board decided to seek continued advice from Williams and DeBordenave. Though the minutes are initially unclear as to whether Mr. Williams and Dr. DeBordenave were library board members, by extrapolating remarks from other meeting minutes, I concluded that they were. Again, however, no action was taken, and Blacks continued to be excluded from the Alexandria Library.

In response to the continuing refusal to grant Black citizens library access, Tucker launched the first of a two-pronged strategy to challenge the institutionalization of racial discrimination at the Alexandria Library. On Friday, March 17, 1939, four days after the regularly scheduled March library board meeting, Samuel Tucker accompanied his friend, retired army sergeant George Wilson, to the Alexandria Library. Functioning as Wilson's attorney, Tucker filled out an application for a library card on Wilson's behalf. (Archival resources offer no explanation as to why Wilson did not fill out his own application.) At this time Tucker did not himself apply for a card because he wanted to be available to serve as Wilson's attorney when the request was denied. Sure enough, Sue Fox, the assistant librarian on duty that day, rejected Wilson's application and told him that the library was restricted to Whites. Tucker then contacted the head librarian, Katharine H. Scoggin, to confirm the rules regarding Black access to the facility. After Scoggin corroborated Fox's explanation of library policy, Tucker filed a writ of mandamus on Wilson's behalf, demanding that Scoggin and the library board accept Wilson's request for library privileges. The city's corporation court then took the matter under advisement.[4]

At the April board meeting, Smoot said that she "had been looking into the question of a colored library" and had spoken to Williams and DeBordenave "but had received no encouragement . . . for the prospect of establishing a library at [the Blacks-only] Parker-Gray High School."[5] Another board member, Mrs. G. H. Outwater, said that she and Scoggin had looked into establishing "an annex, connected with [the] main library building, for colored citizens, at a cost of approximately $2,000, with $250 more a year for books and expenses, said annex to be opened two afternoons and two evenings a week."[6] Outwater then suggested that the board present her proposition to the city council's library committee and "leave the responsibility [for decision making] to them."[7] However, she felt that the board should go "on the record as having a plan to present to [the] Library Committee of City Council, . . . and recommending adoption of said plan as the best means of facilitating library work among the colored people of [the] town."[8] The board endorsed her recommendation. Archival sources do not make it clear if the board had the authority at that time to make an independent and definitive decision about Black use of the library. However, it certainly had the authority to present a strong case to the library committee on behalf of Black residents, and it chose not to do so.

At the May library board meeting, Smoot again broached the issue of the "colored library situation" and said that Dr. Lowrie, a board member, had met with the city council's library committee. At that time the city manager, Carl Budwesky, had indicated his preference for a separate library rather than an annex. Smoot now told the board that "the Interracial Committee had endorsed [the] Library's plan for an annex, but had requested that the same entrance be used for both races."[9] By "Interracial Committee," she was probably referring to a group of concerned citizens who had little influence and no decision-making authority but could give the actual decision makers a community perspective on the issue to claim they had sought community feedback. The meeting minutes do not mention a separate Black entrance for the proposed annex. Nevertheless, it is reasonable to assume that the board had found the idea of a common entrance unacceptable because Outwater then advised formulating a plan, accompanied by an itemization of expenses, for the establishment of a separate library for Blacks and submitting it to the city council.[10] At the June board meeting, a Mr. Lamond said that the city manager had promised to respond to the board's plan for a separate Black library, but as of that day no report had been received.[11] Like the library board, the city council hesitated to commit to providing library services for Black Alexandrians. That hesitation was tantamount to a refusal.

While Tucker and Wilson awaited a ruling on the writ, Tucker executed the second prong of his strategy to challenge the library's discriminatory policies: a sit-in demonstration at the library. He expected that the protesters would be arrested for attempting to integrate the library, and he likely anticipated that legal action would be required. In advance of his implementation of the tactic, Tucker met with his mentor, Charles Hamilton Houston, to discuss the planned protest. During their meeting, Houston indicated that he had not considered that libraries could be used as sites to contest segregation. His initial response was to attempt to dissuade Tucker from initiating the sit-in; but when Tucker refused to relent, Houston advised him to ensure that the strategy was legally sound. According to a later article in the *Pittsburgh Courier*, "the NAACP recognized the importance of Attorney Tucker's fight, and Charles Houston, Leon Ransome and other members of the association's staff assisted him in consultations."[12]

Tucker and his brother Otto recruited eleven young Black men to participate in the public protest. All lived in Alexandria, and all were either personal acquaintances of the Tuckers or community members who were familiar with the Tucker family's commitment to civil rights activism. Dorothy Evans Turner, the sister of protest participant William "Buddy" Evans, recalled that Tucker had been her family's attorney. During multiple meetings in the Old Town office he shared with his father and Tom Watson, Tucker secretly prepared the men for the sit-in, teaching them civil-disobedience tactics to forestall any possibility that they could be accused of disorderly conduct by the librarian or the police.[13] Tucker emphasized that the recruits should be properly attired, exhibit good manners, and resist the temptation to respond to any remarks by library employees or the police. Buddy Evans later said, "The whole setup was that we would each sit at a different table in the library and read a book, and that we would remain silent the whole time so they couldn't arrest us for disorderly conduct."[14] In fact, in preparation for the sit-in, Tucker also insisted that the recruits dress and behave appropriately while attending the planning sessions. Tucker emphasized appropriate dress and decorum to avoid legal problems; but August Meier, Elliott Rudwick, and Francis L. Broderick also contend that instructions such as "look my best," "refrain from boisterous or offensive language," and "do or say nothing which will [cause embarrassment]" were indicators of the middle-class values of early sit-in demonstrators.[15]

Tucker anticipated that the men would be arrested, and he planned to meet them at the police station, arrange their bond and release, and serve as their attorney during the subsequent hearings. Bobby Strange, the youngest of the eleven recruits, was fourteen at the time of the sit-in. His duty was to stand outside the library and serve as a runner, sprinting back and forth to Tucker's law office, three blocks away, with ongoing reports of library and police activities. Because Bobby Strange would not actually participate in the demonstration, he would not be subject to arrest or prosecution.[16]

On the morning of Monday, August 21, 1939, only six of the original eleven arrived for the protest. The parents of four of the missing men were concerned about their sons' safety and refused to allow them to participate. According to Audrey P. Davis (no relation to Gladys Howard Davis), director of the Alexandria Black History Museum, the fifth recruit overslept and missed the protest. Evans recalled that his father felt the protest was "a stupid thing to do," but the young man decided to participate nonetheless: "Sure, I was afraid when I first went in, but we had made up our minds and I knew I had to do it. . . . At that particular time, I didn't realize it would be such a big event. I just thought I was doing something to get a library for the black people in Alexandria."[17] In a later interview with William Elwood, he said, "It was something that had to be done and someone had to do it and if everybody said no, it never would have gotten done." But he acknowledged to a *Washington Post* staff writer that he and the other participants feared the potential repercussions from their actions but were committed to the effort.[18]

With Bobby Strange remaining outside, the protest participants began to enact Tucker's plan. One by one, in five-minute intervals, four of the five courteous, well-dressed men entered the Alexandria Library: Otto Lee Tucker, age twenty-two; Morris L. Murray, age twenty-two; Edward Gaddis, age twenty-one; and Clarence "Buck" Strange, age twenty. Otto Tucker was the first to enter the library; he was followed five minutes later by Morris Murray. Each man walked to the library's circulation desk and politely requested a library card. The fifth young man, William "Buddy" Evans, age nineteen and still in high school, inadvertently bypassed the circulation desk and went directly to a library shelf.[19] The *Alexandria Gazette*, which reported on the sit-in and the protesters' subsequent arrests, printed the men's names, ages, and addresses on the front page of the paper in three separate articles. Given that the protest was a pronounced deviation from the era's normalized behavior, it may seem surprising that the protesters suffered no backlash from other Alexandrians either Black or White. Yet as Lovell A. Lee explained, "segregation and racism were institutionalized [in the city], but in spite of that there were friendly relationships between Whites and Blacks [who] lived in harmony because Blacks knew their place."[20]

As expected, Alice Green, the assistant librarian on duty, denied each man's request for a library card and told him that library policies restricted use of the facility and its resources to Whites. Each man then respectfully thanked Green for her time and attention, also as instructed by Tucker, before proceeding to the library shelves. Ignoring the incredulous glares of the White patrons, each young man followed Tucker's strict directives to select a book at random, take a seat alone at a table, and silently begin to read. Although Evans had bypassed the circulation desk, he, too, chose a book, sat, and read.

White patrons quickly began lodging complaints about the situation.[21] After trying and failing to persuade the demonstrators to leave, Green summoned Robert William Adam, another assistant librarian, and asked him to summon the head librarian, Katharine Scoggin, who resided on the second floor of the library. Scoggin came downstairs and attempted to persuade the protesters to leave the library; but when the silent young men persisted in their reading, she telephoned the city manager, Carl Budwesky, and the captain of police, John S. Arnold, to discuss the unfolding drama. Arnold dispatched two officers to the library, John F. Kelley and John C. Wilkerson, to handle the "commotion."[22]

Upon their arrival at the library, Kelley and Wilkerson approached the protesters and asked them to leave, although, in his testimony at the hearing, Kelley admitted that he never told the men *why* they should go though "he knew the library did not issue books to colored persons."[23] Only Evans answered the officers—an error, as Tucker had instructed the men not to respond to any remarks by librarians or police and thus potentially jeopardize his defense of the case.

"What would happen if we don't leave?" Evans asked.

Kelley replied, "I am sorry, but I shall have to arrest you then."

Evans retorted, "Well, we are staying."[24]

The officers again asked the protesters to leave, but the men remained seated, silent, and composed. As Bobby Strange later recalled, "People just stared when we walked in. They were amazed that we would go there. When the police came, they weren't sure what to do, either."[25] The protesters remained in the library for about an hour, and then Kelley and Wilkerson quietly escorted them from the building to the police court, where they were arraigned (see fig. 6). As the arrested men emerged from the library, Bobby Strange raced to notify Tucker that more than two hundred spectators had assembled outside the library.[26]

Prior to the sit-in, media-savvy Tucker had alerted local and national Black and White newspapers about the upcoming protest to ensure coverage of the event. The *Alexandria Gazette* provided modest coverage of the protest, and articles about the demonstration also appeared in the *Washington Times-Herald*, the *Washington Post*, the *Chicago Defender*, and the *Washington Tribune*.[27] The Black press continued to cover events as they unfolded; but for the most part, the protest and its aftermath received scant attention in the White press, which was focused on the Molotov-Ribbentrop Pact and the impending war. There is no doubt that this displacement contributed to the erasure of the demonstration from national public memory.

In a later interview, Tucker recalled that city officials tried to contact the city's attorney, Armistead Boothe, for advice about what to do with the protesters. Boothe, however, was out of town and could not be reached, so they eventually decided to arrest the men on a charge of trespassing. As planned, Tucker met the demonstrators at the police court.[28] At the arraignment, Tucker charged that the absence of a conspicuous ordinance excluding Blacks from the library supported his clients' right to use the facility. He convinced the authorities that the

Figure 6. "Sit-in Demonstrators Escorted from the Alexandria Library," photographer unidentified [possibly Florence Murray], for "Young Alexandria Goes to Bat," *Washington Tribune*, August 26, 1939, n.p. The caption reads: "The five young men above are being escorted to the police court, Monday, August 21, 1939, by Policeman John F. Kelley who placed them under arrest for reading in the City Library, which Alexandria city authorities contend is for white persons only. Left to right, they are (front row) Morris L. Murray and Clarence Strange; (back row) William Evans, Otto L. Tucker, Edward Gaddis, and Officer Kelley. The youths are making a test case of the library affair." In the collection of the Alexandria Black History Museum, Alexandria, Virginia. Reprinted with permission.

men had broken no trespassing laws, so the charge was amended to disorderly conduct, which Tucker knew he could persuasively fight, given the men's quiet, polite behavior during the sit-in. He posted their bonds, and they were released, with a hearing scheduled at the court for the following day.[29]

On Tuesday, August 22, 1939, the five protesters appeared before Judge James Reece Duncan for their first hearing. Tucker had requested that they be brought to trial one at a time, saying that "he would stand by any decision handed down in the case of the first one tried." That person turned out to be Morris Murray.[30] At the hearing, the city attorney, Boothe, and the defense attorney, Tucker, questioned and cross-questioned Officers Kelley and Wilkerson and the library assistant, Adam. All readily acknowledged that the young protesters had been quiet and orderly. Kelley also acknowledged that the men had been properly attired and had not destroyed any property. Tucker asked, "Then they were disorderly because they were black?"[31] In response, Kelley "admitted that the only disorder in question was because the men were members of the 'Race' and the library was for white people." Tucker then charged that, in the absence of evidence of disorderly conduct, the men had been denied library use solely on the basis of their race.[32] He turned to the head librarian, Scoggin, asking "if it were true that had the defendants been white and acting as they did, would they [have been] forcibly removed?" She said they would not have been removed.[33] According to an article in the *Pittsburgh Courier*, her reply "practically [admitted] that the cause for the arrest was a matter of color and not a violation of any city ordinance."[34] The library employees also testified that the demonstrators had been refused library cards because "the Alexandria Library Board, which controls the semi-public institution, had ordered that books were not to be loaned to colored residents."[35] Tucker later maintained that the central challenge in the case had been based on two key questions: "If they had been white, would they have been asked to leave? If they had been white, would they have been arrested?"[36]

Following this questioning, Boothe "asked for more time to study the case, since the testimony raised doubts about the 'disorderly conduct' charge."[37] Judge Duncan also conceded "that he saw no reason for a charge of disorderly conduct."[38] According to the *Pittsburgh Courier*, the judge commented, "There seems to be no evidence of disorderly conduct here, but it is a matter of constitutional privileges."[39] Nevertheless, he issued no ruling, and the charge of disorderly conduct was upheld pending a continuance, requested by Boothe, to submit legal authorities on the case. Boothe also noted that a writ filed on behalf of George Wilson was pending in the corporation court. An article in the *Washington Post* reported that "Tucker said as far as he knew the 'sit-down' was not connected with Wilson's petition and to his knowledge the youths were acting on their own initiative."[40] Judge Duncan continued the case, pending arguments, and scheduled the next hearing for the following Tuesday. The demonstrators were then "released on their own recognizance."[41] The *Pittsburgh Courier* reported that "the case is attracting considerable [attention] as it has a direct bearing on the jim crow laws of the Old Dominion state and as Judge Duncan pointed out, affected the constitutional rights of citizens."[42]

On August 27, members of the library board met at the home of Mrs. Albert A. Smoot to discuss the sit-in demonstration and its ramifications for the city and the library.[43] Armistead Boothe read aloud a statement of the board's current position regarding Black Alexandrians' use of the library and of a proposed, separate branch for Blacks.[44] Members then made three decisions at the meeting. First, admission to the Alexandria Library would be restricted to "library members," a policy that underscored its White exclusivity because Blacks were not permitted to apply for library cards. Second, a sign would be posted at the library indicating that the facility was reserved for the exclusive use of members. Third, no employee would be left alone to staff the building.[45]

On the following day, the *Alexandria Gazette* published a lengthy statement under Smoot's name outlining the "facts" of the situation. (According to J. Douglas Smith, the statement of the position of the library board credited to Smoot was actually drafted by Boothe.)[46] The statement claimed that "shortly after the [Alexandria Library] opened, the Library Board appointed a committee to meet with a number of prominent colored citizens of Alexandria" but did not mention either the names or the affiliations of these citizens.[47] In the opinion of this particular group of Black Alexandrians, the protest was unwarranted and that any discussions about the establishment of a Black branch would be overshadowed by the "tremendous immediate need" for a boys' club and community center.[48] As a result, board and city council members had decided to consider the provision of library privileges to African Americans only when Blacks made a "real demand" for a library—which, by implication, would be a segregated facility. Apparently, the direct-action protest for library privileges at the Alexandria Library did not constitute a "real demand." In addition, board members were choosing to ignore their own previous acknowledgment of the need for Black library services as documented in their April 10 meeting minutes.[49] In the intervening months, the board had, in fact, been seeking information about "erecting and administering a colored library" from Richmond, Roanoke, Lynchburg, Danville, and Petersburg, all of which had long histories of racial discrimination and segregation.[50] Thus, while Smoot's statement emphasized ongoing discussions of separate service for Black citizens, it failed to mention that those discussions had produced no results except to continue to exclude Blacks.

Smoot's article asserts that no public funds had ever been spent on the Alexandria Library and that funds donated by African Americans for the construction of a Black library were actually intended for the protesters' "court expenses or attorney's fees," not for a facility of their own. Yet on August 22, the day after the demonstration, the *Washington Times-Herald* had accurately reported that "[the library's] operation . . . is financed principally by the city through an agreement with the [library] association."[51] It was always clear that the city council was appropriating municipal tax revenue to support and operate the library. When the article downplayed the importance of Black donations, it likewise failed to note that Dr. and Mrs. Barrett had donated funds to construct the Alexandria Library building, that the site had been acquired through a nominal long-term lease from the Alexandria Monthly Meeting, and that the collection included a substantial number of books acquired through donation. In other words, monetary and tangible donations to establish a free public library for Whites were perfectly acceptable, but donations from Blacks to finance

a free public library of their own were ignored or belittled. The article closed by snidely referring to both the sit-in and the writ filed on
behalf of George Wilson as "steps taken in court by some over-zealous
persons"—a thinly veiled sneer at Tucker.[52]

On August 28, the *Washington Tribune* and the *Alexandria Gazette*
reported that Judge Duncan would hear the continued sit-in case on
the following day, and the *Tribune* included a reference to the writ of
mandamus filed by Tucker on behalf of Wilson.[53] William Evans was
the designated protester who would be tried at the August 29 hearing. This session was far longer and more involved than Murray's had
been.[54] Before the hearing began, Tucker had agreed that the verdict for
all five demonstrators would be based on the outcome of Evans's case
because Judge Duncan had issued no ruling during Murray's earlier
hearing. This time, however, Evans's father chose to retain T. Brooke
Howard, a local White attorney who was also his employer, to defend
his son. Unbeknownst to Tucker, William Evans was on probation for
an assault conviction, and his father likely feared that his participation
in the protest would lead to jail time. This was probably why Evans's
father had discouraged his son's involvement from the beginning. After
joining the case, Howard arranged to sever Evans's trial from the trial of
the other four protesters, whom Tucker continued to defend. Dorothy
Evans Turner told me that her brother had wanted Tucker to represent
him but was overruled by his father. Whatever the truth of the matter,
Evans's subsequent responses to questioning potentially jeopardized
Tucker's defense of his fellow protesters. For example, Evans stated that
"he had been requested by another man to make the trip to the library"
and said that Tucker had planned the sit-in demonstration. After that
assertion, Judge Duncan queried Tucker about his involvement in the
protest, and Tucker retorted that *he* was not on trial.[55]

Witnesses for the second hearing included Mrs. Albert A. Smoot and
Officer Kelley. Smoot testified about the rules for the operation and use
of the library, and Kelley testified about the circumstances in the library
on the day the demonstrators were arrested. The prosecutor, Boothe,

maintained that the men had not been entitled to use the library because it was not a "public" space—which, as vice president of the library board, he knew was a false argument. He further charged that Virginia law had separated the races, so the defendants should not have assumed that the library was a facility available for use by Blacks.[56] Tucker responded by leveraging Judge Duncan's first-hearing pronouncement that the case was based on "constitutional privileges." He challenged Boothe's argument that the demonstrators were not entitled to use the library based solely on their race, stating that segregation was a violation of the equal-protection clause of the Fourteenth Amendment to the U.S. Constitution. Boothe replied that the case was about disorderly conduct, not the Constitution, despite the fact that multiple witnesses had testified that the protesters were not disorderly.[57] In the first hearing, Boothe had dismissed Tucker's reference to the equal-protection clause of the Fourteenth Amendment, but now he rekindled sectional divisiveness, weakly arguing that "a carpet-bagging government in the southern states forced the vote [for the Fourteenth and Fifteenth amendments] on the white population of the South."[58] By maintaining that White Virginians were not bound to accept the universal freedoms granted by those amendments because their enactment had been coerced, he deeply offended Black citizens, some of whom had previously supported him, and he lost credibility with many of them.[59]

In response to the defense and prosecutorial arguments, Judge Duncan stated that the issue was whether or not there had been a breach of the peace—a significant shift from his original contention that the case was about "constitutional privileges." Boothe then said that the protesters should have investigated whether the city intended to construct a Black branch before they proceeded with their sit-in demonstration.[60] Judge Duncan, however, was still reluctant to rule on the case, given that the charge of disorderly conduct was so tenuous. He issued Boothe another continuance until September 1 so that the prosecutor could search for and submit legal authorities on the charge of "breach of the peace," which might be easier to prove.[61]

Several Black luminaries appeared at the third hearing of the sit-in protesters, including Leon A. Ransom and Henry Lincoln Johnson, both Howard law professors, and William H. Hastie, a federal judge. All three were associated with the NAACP's legal defense team, which had evidently come to recognize the significance of the library sit-in case. But they and the crowds in attendance were sorely disappointed because Judge Duncan left the courtroom after calling a series of minor preliminary cases. After issuing the continuance at the end of the second hearing, he never again heard arguments for or against the library demonstrators. Instead, Tucker and Boothe joined the judge in his chambers. When Tucker returned to the courtroom, he abruptly left with his four defendants, followed by the witnesses and the spectators. Once outside, he announced that he had promised not to speak about the matter at hand. On September 2, the *Alexandria Gazette* reported that the judge had not yet received the requested authorities regarding breach of the peace from Boothe, which he needed to study before he could issue a decision.[62] The *Chicago Defender* reported that the judge wanted additional time to conduct his own search of legal authorities on the subject because it was clear that the charge of disorderly conduct could not be proved and that he wanted the defense and the prosecution to submit briefs to stay the case. The *Pittsburgh Courier*, however, reported that Tucker and Boothe had informed their clients that the trial had been "indefinitely postponed."[63]

On September 23, the *Chicago Defender* published coverage of the briefs that the defense and prosecution attorneys had filed in police court during the week of September 11, which the judge had requested at the conclusion of the second hearing.[64] Boothe's brief was submitted first, and Tucker's was submitted in response. The *Defender*'s account of Boothe's brief was terse. Citing the case of *People v. Galpern in New York*, Boothe argued that the question William Evans posed to the police during the sit-in—"What would happen if we don't leave?"—constituted disorderly conduct because it represented a failure to obey an officer. He also "contend[ed] that a[n unspecified] case in South Carolina established the grounds that any language used by the defendant which was calculated to produce disorder and to disturb the quiet and peace was unlawful and considered to be disorderly conduct, even though no one was disturbed."[65]

The *Defender* gave far more space to Tucker's brief. To frame his response to Boothe's legal arguments, Tucker used the case of his brother Otto, who, he wrote, "has the right to sit and read in the library [and] there is nothing left for judicial determination unless we can find that: (1) the police officer's order that [Otto] Tucker should leave the library was clothed with authority of the law, or (2) the manner in which [Otto Tucker] exercised the right we are assuming him to have had was in fact disorderly and in fact did breach the peace."[66] The *Defender* reported "that upon the assumption that the young man has a right to sit and read, the police officer was not only without authority of law to order him to leave, but that his attempt to make him leave was unlawful and punishable under criminal law, and actionable under the civil laws of the state."[67] Moreover, "concerning the second point, [Otto Tucker] declares that the evidence shows that the only objectionable feature about the entire incident was that [he] is colored, and that in the absence of a statute requiring the court to do so, 'we cannot allow his racial identity to enter into the consideration of this case.'"[68] According to Tucker's brief,

> One who without invitation quietly enters a library though privately owned and operated, and does no more than sit and read therein is neither guilty of disorderly conduct, nor of conduct tending to breach of the peace (until he refuses to leave upon request of the owner), nor of any offense approaching the magnitude of a crime; and his innocence is in no wise altered by the fact that he may be a colored man and that the definitely known policy of the library is to accommodate white people only. . . . There is no statute or ordinance under which such act—amounting to no more than a trespass if any offense at all—when committed by a person of one race, can be construed as a crime when committed by a person of another race; and certainly such discrimination is unknown in common law.[69]

The *Defender* concluded with a summary of Tucker's argument enjoining the city of Alexandria to give Black citizens access to the public library maintained at "considerable" public expense: "Where the municipality has undertaken the function of providing public library facilities not only does the law give to every citizen the right to the use thereof . . . but the law enjoins the municipality from denying to any citizen access to any building which may be dedicated for such public use, regardless of his race or color."[70]

From the beginning, Judge Duncan seemed reluctant to side with either the prosecution or the defense. By issuing Boothe multiple continuances, he was simply using *prosecutorial discretion*—standard legal protocol—that allows local judges and prosecutors to amend legal charges against defendants. As attorney Barbara Ann Rowan has explained, "local judges and local prosecutors are political appointees or elected officials, so some element of public pressure can be implied in the decision to charge or not to charge and even what to charge."[71] Community sentiment, therefore, is a critical component of local prosecutions. In any event, Judge Duncan never issued a ruling on either the requested briefs or the case of the sit-in demonstrators. None of them served any time in jail, nor were they obligated to pay any fines.[72]

The numerous continuances and brief submissions did, however, give the city manager and the city council time to investigate the prospects of a separate-and-unequal Black branch. During the week of September 11, City Manager Carl Budwesky submitted a report to the council estimating the cost of construction at $3,950. Budwesky also recommended that the city allocate a budget of $1,750 for annual maintenance of the facility.[73] While the council was considering the proposal, it ordered a second estimate, which put total construction costs at $3,500. The council eventually decided to defer action on the project because it hoped to secure project financing from a federal housing program rather than appropriate municipal funds.[74] At its September 26 meeting, the council's library committee recommended the purchase of a tract of land to be used for the site of the Black library but advised that the purchase be postponed "until such time as the City Manager can ascertain from the Housing Authority the prospects of including the library in the colored housing project." In other words, city officials persisted in their attempts to avoid desegregating the Alexandria Library and allocating municipal funds for a separate Black branch.[75]

That same week, Judge William Pape Woolls issued his initial ruling on the writ of mandamus that Tucker had filed on behalf of George Wilson. (Earlier arguments on the writ had been heard on July 10.)[76] In his decision, Woolls upheld the demurrer filed by Boothe, ruling that until Wilson "identifies himself to the librarian as a citizen entitled to use and enjoy the library there was no duty on the librarian to issue a reading card." Woolls's decision implied that, if Wilson had properly identified himself and provided proof of residency in Alexandria, he would have been granted a reading card. There is no available primary-source documentation explaining why Wilson did not do this. Even if specific elements of the application had confused him, Tucker had been present for assistance.[77] The judge's ruling concluded with a directive to Tucker: "If you will draw a decree embracing the above opinion, I will be glad to enter it."[78] He continued:

> When one is required to perform a ministerial act or duty under certain conditions after being apprised of the existence of such conditions, and refuses to do so, mandamus will require that it be done. . . . Pleadings do not [allege] that George Wilson identified himself to the librarian to use and enjoy the library . . . and until this was done, there was no duty on the librarian to issue a reading card. As there has, from the pleading, been no refusal by the librarian to perform a required duty, mandamus will not lie, and the demurrer to the petition is therefore sustained.[79]

A continuance was issued in the Wilson case until December 11, to enable Tucker to amend the submitted writ. According to the *Chicago Defender*, Wilson's case, which was heard in Alexandria's corporation court, was unusual because it would be heard by a jury, whereas most cases that involve civil liberties or constitutional rights are decided by a judge. The *Alexandria Gazette*, however, reported that the case would be heard and decided by Judge Woolls alone.

On December 11, Tucker was late for the court session. After waiting twenty minutes for him to arrive, the judge continued the case to the court's next session, later in the week. When Tucker finally appeared, he explained that Boothe had told him that two cases would precede Wilson's so he had expected to be on time to defend him.[80] Primary sources do not show that Boothe and Tucker spoke on the matter or that Tucker intentionally arrived late. However, it is unlikely that he would have made such an assertion while Boothe was on hand to refute it if it had not been true. During the hearings on the sit-in case, Tucker and Boothe became friendly colleagues—but not friends—and were accustomed to consulting with one another. It is probable, therefore, that Tucker's explanation about the scheduling was accurate.[81]

On January 10, 1940, Judge Woolls announced a final decision in corporation court regarding the Wilson writ of mandamus case. Though he ultimately denied the plaintiff's petition, Woolls indicated that "the *writ* would have [been] issued had the applicant complied with library regulations in applying for his card, and that library officials might be forced to issue reading cards to colored citizens who follow the correct procedure in applying in the future." In effect, he ruled that Scoggin had denied Wilson's application because Tucker had filled it out and because he had failed to identify himself and provide evidence of residence in Alexandria—*not* because of his race—which, technically and legally, authorized Black use of the Alexandria Library. The *Alexandria Gazette* published the full text of Woolls's decision in its January 11 coverage of the case.[82] In his ruling, Woolls wrote:

> In this case there has not been introduced any evidence that the Alexandria Library Association has any regulations limiting the library's use and facilities to the white race. Also, there is no provision or covenant to this effect in the joint agreement to which City of Alexandria and the Alexandria Library Association are

parties. On the contrary the evidence shows that under the rules and regulations of the Alexandria Library Association those entitled to its benefits are "persons living in the City of Alexandria or tax payers in Alexandria, who fill out an application and give a local reference." Inasmuch as the City Council has not provided a separate library for the colored race, upon a proper showing mandamus would lie to require the librarian to issue reading cards and facilities to such members of the colored race as come within the above description. . . . However, the facts as shown do not permit or justify the issuance of the writ in this case. The petitioner or relater must have a legal right, and in order to have this right he must have complied with the rules as promulgated or adopted. One of these rules is that he must fill out an application and give a local reference before he has the right to a card to withdraw books. This he did not do, and for this reason the petition for *mandamus* will be dismissed at the cost of the petitioner.[83]

As Florence Murray later explained in *The Negro Handbook*, "since Sergt. Wilson's racial identity was not mentioned in his petition, the question of race was not brought up in the arguments of the plaintiff's counsel nor in the judge's decision."[84]

Black Alexandrians saw the ruling as a victory. Though Woolls's decision received scant media coverage, the news was quickly disseminated throughout the Black community. Within days, two Black citizens applied for library cards at the Alexandria Library. Five-year city resident Dorothy Pierce was the first. A French teacher and the librarian at Parker-Gray High School, she was a graduate of Howard University and had also completed a library science course at Hampton Institute. Although the librarian on duty treated her cordially, she was asked to wait because the "colored branch would be opened in a month." Pierce replied that she needed the material immediately, so she was allowed to complete an application and was told she would receive an answer shortly.[85] There is no archival information about whether she ever received a response, and no library board meeting minutes mention her application.

On January 11, the day after Judge Woolls's ruling on Wilson's writ of mandamus, the library board held an emergency meeting. Members feared the ruling would encourage Blacks to apply for library cards, and they wanted to avoid an onslaught of unwelcome visitors.[86] Scoggin and Budwesky also attended the meeting. Scoggin reported that newly allocated funds had enabled her to hire additional staff members to check the references of prospective borrowers; presumably, she and the board were particularly concerned about prospective applications from Black users. After both the librarian and several board members expressed their concerns about library rules and regulations, the board passed the following resolution:

> Only persons to whom library cards have been issued shall be entitled to withdraw books to read in the reading room or otherwise to use library facilities. Library cards shall be issued to any person living in Alexandria or any taxpayer in Alexandria who shall fill out an application, give a local reference, and give the Librarian a reasonable time within which to verify information contained in the application and reference.[87]

This requirement for "reasonable time" was an obvious ploy to delay processing applications from prospective Black patrons until the city could make alternative library arrangements for them.

On January 12, the city council also held an emergency meeting, where it approved the allocation of $2,500 to be used for the construction of a segregated Black library "upon its first consideration."[88] The appropriation was $1,450 less than the sum recommended by the city manager in August 1939 and also $1,000 less than the $3,500 recommended in the subsequent survey commissioned by the city council in September 1939 in the two construction estimates.[89] According to the *Alexandria Gazette*, negotiations for a site were underway, and one was particularly appealing to the library board. The site appropriation was slated to be presented to the city council for final passage on January 23.[90]

On January 22, the library board held its third meeting of the month, this time to discuss the new Black branch. According to the minutes,

> Miss Scoggin stated that letters are being sent to all references, that a file is being kept, and that she is to write a letter to each colored applicant enclosing [a] copy of a promised letter from Mr. Budwesky saying that said colored applicant may register in Library building, but that no cards will be issued to them, nor can books be withdrawn by them until the new Colored Library, in process of erection, [will] be opened. . . . If [the] person applying is not known to one of the Librarians, and is not in telephone directory [so] that his references [can] be verified [staff can try] consulting the City directory instead of [the] telephone directory.[91]

Presumably, these exaggerated concerns about local references pertained specifically to Black applicants, though the minutes made no explicit mention of "Colored persons."[92]

Scoggin announced that Dorothy Pierce had applied for the position of librarian at the Black branch, and the board instructed her to handle the application "as she saw fit."[93] But in spite of her formidable qualifications, Pierce was not hired. It is reasonable to assume that her eagerness to apply for a library card labeled her as a potential troublemaker. Clearly, she was well aware of the history of the Alexandria Library, the sit-in demonstration, and the board's unyielding position on the subject of desegregation. Meanwhile, on January 23, the city council resolved to appropriate $2,500 for construction costs for the new Black branch. On February 27, it then resolved to spend $1,941.50 on equipment for the branch, which also included the purchase of library materials.[94]

Tucker and Wilson returned to the library on January 30 to resubmit library-card applications, but Scoggin merely offered them library cards that could be used only in the proposed Black branch. Outraged, Tucker wrote a stern letter to the librarian in which he declared, "I refuse and will always refuse to accept a card to be used at the library to be constructed and operated at Alfred and Wythe Streets in lieu of a card to be used at the existing library on Queen Street for which I have made application" (see fig. 7).[95]

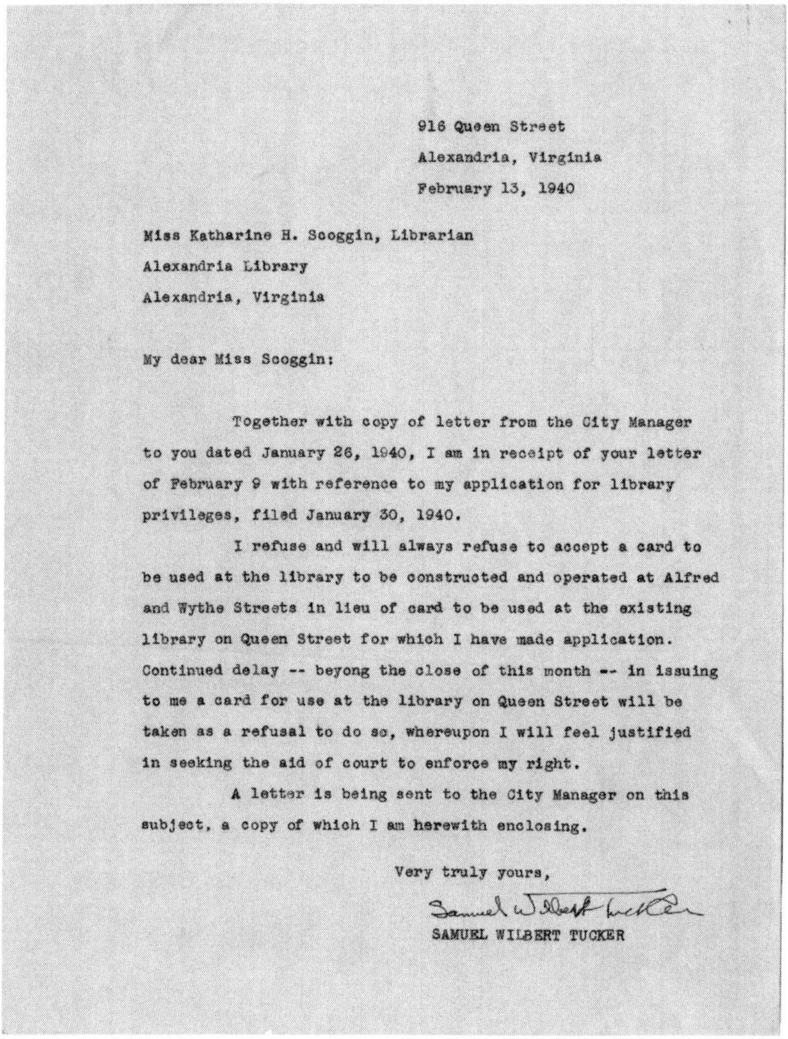

916 Queen Street
Alexandria, Virginia
February 13, 1940

Miss Katharine H. Scoggin, Librarian
Alexandria Library
Alexandria, Virginia

My dear Miss Scoggin:

Together with copy of letter from the City Manager to you dated January 26, 1940, I am in receipt of your letter of February 9 with reference to my application for library privileges, filed January 30, 1940.

I refuse and will always refuse to accept a card to be used at the library to be constructed and operated at Alfred and Wythe Streets in lieu of card to be used at the existing library on Queen Street for which I have made application. Continued delay -- beyong the close of this month -- in issuing to me a card for use at the library on Queen Street will be taken as a refusal to do so, whereupon I will feel justified in seeking the aid of court to enforce my right.

A letter is being sent to the City Manager on this subject, a copy of which I am herewith enclosing.

Very truly yours,

SAMUEL WILBERT TUCKER

Figure 7. Samuel Wilbert Tucker, letter to Katharine H. Scoggin, February 13, 1940, Alexandria Library Company, records, 1937– , box 98J, folder 2, Alexandria Library Special Collections, Alexandria, VA. Reprinted with permission.

Some of the city's African American residents were heartened by the prospect of gaining access to their own library, regardless of any inherent inequities. Many others, however, shared Tucker's anger and resentment; they, too, refused to accept the Jim Crow compromises embodied in the separate-and-unequal Black branch. Tucker

S. W. TUCKER
ATTORNEY AND COUNSELLOR AT LAW
901 PRINCESS STREET
ALEXANDRIA, VIRGINIA

February 13, 1940

Mr. Carl Budwesky
City Manager
Alexandria, Virginia

My dear sir:

      I have copy of your letter dated January 26, 1940, to Miss Katharine H. Scoggin, Librarian, Alexandria Library, discussing the policy to be followed with reference to issuance of library cards to colored residents of this City. I am writing to you in response to Miss Scoggin's consequent failure to issue cards for the library on Queen Street to Sgt. George Wilson, whom I represent as counsel, and to me. Applications for such cards have been duly made and are admitted to be in proper form, etc.

      Each of us has this day advised the Librarian that he will always refuse to accept a card to be used at the library to be constructed and operated at Alfred and Wythe Streets in lieu of card to be used at the existing library on Queen Street; and that continued failure -- beyond the end of this month -- to issue card for which application has been made will be taken as a refusal so to do whereupon relief by mandamus will be sought at the hand of the court.

      Just now, I do not think it necessary to discuss the adequacy or equality of accomodations to be afforded at Alfred and Wythe Streets. I think our position is well fortified by those fundamental rights of the citizen which exist as the basis and foundation of government. Any attempt at segregation contravenes the basic and underlying principle of the common law -- that the purpose of government is to secure the greatest good to the greatest number.

      In the United States, since the adoption of the Fourteenth Amendment to the Federal Constitution, the courts have uniformly declared that in the absence of specific constitutional or statutory authority, municipalities are without power to deny a citizen -- solely on account of his race -- access to any building or other facilities maintained by public funds. Pertinent cases dealing with public schools are numerous. See 11 C. J. 807 CIVIL RIGHTS Section 14, note 74; 56 C. J. 808 SCHOOLS AND SCHOOL DISTRICTS, Section 983, notes 70 and 75. With specific regard to public libraries in a city where separate libraries were maintained for white and colored people, this principle was twice declared by the West Virginia Court as controlling in Brown vs. Board of Education of Charleston Independent School District, 106 W. Va., 476, 146 S. E. 389, 64 A. L. R. 297.

Figure 8. Samuel Wilbert Tucker, letter to Carl Budwesky, February 13, 1940, Alexandria Library Company, records, 1937– , box 98J, folder 2, Alexandria Library Special Collections, Alexandria, VA. Reprinted with permission.

also forwarded a second angry letter, complete with case law citations, to Budwesky, reminding the city manager of his civil rights as an American citizen as stipulated by federal law (see fig. 8).[96] He sent copies of that letter to the city council and to the city attorney, Armistead Boothe.

Tucker planned to appeal Wilson's case but contracted the flu shortly after Woolls's final ruling. During his month-long illness, a group of Black Alexandrians met with city officials and assured them that a segregated library was an acceptable alternative to the desegregation of the Alexandria Library. Given that neither the library board nor city officials wanted to desegregate the main library, they enthusiastically welcomed this news. However, the preemptive gesture effectively undermined Tucker's efforts to force the city to desegregate its only public library.[97] In an interview, Tucker's younger sister Elsie Tucker Thomas derisively referred to this unidentified group as "do-gooders." The archives provide no clue about whether they were the same people who had met previously with board members and urged the construction of a boys' club and community center for African American children rather than a public library.[98]

To circumvent desegregation of the Whites-only Alexandria Library, the Robert H. Robinson Library was hastily constructed as the system's Black branch. At the board's February 12 meeting, Scoggin reported that the city council had chosen the branch's name to honor a Methodist minister and formerly enslaved man who was the grandson of Caroline Branham, Martha Washington's personal maid.[99] There is no evidence that officials made any effort to consult with Alexandria's Black community about the name choice. At the same board meeting, Scoggin also announced that she had hired Evelyn Roper Beam, a Black librarian, to oversee the Robinson Library. Beam, like Pierce, had earned her library degree from Hampton Institute and had also received a librarian's certificate from the Commonwealth of Virginia. She had taught library science at Atlanta University and had worked at the Hampton Institute's library and the Newport News High School's library as well as in a facility in South Carolina. Her familiarity with the service needs of both adults and youths made her an ideal choice to head the new library. However, in spite of her stellar credentials, her years of professional experience, and her full-time status, she was paid far less than the White librarians in the system. The meeting minutes record that Scoggin hired Beam at a Jim Crow salary of $720 per year.[100] In contrast, the minutes for a meeting on December 11, 1939, note that Ellen Coolidge Burke, a White employee, was paid $1,940 per year for work as a part-time cataloger and assistant librarian.[101]

Local newspapers published regular updates about the building's construction progress.[102] On March 4, for example, the *Alexandria Gazette* outlined structural elements yet to be completed at the new branch library and mentioned that the finished space would house a single reading room, a small office for the librarian, a lavatory, and a small area for a janitor. Compared with the Alexandria Library, which was far larger than the Black branch, the Robinson Library shelving and reading spaces would be extremely limited, and there would be no dedicated space for children. The spacious and well-appointed Alexandria Library, on the other hand, featured a reference room, a circulating library, a rare-book room, a children's room, and a meeting room. The frontage of the facility measured sixty-five feet and the depth was fifty feet; the ceiling height was fifteen feet. The *Gazette*'s March 6 update enumerated the branch's architectural details, profiled its namesake and the new librarian, and summarized its organizational relationship with the Alexandria Library. On March 20, the *Gazette* published a photograph of the new library captioned "Library Branch Near Completion" as well as a picture of Beam.[103] This brief news item, however, was overshadowed by a detailed companion article in which Katharine Scoggin reported impressive circulation statistics for the White library.[104]

The branch's total cost included appropriations of $2,500 for construction expenses, $750 for the site purchase, $1,941.50 for books and equipment, and $1,750 for annual operating costs—considerably less than the cost of building, stocking, and maintaining the White library. (A total of $7,500 had been appropriated for equipment for the Alexandria Library—286 percent more than the appropriation for books *and* equipment for the Black branch.)[105] It is unclear if Beam's and the janitor's salaries were included in the branch's operating costs. The architect Ward Brown had designed the modest, one-room, colonial-style brick building, and it was equipped by Remington-Rand—the same company that had equipped the Alexandria Library. In addition to books, the figure for equipment expenses included a typewriter and accessories, a telephone, a library catalog and catalog cards, library-book cards and sleeves, and library-application materials. Whether it also included library furniture and shelving is unclear, though we do know that, like most of the books, the furniture was used.[106] In the *Pittsburgh Courier*, Ted Poston described the Robinson Library as "modest" and reported that there were "better facilities in the capital."[107] During a 1999 interview, Katharine Martyn née Scoggin readily admitted that the two city libraries were not equal, but she hastened to add that the Black library was "attractive." Even sixty years later, she was still insisting that Blacks could have used the District of Columbia libraries, not their own city institution, if they had been "serious readers" (see figs. 9, 10, 11, and 12).[108]

Figure 9. Exterior view of the large and well-appointed Alexandria Library, 2021, photograph by Cal Powell. © 2021 by Cal Powell. Reprinted with permission.

At a board meeting on March 11, (Scoggin) Martyn described the preparations for the Robinson Library and read an itemized list of expenses. According to the minutes, the branch would be considered "part of [the] Alexandria Library system, and . . . be administered by the Board of Directors of the Alexandria Library, . . . under the supervision of Miss Scoggin."[109] The minutes noted that a resolution to that effect would be offered at the next day's city council meeting.

At the April 8 library board meeting, (Scoggin) Martyn announced tentative plans for the opening of the Robinson Library on April 22. She said that city council members had been invited to attend the opening and suggested that library board members should also be present.[110] It is noteworthy that Scoggin was more concerned that the board members attend the opening in order to receive the council rather than as a show of their support for the new branch and the community members it

Figure 10. "Robert H. Robinson Library with Miss Bracie entering, circa 1940," photographer unknown. In the collection of the Alexandria Black History Museum, Alexandria, VA. Reprinted with permission.

Figure 11. Interior view of the spacious, light-filled Alexandria Library, 1937, photographer unknown, MS335 Alexandria Library Book 001 002. Alexandria Library Special Collections, Alexandria, VA. Reprinted with permission.

would serve. The May 13 minutes make no further mention of board or council attendance at the branch opening.[111]

The Black branch project was rushed through construction, opening less than a year after the August 21, 1939, sit-in and less than four months after Judge Woolls's ruling on Wilson's writ of mandamus.[112] On Tuesday, April 23, 1940, the Robert H. Robinson Library opened at 9:00 a.m. for community inspection; and on the following day, between 2:00 and 6:00 p.m., prospective patrons were invited to register for library cards. According to the *Alexandria Gazette*, "[the branch's] collection of books written by negroes for negroes is quite good."[113] Black patrons, however, disputed that claim. Jesse Jennings recalled, "The history books did not include blacks." Lovell A. Lee could not remember if there were books by Black authors in the library; but when asked if the history books accurately portrayed Black lived experience, he quickly replied, "There weren't many books about Black history."[114]

Figure 12. Interior view of the cramped Robinson Library. "Robinson Library Librarian Mrs. Murphy S. Carr [Sara Murphy Carr], April 1946," photographer unknown, MS335 Alexandria Library Book 002 497. Alexandria Library Special Collections, Alexandria, VA. Reprinted with permission.

Library historian Cheryl Knott notes that "public librarians tended to shape local collections according to [evolving] standards of taste and appropriateness. . . . The result was a tension between the potential for change that a black library represented and the pressure toward stasis apparent in a collection that supported the status quo."[115] Thus, White collection developers often based their acquisition choices on titles that reflected their assumptions and expectations about Black readers or on a desire to maintain the social and cultural status quo. Titles purchased for African Americans did not necessarily reflect the realities of Black lived experience, nor did they encourage the racial pride that was more likely to be conveyed in books acquired by Black librarians who were able to participate in collection-development decisions. Whether Beam was allowed to select reading materials is not known. Recalling her childhood reading choices at the Robinson Library, Lillian S. Patterson told me, "I didn't read history books. I primarily read fiction that was not related to my schoolwork. I liked upbeat stories about teenagers. I also liked novels that were love stories." But she had to take what she could get: the donated books that constituted a sizable portion of the Robinson collection reflected the tastes and interests of their White donors rather than the needs or desires of Black library users. Castoffs from the Alexandria Library, another sizable portion of the Robinson Library resources, consisted of unwanted, used, or dated books deemed unsuitable for White patrons.[116] Still, many members of the community were pleased to have access to a library. Lovell Lee said, "[As children] we went to the library often because it was right across the street from my school [Parker-Gray Elementary]. . . . My brother and I patronized the library, but our parents didn't. It was a small library, but they had books of interest to children. I liked books about the West, cowboys, and animals."[117]

The original Robinson Library collection included approximately 1,500 titles, though their categories and sample titles were not recorded. This meager figure stands in stark contrast to the White library. When the Alexandria Library opened, it housed approximately 10,000 books, including approximately 3,000 titles that dated from the original 1794 subscription library.[118] The archives make no mention of magazines in the Robinson Library, though the branch probably stocked them because they were always popular with adults. While Gladys Howard Davis stated that all of the library's books were new, other interviewees remarked that the majority of the Robinson's books were donated or castoffs from the White library. Library board meeting minutes corroborate the recollections of these other interviewees. Ferdinand T. Day told me, "The books were used. I remember a young boy who had a book in which someone had written their name." Lillian Patterson said, "The pattern of the day was to provide Blacks with used rather than new books. . . . The books provided by the city . . . at my school [Parker-Gray Elementary] were used. The books at the Robinson Library were likely used, but they were in good condition."[119] In an article published in *Alexandria Life* on the sixtieth anniversary of the sit-in, a Parker-Gray neighborhood mother recalled, "People do not understand what it is like to explain white books and black books to a child . . . those tattered, out-of-date, hand-me-down books." In the same article, Jesse Jennings commented, "Books at the Robinson Library were considered new to us, but they were literally used books, substandard. We did not have access to newly-published books."[120]

At first, the new Robinson Library was open for only thirty hours per week: Monday through Friday 2:00 to 6:00 p.m., plus evening hours of 7:00 to 9:00 p.m. on Tuesday and Thursday, and Saturday hours of 9:00 a.m. to 3:00 p.m. Even though those hours were already insufficient for working Black adults, beginning in 1944 the operational hours were further shortened: 2:00 to 7:00 p.m., Monday through Friday, and 9:00 a.m. to 1:00 p.m. on Saturday—a one-hour reduction in service per week. In contrast, the Alexandria Library's hours of operation were far more patron-friendly. On Monday, Wednesday, Friday, and Saturday, the facility was open from 9:00 a.m. to 9:00 p.m.; on Tuesday and Thursday, the hours were 9:00 a.m. to 6:00 p.m.—a total of fifty-six hours per week. The main library's dedicated children's room was open from 3:00 to 6:00 p.m. Monday through Friday, and 9:00 a.m. to 6:00 p.m. on Saturday.[121]

At the library board's June 10, 1940, meeting, (Scoggin) Martyn reported that 254 patrons had applied for library cards at the Robinson Library and that circulation had already reached 1,030 books.[122] At the September 18 meeting, she announced that the branch's circulation had reached 2,848 books and that there had been a "decided increase" in adult use of the facility. At the October 14 meeting, she reported that circulation at the Alexandria Library now totaled 4,832 while circulation at the Black branch had decreased to 932 books and magazines. On November 18, she said that circulation at the Alexandria Library had reached 5,470 and that 211 new books had been added to the collection, whereas circulation at the Robinson Library totaled 1,243 and 81 "new" books had been added. The minutes make no mention of whether those "new" books had been newly purchased specifically for the branch or whether they were castoffs from the main library or donated materials.[123]

At the September 18 board meeting, there was a proposal that the city council appropriate $10,500 for the annual operation and expenses of the Alexandria and Robinson libraries. The following increases were suggested and accepted:

Janitor for both libraries: from $270 to $300 yearly
"Colored" assistant librarian: from $60 to $65 monthly
Ellen Coolidge Burke: part-time cataloger and assistant librarian:
     from $420 to $840 yearly
Books: from $1,700 to $1,800 yearly
Telephone: from $72 to $75 yearly
Supplies for both libraries: from $260 to $300 yearly[124]

This was the only mention of a Black assistant librarian in the library board meeting minutes. All of the other minutes referred to Evelyn Beam as the Robinson "Librarian," and she was the only known Black Alexandria Library system employee during the era. Privacy laws prohibit access to employee records, so we can only speculate on where this Black assistant librarian might have worked. Given Robinson's limited hours of operation, it is unlikely that the branch needed an aide at the time. The first known African American paraprofessional was not hired to work at the Black branch until 1947. On the other hand, the expansive hours of operation at the Alexandria Library would have required greater employee coverage, and the facility already employed four White assistant librarians: Alice Green, Sue Fox, Ellen Coolidge Burke, and Robert William Adam. While it is possible that a Black assistant was hired to work at the Alexandria Library, it is unlikely. However, if that were the case, it is also unlikely that the employee would have worked in the public areas of the library. More likely, "colored" assistant librarian referred to Beam. In any case, that salary and the salary of the Black janitor contrast starkly with Burke's, the White part-time cataloger and assistant librarian mentioned on the increase list.

According to the December 9 library board meeting minutes, an unnamed board officer met with Budwesky to discuss "ultimate salary goals." The following objectives were proposed:

Librarian, $2,400 annually

Assistant librarian, $1,500 annually (there is no mention of the
identity or employment site of this assistant)

Cataloger and assistant librarian, $1,200 annually

The ultimate salary objective for the Robinson librarian was proposed at $1,200 annually—50 percent of the White librarian's salary, 80 percent of the White assistant librarian's, and on par with the part-time White cataloger and assistant librarian's. Again, the contrasts are stark. The minutes also note that Scoggin had reduced her hours at the Alexandria Library to half time due to illness in her family. An assistant librarian named Mary Lloyd, not mentioned in previous minutes, added Scoggin's eliminated hours to her schedule.[125]

Though no specific details were recorded, the resignation of Scoggin was discussed at the January 13, 1941, board meeting.[126] Elizabeth Watson was selected to succeed her as the new Alexandria Library librarian and the city's library director. In addition, several salary increases were announced:

Ellen Coolidge Burke, cataloger and assistant librarian: from $70
to $80 monthly

Sue Fox, assistant librarian, from $90 to $95 monthly

Robert William Adam, assistant librarian, from $50 to $60
monthly

Evelyn Roper Beam, the Robinson librarian, from $65 to $70
monthly

Janitor for both libraries, from $25 to $32.50 monthly

Again, the disparity is striking.[127]

These kinds of inequities persisted long after the Black branch was constructed. The physical surroundings of the two properties are a case in point. The grounds of the Alexandria Library had been fully landscaped by the Alexandria Garden Club and were well maintained. Scoggin, to do her justice, did repeatedly request funding to landscape the Robinson Library grounds, but the board routinely refused. Finally, at their March 10 meeting, members consented to pay "no more than $20" for Robinson Library shrubbery.[128] Less than two weeks before the celebration to commemorate the branch's one-year anniversary, its appearance still was not considered a priority. On April 14, board members decided they could not afford to seed the Robinson yard because it had no topsoil. They never considered the possibility of spreading topsoil and then seeding the yard.[129]

Another example of inequity was the lack of consistency in the quality of the staffing. The exact date when Beam left her position as the Robinson's librarian is unknown, but subsequent meeting minutes indicate that she was no longer employed as of November 1942. While she was seeking a replacement, Elizabeth Watson hired a high school student to oversee Robinson Library services, presumably a Black student from Parker-Gray.[130] Apparently, Watson was unable or unwilling to have one of her White assistant librarians work on an interim basis at the Robinson Library until a full-time, credentialed, Black librarian could be hired. This inadequate staffing solution contrasts significantly with board members' long-standing concerns about maintaining the "high standing" of the Alexandria Library and its staff certifications.[131] Hazel Miller, a new permanent, credentialed librarian, was hired for the Robinson Library later in 1942.[132]

At the board meeting on April 23, 1941, which was also the one-year anniversary of the opening of the Robert H. Robinson Library, Elizabeth Watson reported that the facility was offering excellent services and attracting significant patronage. According to the *Alexandria Gazette*, six hundred Black citizens, 12 percent of the city's total Black population, had library cards. Half of these registered patrons were elementary and high school students who used the branch's resources to support their schoolwork. Circulation equaled approximately twenty books per patron. To commemorate its anniversary, the Robinson Library hosted an open house that featured a traveling exhibition of work by African artists, on loan from the prestigious William E. Harmon Foundation, which sponsored traveling exhibitions nationally and internationally and awarded monetary prizes and medals to artists. Beam probably made arrangements for the exhibition; she was far more likely than any other Alexandria official to have known of the foundation and its work.[133] The festivities were all but ignored by the Alexandria Library Association. The May 12 meeting minutes make only a cursory mention of the anniversary, and there is no indication that any board members, library staff members, or city council members were in attendance.[134]

Hazel Miller was succeeded in 1944 by Sara Murphy Carr, another credentialed librarian, who held the position for four years, until leaving to get married. Carr was replaced by Minnie N. Fuller, who was also a credentialed Black librarian, and who worked at the Robinson Library from 1948 to 1962.

In 1947, Gladys Howard Davis, a Black Alexandrian, began work at the Robinson Library as a paraprofessional library assistant, and she continued to work in the system for sixty-one years.[135] When interviewed for this book, she explained that her duties at the Robinson Library included administrative tasks such as helping patrons apply for library cards, typing library cards, and processing incoming and outgoing books. She also oversaw the children's story hours, helped students with book reports, and facilitated a weekly book discussion club for adults. If users wanted specific books not available at the Black branch, Davis would request them from the Alexandria Library. Because Blacks were still barred from the White library, those books would be pulled from the shelves of the library and held for Davis to pick up. She remarked that the Alexandria Library librarians "were always nice and were always fair-minded about loan policies" and "would suggest other titles that might be of interest [to Black patrons]." It is impossible to know, however, if they were genuinely being nice or were working to ensure that Robinson Library patrons would remain satisfied with the existing library arrangements. Lovell Lee told me that "books from the Alexandria Library weren't delivered quickly."[136]

It is not clear if the Robinson Library had a complete copy of the Alexandria Library's catalog from which patrons could choose titles that best served their needs and interests. When I asked Lovell Lee, he said, "I don't think they did." We do know that new books intended for the Robinson Library were cataloged and that used titles were recataloged by the Alexandria Library's staff. However, this does not mean that such resources were available for Robinson Library patrons to peruse. Without a book catalog, they would have been doubly penalized—first, in their reliance on a small and inferior Black branch; second, in their lack of knowledge about all of the available resources. Although Alexandria Library librarians did recommend titles to Robinson Library patrons, they did not communicate with users directly so they may not have known precisely which titles would be most appropriate. It is doubtful that Gladys Davis would have had direct knowledge of the available titles because she was likely not allowed to spend time in the Alexandria Library perusing the catalog or shelves. When I asked her about policies for borrowing books, she said that the same policies applied to patrons of both libraries. Users could borrow four books at a time. Loan time was initially four days, though that was later increased to ten. Reference books that Black users needed were available for overnight loans, and Davis would retrieve and return them from the Alexandria Library.[137]

In 1950, the Robert H. Robinson Library celebrated its tenth anniversary, and its librarian, Minnie N. Fuller, covered the festivities in her May report. She noted that Evelyn Beam, the branch's first librarian and now a librarian at the Library of Congress, was one of five featured speakers.[138] Five years later, Fuller reported that several city council members, on a tour of the city, had had automobile trouble and stopped at the Robinson Library to use the telephone. Fuller took the opportunity to show the men the facility's crowded condition.[139] On May 21, 1956, the library board held its monthly meeting at the Robinson Library for the first time in the facility's history. The Robinson staff was delighted to host the honored guests who, within an hour of their arrival, decided to redecorate the interior of the building. The following month, the branch underwent a complete cosmetic renovation but not a much-needed and long-overdue expansion. Fuller and Gladys Davis worked at the Alexandria Library while the work at the Robinson was in progress.[140]

The Alexandria Library and the Robinson Library both offered their patrons special programs and activities in addition to organized information and resources. Such programming was especially beneficial for Black children, who had fewer recreational outlets than White children. Shirley M. Lee, for example, remarked that she "enjoyed storytelling hour [at the Robinson Library] when the Librarian would read to us." Her husband, Lovell, remembered "attending events during which the [Robinson] librarian would read books about Black luminaries such as George Washington Carver and Booker T. Washington."[141] In 1958 and 1959, the branch's monthly reports included news about special activities in addition to library statistics such as circulation and registration figures and book and magazine acquisitions. Of note were the Tuesday-morning film screenings for Black seventh graders from the segregated Charles Houston and Lyles-Crouch elementary schools, which were held at the Alexandria Library with the support and encouragement of Ellen Coolidge Burke. Otherwise, there is no evidence that, prior to desegregation, Black elementary students were brought to the White library for any other special programs. Likewise, while Fuller sometimes aided the Alexandria Library assistant librarians during story hours for White children, no White assistant librarians from the Alexandria Library seem to have helped a Robinson librarian with programs for Black children.[142]

The Robinson librarians, like the community's Black teachers, served as local leaders as well as mentors and role models. The Library Company's 1959–60 annual report shows that Fuller organized story hours, puppet shows, and a reading club for the Robinson's juvenile patrons and led a story hour at the School for Retarded Children.[143] In addition, she judged community oratory contests; and in 1959, she participated in Negro History–Brotherhood Week at Lyles-Crouch Elementary School, where she read aloud a children's story she had written.[144] Meanwhile, Burke, who had begun her career at the Alexandria Library in 1939 as a part-time cataloger and assistant librarian, was now the system's director of libraries (1948–69). As director, Burke was responsible for implementing one of Virginia's first bookmobile services. She was also an active participant with the local branch of the interracial Urban League and with the Southern Regional Council, which was dedicated to the promotion of racial justice, the protection of democratic rights, and the expansion of civic participation in the South. In a series of letters from May 1963, Burke wrote that she was pleased when "the Alexandria Library became fully integrated. (As it should have been from the beginning.)"[145]

In 1954, the Commonwealth of Virginia had implemented a policy of "Massive Resistance" in opposition to the Supreme Court ruling in *Brown v. Board of Education* that had mandated school desegregation. According to the *Alexandria Gazette*, Alexandria complied with Virginia's policy and "virtually ignored the case completely." In early 1959, "the School Board was taken to court and on January 23, 1959, . . . Judge Albert V. Bryan ordered Alexandria city schools to start integrating." Anticipating a similar judgment, the Alexandria Library quickly began its own process of desegregation and began to admit Black adults and high school students into its main facility. However, because younger children were still barred, a policy of de facto segregation remained in effect. Various sources cite January or February as the library's desegregation start date. In any case, the library board intended to act before the school system did, and the schools in Alexandria were not integrated before February.[146]

At first, the Alexandria Library did not widely publicize the availability of its services for Black high school students and adults. By this time, few of them patronized the Robinson Library, so the powers-that-be probably regarded their presence at the main library as a minimal threat to the established order. Then, in May 1962, Fuller resigned as Robinson librarian. She was briefly replaced in June by Jeanne G. Plitt—a significant change from the previous refusal or unwillingness to have a White employee from the Alexandria Library assigned to the Black branch. The Robinson Library was now functioning exclusively as a children's library, and Gladys Davis continued to work there as a paraprofessional assistant. The secrecy of the library's accessibility, however, was not total because Ellen Burke encouraged Davis to disseminate the news that the Black community now had access to the main branch.[147]

By July 1962, the Alexandria Library was fully integrated, and the separate children's facility was no longer necessary. Davis shifted her focus to operating the bookmobile. After Burke retired in 1969, Plitt took over as director of libraries (1969–92), and bookmobile services were ended. The former Robinson Library was converted to a community center, and Davis was transferred to a behind-the-scenes position at the Alexandria Library. Years later, she moved into more public areas of the library and made the children's department her area of specialization.[148]

When I asked if Black citizens were satisfied with having a segregated library or would have preferred from the beginning to use the Alexandria Library, Davis said that patrons "were very happy and grateful to have access to a library."[149] Although his cousin, William Evans, was a sit-in protester, Ferdinand Day echoed Davis's assessment: "My family patronized the library. The community was very happy and grateful to have a library. . . . We used the library as a venue for community meetings and as a place to have a sounding board to share ideas and plans."[150] Day specifically mentioned the meetings of the Secret Seven, a group of seven Black Alexandrian men who were activists in the community and who regularly assembled at the library to work to improve life for African American residents. He nonetheless added, "Citizens were generally proud of Mr. Tucker and the young men who had the courage and foresight to plan and carry out the sit-in."[151] Lillian Patterson recalled that "she, her siblings, and her parents went to the Robinson Library" and said that "the library was well-patronized," though "[her] father also went to the public library in Washington, D.C."[152] Evans's sister, Dorothy Evans Turner, however, remained angry: "No member of the Evans family ever patronized the Robinson Library, because [we] all supported Tucker's position of not patronizing a library conceived as a segregated Black library."[153] Likewise, Elsie Tucker Thomas stated that no one from her family ever used the Robinson Library and that others in the neighborhood shared her family's resentment toward the Jim Crow facility.[154]

In a 1981 memorandum to Alexandria's city manager, Douglas Harman, the library system's director, Jeanne Plitt, made three significant assertions.[155] First, she stated that the system was "quietly integrated in the 1940s." It is true that Beam began working at the Robinson Library in 1940, so technically the system was integrated that year. But the staff of the Alexandria Library remained all White, and any further integration initiatives during the decade were strictly controlled. Sara Murphy Carr, served as the Robinson librarian until 1948. There is no evidence that any Black staff member worked in the Alexandria Library.[156] Small steps, however, were taken. In April 1948, the board's meeting minutes note, "It was agreed that the Librarian of the Robert Robinson Library be invited to make her report to the Executive Board in person." Previously, the White library director had presented all of the reports from the Robinson Library. Surprisingly, those same meeting minutes also report, "It was suggested that colored members be sought for the [Alexandria Library] Society as vacancies occur."[157] Later that year, Carr made her first in-person presentation to the board.[158] In a 1990 article in the *Alexandria Journal* Plitt reiterated her claims about the system's 1940s integration initiative. This time she went even further, calling the Alexandria Library the first integrated library in Virginia. As shown in table 2, this assertion is not true.[159] Staffing changes notwithstanding, the Alexandria Library continued to function as a Whites-only facility, and the Robinson Library continued to function as the city's Black branch.

Second, Plitt told Harman that, in 1959, the Robinson Library ceased operation as a full-service library and became a children's library and bookmobile station. Services to adult and high school patrons were eliminated because those membership registrations were stagnant and the majority of the branch's patrons were children. When adult services were eliminated, the adult books from the Robinson Library were re-cataloged and transferred to the mezzanine at the Alexandria Library. There is no record of what happened to the children's books when the Robinson Library was closed entirely to the public in 1962. Perhaps the children's books also went to the Alexandria Library, or perhaps they were used to stock the bookmobile.

Some of Plitt's second contention is true: primary sources confirm that the facility became exclusively a children's library in February 1959.[160] But a 1968 summary history of the Alexandria Library says that bookmobile service began in 1962, not 1959, which was also the year that the branch closed entirely. The library's annual reports confirm these dates.[161]

Third, Plitt told Harmon that the Robinson Library and the bookmobile ceased all operation in 1969. Given that sources show that the library was closed as a full-service Black branch before 1969, I believe that she meant that it ceased to function as the bookmobile headquarters that year.[162]

The facility that originally functioned as the Robinson Library reopened in 1983 as the Alexandria Black History Resource Center (ABHRC). In 1987, the city council placed the center's operation under the direction of the Office of Historic Alexandria, which is tasked with "enhanc[ing] the quality of life for City residents and visitors by preserving and interpreting Alexandria's historic properties, archaeological sites, cultural resources, artifact collections, objects, archives, records, and personal stories, and by encouraging audiences to appreciate Alexandria's diverse historic heritage and its place within the broader context of American history."[163] Although the Alexandria Library was extensively renovated in 1956 and 1964, the expansion and renovation of the ABHRC was not undertaken until 1988, after nearly half a century of intentional and unconscionable neglect. The ABHRC reopened in 1989, and the space that comprised the original Robinson Library now houses "Securing the Blessings of Liberty," a permanent exhibition of Alexandria's Black history. The addition, known as the Parker-Gray Gallery, features changing exhibitions of art, artifacts, and various Black historical materials. The building now has enough room for lectures, panel discussions, and documentary film screenings—all of which would have been impossible in the cramped Robinson Library.

In June 1995, the ABHRC opened the Alexandria African American Heritage Park, an eight-acre lot surrounded by a preserved nineteenth-century cemetery for formerly enslaved Black men, women, and children. Six of the twenty-one graves feature the original headstones on the original burial sites. The Watson Reading Room, a small, noncirculating, publicly available research facility, was built on the lot adjacent to the former Robinson Library. Opened in October 1995, it houses a collection of nearly 4,000 books, videos and DVDs, documents, and periodicals on African and African American history and culture. In 2004, the ABHRC was renamed the Alexandria Black History Museum, and it continues to focus on educational programs and community events. In 2012, the museum joined the 3 percent of all U.S. museums to be nationally accredited by the American Alliance of Museums. Audrey P. Davis, the current director, has worked at the museum and its predecessor institutions for more than twenty-five years.[164]

In 1989, to commemorate the fiftieth anniversary of the Alexandria Library sit-in, the Alexandria Society for the Preservation of Black Heritage, which had been founded in August 1980, established the Annie B. Rose Foundation. Among other services, the foundation offers "stipends for students to do research; training of tour guides and museum guides; workshops for genealogy studies; matching grant funds for exhibits; [an] Annie B. Rose lecture series; [and] exposure for students of the arts."[165] The anniversary was the first of a number of subsequent public ceremonies that the Alexandria Black History Museum organized to commemorate the sit-in. City of Alexandria, the library board, and city and library officials gathered to stage a reenactment of the protest, and a plaque was installed in the foyer of the Alexandria Library, now known as the Kate Waller Barrett Branch. In 1990, a *Washington Post* article recounted the history of the sit-in. Then, in 1999, another reenactment was staged on the sixtieth anniversary of the protest, and the *Washington Post*, the *Washington Times*, the *Alexandria Gazette Packet*, *Alexandria Life*, and the *Journal of Blacks in Higher Education* all covered the event. In 2009, the *Alexandria Gazette Packet* and the *Washington Post* provided coverage of the seventieth anniversary of the protest. That year the Alexandria Library System, under the aegis of its first Black director, Rose T. Dawson, finally became involved in helping to plan these commemorative events.[166]

In 2013, on the seventy-fourth anniversary, the *Alexandria Times* published a series of articles about Samuel Tucker. Then, in early 2014, in anticipation of the upcoming seventy-fifth anniversary, the ABHM premiered its exhibition "Sit Down and Take a Stand," which chronicled the event. Later that year, on the morning of Thursday, August 21—the exact anniversary of the original protest—officials from the Alexandria Library System and representatives of the city ceremonially unveiled a state historical marker honoring Tucker and the five demonstrators. The marker was installed on North Washington Street, around the corner from the library building, which unfortunately obfuscates its context. I inquired about the marker's placement and was told that infrastructure issues prevented installation on Queen Street in front of the library. Sadly, the current placement does little to underscore the history of either the library or the sit-in. A second, more informative marker has since been installed at the entryway to the library, but it is not visible from the street. Dawson hosted the ceremony, and the keynote speakers were Patricia Timmons-Goodson, who served on the U.S. Commission on Civil Rights and was a retired North Carolina Supreme Court justice, and Frank Smith, director of the African American Civil War Museum. A highlight of the program was the reading of the Commonwealth of Virginia's house joint resolution 418 commemorating the anniversary. Letters of congratulations came from the Black Caucus of the American Library Association and the NAACP, and the event was well covered by local media.[167]

In the years following the library demonstration, Otto Tucker was the only one of the five sit-in protestors who remained actively involved in issues of social justice and civil equality. He also seems to have been the only one who attended college. Following in his brother Samuel's footsteps, he graduated from Armstrong Technical High School and earned his baccalaureate and law degrees from Howard University. Otto married Louise Buncamper in 1939; and in 1940, the same year he left the university, he began working as a clerk for his father, Samuel A. Tucker, Jr. After serving in the military, he passed the Virginia bar exam in 1946 and practiced law in Alexandria in the same office occupied by Tom Watson, his brother Samuel, and their father. In addition to his private practice, he served on the legal staff of the state conference of the NAACP. Otto later accepted a position in Milwaukee, where he directed a program that provided legal services to the poor and he provided similar services in Montréal. He returned to Alexandria when his health began to fail and died in 1988 at the age of seventy-one.[168]

In 1940, when the Robert Robinson Library was constructed, both Clarence and Robert Strange were employed by Alexandria Hospital. By 1942, Clarence no longer resided in Alexandria and was likely serving in the military. Eventually, he returned to the city and in 1947 was a federal employee. In 1942, Robert Strange worked at the Community Drug Store. By 1945, he was no longer living in Alexandria; but by 1947, he was back and was enrolled as a student in Alexandria. The brothers were purportedly involved in another civil rights protest in Alexandria, but there is no available evidence supporting or refuting that claim.

After the sit-in, Edward Gaddis was also working for Alexandria Hospital. By 1942, he no longer resided in Alexandria and was likely serving in the military.

In 1936, before the sit-in, Morris Murray was already working as a printer; and by 1940, he was employed as a linotype operator. He joined the army in 1942 and by 1947 was no longer living in Alexandria.

William Evans was still in high school at the time of the sit-in. In a 1990 article in the *Alexandria Journal*, he recalled that "it was difficult for blacks to get good jobs [after high school]. . . . The best jobs available to blacks were as clerks or messengers. There were very few administrative jobs."[169] So Evans joined the army; and "as part of the Army's special services division, he traveled to Italy, France, Africa and Germany arranging entertainment for the troops."[170] Afterward, he returned to Alexandria. At the time of his interview, Evans was sixty-nine years old and still living in Alexandria. He was the only known surviving protester.[171]

Asked if he remembered how his parents had reacted to the sit-in, Lovell Lee told me:

> The protest was a first step, a momentous step, and people must have spoken of it. Surprisingly, my parents never talked about it.

I knew Clarence and Robert Strange—two of the protesters. My family and their family attended the same church and their house was around the corner from the church. My father took me around the neighborhood on weekend visits to Alexandria where my grandparents lived. Clarence and Robert never spoke of the sit-in.

I next asked Lee why he thought people were so silent about the demonstration and whether he thought city residents were concerned about upsetting the harmony that existed between Whites and Blacks because the demonstrators' actions deviated from normalized behavioral practices. He responded, "I think the silence was because people didn't think the protest was such a big deal and they just moved on with their lives. They didn't have the hindsight that we do now."[172]

CHAPTER EIGHT

# What Happened?
# What Changed?

The story of the 1939 sit-in demonstration to desegregate the Alexandria Library is the microhistory of a local Black community agitating for change. It is also the microhistory of the agitators—Samuel Wilbert Tucker, the architect of the protest; and Otto Lee Tucker, Morris L. Murray, Clarence Strange, Edward Gaddis, and William Evans, the five protesters. All tried to use their personal agency to force the city's legal system to dismantle the de facto and de jure discrimination that barred Blacks from the library.[1] Although their efforts were unsuccessful and full integration of the Alexandria Library was deferred for another twenty-three years, Tucker's legal strategies established precedents for subsequent local, regional, and national civil rights initiatives. This dramatic, direct-action effort revealed that the library was a microcosmic physical place and social space that epitomized Jim Crow segregation and Alexandria's community values and showed, in stark relief, the societal boundaries between the city's Black and White citizens. The protestors' activism was also embedded in the macro realm of southern society, culture, history, and mores, including the region's public library development. As August Meier and Elliott Rudwick contend, "Rarely were frontal assaults made on the issue of segregation itself." Yet before the Alexandria Library sit-in, no southern public library had been the focus of a demonstration aimed directly at desegregation, and never before had a library been the site of a direct-action demand for full and equitable Black access to services and collections. That would all change in the coming decades.[2]

Throughout the legal hearings associated with the demonstration, Armistead Boothe and Samuel Tucker waged a tactical tug-of-war.

154

Neither attorney wanted the protesters to be indicted, but each played his role in the confrontation with established racial, social, cultural, historical, intellectual, economic, political, and judicial mores. Boothe, the scion of one of the city's oldest and most prominent families, personified tradition, continuity, and the status quo. As city attorney and vice president of the library board, he vigorously prosecuted the demonstrators and forcefully represented the interests of city and library officials. His exuberance led him to present questionable arguments rejecting the Fourteenth and Fifteenth amendments, though his daughter, Julie B. Perry, later said that her father was a staunch supporter of the U.S. Constitution and endorsed education for all citizens. Boothe's constitutional arguments were at odds with his reputation in the Black community "as a man who was fair and square in all of his undertakings." The *Chicago Defender* reported that one of the city's Black residents "went so far as to publish a small hometown journal devoted entirely to Mr. Booth[e] and urging the citizens to cast their vote for him" in an upcoming election. In an article in the *Virginia Law Review*, George Rutherglen described Boothe as a liberal, though that characterization may be applicable only from a southern perspective. Perry herself characterized her father as a moderate.[3]

Tucker, the talented son of educated, middle-class, professional parents who encouraged social activism, embodied the spirit and pursuit of change as well as the opposition to the imperatives of Jim Crow. Tucker's engagement in civil rights activism and his conceptualization and orchestration of the library protest were not anomalies but a reflection of his family legacy. Though he faced the disapprobation of city officials, the library board, White citizens, and the Black community's core of accommodationists, he was willing to confront those challenges because he realized that public libraries were essential components of the city's educational infrastructure, and he was determined to secure equitable access for the city's Black citizens.

In fact, the library protest triggered a public crisis of authority in an iconic local institution that epitomized the ideals that Whites reserved for themselves and denied to Blacks: literacy, education, culture, and power. These ideals underscored and perpetuated the White supremacy and hegemony that were fundamental to southern society as Whites knew it and wanted it preserved. Most southern Whites assumed that a natural and proper racial order separated them from Blacks and specified the only reasonable position of African Americans in the racial hierarchy. To deviate from that hierarchy would obfuscate the laws of nature and society and confound racial and social order. This public crisis of authority also represented a direct threat to the metaphoric symbol of everything that differentiated Whites and Blacks and everything that justified White supremacy and Black subjugation. Many Whites believed that Blacks were incapable of the higher-order critical thinking and cognitive-processing skills required for intellectual, cultural, and aspirational pursuits. Belief in this myth lay behind their automatic assumption that Blacks were suited only for menial endeavors that needed to be supervised by their supposed intellectual superiors, and that they should passively accept their lot.[4]

Before the library sit-in, Whites in Alexandria never anticipated that Blacks would view public library access as a right worth pursuing, nor did they anticipate challenges to their society's normative standards and its de facto and de jure policies. Tucker's decision to situate a civil rights protest in a library was both conceptually novel and prescient because it extended the NAACP's legal achievements in the realm of graduate and professional education to local public library education. Without Tucker's initiative, African Americans who wanted library access would have waited indefinitely for a top-down decision from White city leaders, many of whom were indifferent to their plight and were intent on maintaining existing power relations. In an interview, Elsie Tucker Thomas said, "White people never thought that black people ever needed anything. Now if they need something . . . they're human beings. . . . Why shouldn't we?"[5] Her comment speaks directly to the human condition. As Aldous Huxley wrote, "Every man who knows how to read has it in his power to magnify himself, to multiply the ways in which he exists, to make his life full, significant and interesting." Yet as W. E. B. Du Bois noted, "we daily hear that an education that encourages aspiration, that sets the loftiest of ideals and seeks as an end culture and character rather than bread-winning, is the privilege of white men and the danger and delusion of black."[6] When the library board and the city council originally decided to limit use of the Alexandria Library to Whites and make no alternative provisions for African Americans, they perpetuated inequality and chose to deprive Black Alexandrians of opportunities for self-education, self-empowerment, and participation in civic engagement and the democratic process. Though the library now termed itself a public institution, by barring Blacks it was in fact public in name only. David Sibley refers to such sites as "ambiguous, seemingly public but actually private space."[7] This decision reflected an inconsistency between public rhetoric—the claim that a serious discussion of Black use of the library had taken place—and private communication—the resolution to dismiss an entire group of Alexandrian citizens from a specific municipal service.

In 1937, when the Alexandria Library was established as a free, tax-supported municipal facility, civic engagement joined moral and intellectual advancement as institutional hallmarks. The February 12, 1940, library board minutes, for example, report that Rabbi Hugo Schiff of Alexandria's Congregation Beth El had written to the *Alexandria Gazette* recommending that the city "hold a forum for the discussion of matters pertaining to [the] City, and other subjects of public interest, and suggesting [the] Alexandria Library as [the] place of meeting."[8] The board enthusiastically endorsed his proposal. Rabbi Schiff, the spiritual leader of Congregation Beth El from 1939 through 1949, had been imprisoned in the Dachau concentration camp and was now the Jewish chaplain at Fort Belvoir and vice president of the Alexandria Ministerial Association.[9] Rabbi Schiff's idea about using the library as a site of social interaction and community building emphasized its importance as a "public sphere," which the German philosopher Jürgen Habermas has defined as a physical place and social space for public discourse, transmission of information, and civic engagement, one separate from the government and the marketplace. His theory, however, is flawed. Jane Mansbridge, for example, shows that in basing his public-sphere concept on sites such as eighteenth-century coffee houses, which excluded women and the working class, Habermas circumscribed the place of women and workers in society and contradicted democratic principles that encompass "both common and conflicting interests." Likewise, in discussing the ways in which people "actively construct relations of separation," Susan Bickford notes that while "theorists of the public sphere have stressed its role as a nonstate arena of communicative interaction, a central space of opinion formation . . . [,] the architecture of our urban and suburban lives provides a hostile environment for the development of democratic imagination and participation."[10]

The systemic racist policies that barred Blacks from Alexandria's public library also contradicted democratic principles. African Americans' place in society was circumscribed not only by race but also by gender and class, making them particularly conspicuous in public places and social spaces and especially vulnerable to banishment. White female librarians and library patrons likely perceived the Black, male, sit-in protesters as physical and social threats, even though they were doing nothing more than sitting and reading. These perceived threats were magnified by the standard operational milieu of public libraries in the early decades of the twentieth century, when middle- and upper-class White women typically oversaw these facilities. In other words, libraries were gendered, racialized, and classist spaces managed by people who functioned as agents for White patriarchy, White supremacy, and idealized femininity. As the scholar Gina Schlesselman-Tarango writes:

> Lady Bountiful, an archetype that represents a particular mode of femininity and its supposed moral superiority, is specifically white, female, and middle or upper class. As we work to locate Lady Bountiful in [library and information science] we can begin to see that it was the very qualities associated, not simply with gender, but also whiteness in feminine form that functioned to position her as the ideal library worker.

Cheryl Knott similarly maintains that denying Blacks access to White libraries protected White women's racial superiority, entitlement, and authority as well as White men's perceived need to protect them from a self-created threat. During the sit-in, the White women's complaints about the presence of the protesters was a step toward accusing the men of violating race-based social-contact mores.[11]

In contrast with Habermas, the theorist Ray Oldenburg identifies more egalitarian "third spaces" or "core settings of informal public life . . . beyond the realms of home and work" as sites of democratic social interaction. In these third spaces, individuals engage in voluntary leisure or recreational activities that are fundamental to maintaining public life, local democracy, human connections, and community vitality. Theoretically, libraries could serve as neutral third spaces in which the social activity of reading would create community and where inclusion would be the rule. But in fact, neutrality is impossible: in any situation there is an inequitable distribution of power predicated on social, class, racial, gender, and political hierarchies. Disruptions to systems of power, such as challenges to systemic racism, are required to ensure equity, diversity, and inclusion.[12] Furthermore, Oldenburg's conception of libraries as third spaces does not account for the divergencies and limitations of potential personal interactions in the microenvironment of 1930s Alexandria or the macroenvironment of the Jim Crow South. While interpersonal contacts and activities were possible within distinctly racialized spaces, prohibitions on mingling outside of one's circumscribed place and space reduced the extent of potential contacts and underscored racial differences. Moreover, true neutrality entails temporal and spatial welcome, equity of patron service and experience, and equity of materials selection and availability; but in the contested terrain of the Alexandria Library, elite and nonelite White patrons, staff, and administration felt a sense of entitlement, ownership, and privilege that left no room for Black Alexandrians. According to Wayne A. Wiegand, regular visitors to these physical places and social spaces "play very influential roles in controlling the third place activities of [other] individuals, who over time learn habits of acceptable social behavior and civic responsibility by observing the interactions of others." Wiegand points out that while library spaces have broad, popular appeal for users interested in collections, information services, and personal workspaces, many questions remain about how they provide experiential spaces for public use. In his view, library professionals have neglected to provide a full understanding of "libraries as [multifaceted] places . . . in the [lives of] users," ones that also attract nonusers and enhance human connectedness.[13]

The theorist Lyn H. Lofland posits a "private realm" of intimate relationships, a "parochial realm" in which individuals are united by similitude and interpersonal networks, and a "public realm" where people are unknown or little-known to one another. She defines public realms not as geographical or physical territories but as social ones. Unlike Oldenburg, she maintains that public realms are frequently viewed through a moral lens, and this hierarchical grounding privileges those who perceive themselves to be morally superior. Her theory thus addresses a fundamental tenet of White supremacy—moral superiority—that undergirds systemic racism. By acknowledging society's fixation on the social and cultural differentiation that affects how individuals and groups shape and are shaped by interactions with others, Lofland's theory of the public realm embraces a broader historical and experiential perspective, one that includes both its potential negative aspects and its educative, recreational, intercommunicative, and interactive opportunities.[14]

In Alexandria, Black adults and children had far fewer third spaces or public realms than Whites did because segregation and Jim Crow imperatives excluded them from many settings and opportunities that Whites took for granted. Ferdinand T. Day told me, "There were no places where [Black adults] could go for wholesome entertainment." Although the physical place and social space of the Robinson Library were inferior to those of the Whites-only Alexandria Library, the Black branch provided a quiet and safe environment that was free of explicit and implicit racial biases. Adult patrons could acquire literacy skills, join reading enthusiasts in book groups, socialize with friends and colleagues, and participate in civic engagement and the democratic process through discussions of local and national sociopolitical issues that impacted Black life and the Black community. Black Alexandrians with limited educations could master literacy skills, using their personal agency to enrich their lives and support their children's academic growth. Patrons with diverse socioeconomic and education levels came together in an environment in which the normative standards of the larger White community did not hinder social interaction and learning opportunities. As Day remarked, "the library was a vehicle for the acquisition and dissemination of knowledge and information in the Black community. It provided a central meeting place for citizens to find out about activities in the community. Citizens were better able to gain knowledge to allow them to move forward."[15] Importantly, the Robinson Library was also a nonsectarian communal meeting space. As Julia A. Hersberger, Lou Sau, and Adam L. Murray write, Black churches supplied African American communities with material needs, mutual aid societies, and political platforms, in addition to supporting their faith. But these sectarian benefits, often accompanied denominational rivalry and competition or reinforced class distinctions that created divisiveness in the community. The library was a more neutral and less divisive place and space that supplemented the roles of the churches.[16]

In *Geographies of Exclusion*, David Sibley posits the notion of object relations theory to identify "spatial and social boundary processes [which] separate some groups and individuals from society." He maintains that adherence to established social rules is more likely "when the identity of the community is threatened," as when the racial tension fomented in response to the library sit-in exacerbated the intransigence of Whites about transgressed social boundaries in third spaces.[17] Sibley argues:

> Concern with order, conformity and social homogeneity [is] secured by strengthening the external boundary. . . . This process is seen by the members of the community as a virtuous one—it brings into being a morally superior condition to one where there is mixing because mixing (of social groups and of diverse activities in space) carries the threat of contamination and a challenge to hegemonic values.[18]

In the case of the Alexandria Library System, only rarely did exceptional individuals—for instance, Ellen Coolidge Burke, who directed the system from 1948 to 1969, and Arthur J. Mourot, a president of the library board—attempt to expand spatial, social, and racial boundaries to connect with a broader constituency. That happened, for example, in 1960, when Mourot suggested that the library board members hold their next meeting at the Robinson Library.[19] That meeting marked the first occasion on which the board met at the Robinson Library—a facility constructed twenty-one years earlier.

Susan Bickford posits a political theory of urban settings in which constructed environments, democratic politics, and public life reveal inequitable social dynamics in matters of public policy.[20] Such dynamics demonstrate that the complex relationship between politics and administration—including the administration of public policy—is contingent on established social mores, social and political policies and politics, community attitudes, locale, and era. In the case of the Alexandria Library, the city council's decisions about public policy— under the persuasive leadership of Carl Budwesky—determined that use of the Alexandria Library would continue to be limited to Whites and that a separate-and-unequal library would be built for Blacks. Librarian Katharine H. Scoggin, the library board, and the Alexandria Interracial Committee had preferred the idea of creating a Black annex to the existing library, until the committee insisted that Black visitors to the annex should use the same entrance as Whites.[21] Such an idea was inconceivable to Whites because it would have endowed prospective Black library patrons with social and cultural parity.

Cheryl Knott addresses libraries as constructed environments that reflect both social dynamics and user activism. She contends that "a theory about space as a cultural phenomenon subject to various interpretations and in which social relations are reproduced helps position public libraries as symbolic parts of the built environment within a milieu that shaped and was shaped by gender, race, and class but also by individuals intent on having access to a collection of books and periodicals."[22] As physical, social, and cultural constructs, the Alexandria Library and, later, the Robert H. Robinson Library epitomized places and spaces that affirmed and perpetuated the Jim Crow policies of separate and unequal. They symbolized the ways in which Whites and Blacks navigated social and cultural systems and institutions conceived to ensure both their disengagement and their interdependence. The races of library users and their choice of libraries were examples of such navigation. Like the Alexandria Library, the Robinson Library was subsidized with municipal taxes paid by all Alexandrians. Although constructed for use by Black citizens, it was, technically, open to all Alexandrians. There is no evidence, however, that any Whites ever patronized the facility. Why would they? They knew the Black branch and its collections were inferior to the facility and resources of the Alexandria Library, which was readily accessible even to non-elite Whites. Curiosity would have been White patrons' only motivation for visiting the Black library, an act that would have defied White protocols for acceptable behavior and jeopardized their standing in the community. The visits of White city council and library board members were expressions of power rather than equality, and this would have been the case for *any* Whites who chose to patronize the Robinson Library. By contrast, Blacks had no choice of facilities because the Robinson Library was the only one available to them.

Why do some historical events lead to change, while others change nothing and are forgotten? Although the 1939 library sit-in is relatively unknown within the larger national story of the Civil Rights Movement, the event had a profound impact on the city of Alexandria, the library board, city officials, and the community's White and Black citizens. It not only challenged Commonwealth laws, local public ordinances, and normative standards but also defied hegemonic racial imperatives. For Whites, the sit-in symbolized threats to White supremacy, managed race relations, and acceptable behavioral norms. For Blacks, it symbolized opposition to racial discrimination and the pursuit of civil rights.

Whites regarded the demonstration's outcome as a victory because they were able to accommodate the Black community while preserving racial supremacy, hegemonic hierarchies, and normative mores. Except for the brief time that the protesters were in the public library, Whites were not obliged to share their exclusive place and space with African Americans, and they sacrificed no loss of power, authority, or identity. For Blacks, the sit-in's outcome was a partial victory and a defeat. Although the Robinson Library was conspicuously inferior to the White library in size, construction, and collections, it gave many African Americans their first and only access to library services and resources. For others, the acquisition of a local Black library eliminated the necessity of costly and time-consuming trips to the libraries in the District of Columbia. With the Robinson Library, Black Alexandrians finally acquired a formal structure in their own community where they could utilize individual agency to pursue personal and group goals as well as engage in recreational reading or socializing. For many in the Black community, a Jim Crow library was preferable to no library at all. But other African Americans continued to resent their racist exclusion from the so-called public library that their tax dollars helped to subsidize. Ultimately, therefore, the construction of the Robinson Library was both a qualified victory and a civil rights loss. Moreover, this qualified victory was also recognized by everyone in the African American community as an unqualified victory for the status quo. Though the sit-in had reaffirmed hegemonic rule and White social norms, the protest was one of a series of incremental steps forward in the continuum of civil rights progress at the municipal level. Thus, the sit-in remains a testament to the power of public protest and nonviolent civil disobedience to compel accommodation, if not equity.

Given Alexandria's prevailing political and judicial power dynamics, the success of Tucker's ambitious plan was always remote, despite its sound tactics and Tucker's brilliant legal mind. In this way, the outcome was not unusual. While a number of major judicial achievements supporting social progress were won through the court system, many other attempts failed, especially those that were directly affected by local politics and conservative courts. Legal historian and political scientist Gerald N. Rosenberg argues that significant reform is rarely generated by litigation because courts are typically ineffective and weak. In his chronicle of the U.S. Supreme Court's subversion of equal rights, Lawrence Goldstone agrees.[23] This does not, however, mean that Tucker erred in his decision to stage a civil rights protest in a library. He knew the fight was justified and that he had a slim chance of success. His battle for Black self-determination and self-interest was worth waging, regardless of the odds.

One could argue that the demonstration was largely forgotten because Tucker failed to achieve his objective and the ensuing change was minimal. This argument, however, neglects to acknowledge critical factors that contributed to the demonstration's erasure from all but local memory. Included are the mainstream media's frantic coverage of the impending war, which superseded ongoing news coverage of the sit-in and Tucker's subsequent illness, which prevented him from sustaining his civil rights activism and pursuing further legal challenges. An additional factor was the preemptive undermining of the effort's objective by a group of accommodationist Black Alexandrians. Nevertheless, the 1939 sit-in remains central to understanding the function, meaning, and symbolism of Alexandria's separate-and-unequal libraries. As intellectual and cultural constructs in places and spaces, they defined the city's community values and the social boundaries that shaped interracial relationships.

The Alexandria Library sit-in was significant because it incorporated five interrelated, interdependent challenges. First, the protest overtly opposed established social, historical, cultural, intellectual, institutional, and legal norms conceived to ensure and perpetuate the relegation of Black citizens to subjugation and second-class citizenship. Second, it demanded social equity because it briefly enabled Blacks to share a physical place and social space previously reserved for exclusive use by Whites. Third, it sought the rights of citizens, regardless of race, to pursue aspirational goals. Fourth, it demanded economic equity, through Black access to services that all city residents paid for with their municipal taxes. Finally, it sought judicial equity. Tucker's orchestration of the protest was audacious in its conception and execution because it employed the juridical processes customarily used to exploit Black powerlessness to force city officials to confront an issue they had consciously and intentionally chosen to ignore. This last challenge was crucial, because without Tucker's initiative, White officials would probably have continued to deny Black citizens any form of public library access.

Historian Patterson Toby Graham writes:

The emphasis that black civil rights workers placed on the integration of public libraries throughout the segregated South demonstrated that to them public libraries were not "marginal" cultural institutions but an intrinsic part of the communities' educational infrastructure. Because of their professed democratic nature, public libraries that practiced segregation became symbols of the American racial dilemma.[24]

The sit-in gave White Alexandrians the opportunity to realize the promise of democracy that public libraries embody. They had the chance to enrich their city and benefit its residents by facilitating the development of a better-educated, more informed, and more engaged citizenry. Instead, they remained committed to an idealized southern past and culture that were socially and morally regressive as well as racist. By so doing, they belied the professed mission of public libraries as democratic institutions and intentionally crippled the ethos of *public*.

The physical place and social space of Alexandria's White library mirrored the racialized hierarchy of the larger society in which Blacks were the least empowered citizens in the community. White Alexandrians reacted anxiously to Tucker's civil rights initiative because it necessitated reevaluation of the racial tensions between empowerment and subjugation implicit in *Plessy v. Ferguson* and of the terms and conditions of existing normative standards. Following Judge William Pape Woolls's writ of mandamus ruling, library and city officials were faced with the immediate need to address the possibility that large numbers of Black Alexandrians would legally register as Alexandria Library patrons. They responded by constructing a Black branch that perpetuated inequality and White supremacy, reinforced spatial and social boundaries devised to manage and control race relations, and preserved the racial inviolability of the physical place and social space of the Alexandria Library. As one Black resident later remarked, "[Whites] have neither the resolve nor the stamina to deal with discrimination."[25] Ultimately, the actions of the city's White elite merely deferred the library's eventual desegregation.

According to political sociologist and labor historian Rachel Meyer, sit-in demonstrations have been perceived as both undemocratic (because a minority of workers can "[bring] other workers into the fold") and "quintessentially democratic" (because "the rank and file [act] against corporate and union power alike"). Tucker's sit-in fits the definition of "quintessentially democratic" because it is, in Meyer's words, "a tactic that is more radical than its demands." Scholar Pamela Spence Richards takes this idea further, maintaining that protest against an existing order that impedes intellectual aspirations is "inherently subversive."[26] By proactively using direct action in an effort to desegregate the public library, Tucker and the protesters were challenging not only library and city officials but also the larger Black community, including those individuals who later cooperated with White authorities by accepting the compromise of a separate-and-unequal Jim Crow library.

Tucker's attempt to desegregate the Alexandria Library was unsuccessful in the short term, but its achievements were still significant. It was the first recorded example of a staged sit-in demonstration used as a tactic to pressure a municipality to provide Black citizens with full access to the services and resources of a Whites-only public library. Moreover, it was one of the rare instances in recorded civil rights history in which an all-Black group launched a challenge directly and overtly against the issue of segregation for the benefit of Blacks. Blacks' previous public protests—with or without White allies—had generally involved boycotts or picket lines with the goal of ending discriminatory practices in service treatment or public accommodations. As Meier and Rudwick explain, their objective "was usually not desegregation, but a fairer allocation of the separate arrangements," such as improved seating in theaters. Nearly all of the earlier direct-action protests against Jim Crow segregation occurred in the North, involved Communists and mass-action demonstrations with integrated groups, and were not sustained incidents. The few all-Black for-Blacks direct-action civil rights challenges that took place in the border states or the upper South concerned public accommodations and service provisions; they were not waged directly against segregation. For instance, the successful 1867

Charleston, South Carolina, protests against excluding Blacks from riding inside streetcars were exceptional in that they involved early sit-ins, but their objective was to end inequitable service treatment rather than confront the issue of segregation.[27]

The Alexandria Library sit-in demonstration also anticipated protests in subsequent decades, when Black activists in the South demonstrated for equal access to their local Whites-only libraries. We have no direct evidence of a link between the 1939 library protest and these later actions. However, the Black local and national press continued to report on events associated with the sit-in, so it is highly possible that news of the Alexandria demonstration attracted the attention of other African American community leaders, perhaps inspiring them to engage in discussions with library and municipal officials or to engage in direct-action protests to secure library access for their own Black citizens. The timeline suggests that this may be true. For instance, in Louisville, Kentucky, activists began working in 1942 to integrate the city's public libraries, and their coalition used sit-ins, letters to the editor, and testimony at a library board meeting to persuade the board to integrate gradually between 1948 and 1952. Likewise, in 1949, as the head of the NAACP's Youth Council in Montgomery, Alabama, life-long civil rights activist Rosa Parks trained young people to challenge segregation in the city's public library.[28]

It is also possible that news of Alexandria's library sit-in drew the attention of library boards and officials in other cities. They may have made the move to provide their Black citizens with library access as a way to forestall protracted legal battles and negative media coverage of segregated facilities. Some municipalities may have wanted to protect local business interests by avoiding reportage that may have cast their communities in an unfavorable light. I found evidence suggesting that the Alexandria Library demonstration did have a direct influence on library desegregation activism among Black citizens in another Virginia microenvironment. In 1960, protestors conducted a library sit-in at the Whites-only McKenney Public Library in the city of Petersburg. The Petersburg demonstration was significant on its own, but it was also significant as a continuation of Tucker's involvement in direct-action library desegregation protests. According to Howard G. Cooley, the son of Robert H. Cooley, Jr., a lawyer involved with the action, the Alexandria Library sit-in was the inspiration for the Petersburg protest. Cooley's father had been Tucker's friend and legal colleague, and there is strong circumstantial evidence that the two civil rights attorneys had discussed the Alexandria demonstration. Howard Cooley said that his father had spoken to him directly about the Alexandria protest; and during a 1985 interview, both Samuel and Otto Tucker mentioned the Petersburg protest and Samuel's involvement with it.[29]

The location and the atmosphere of Alexandria and the attitudes and sensibilities of its citizenry also played unique roles in the unfolding drama. Given its proximity to Washington, D.C., the city had close ties to national issues through Black and White media as well as government interests. Its citizenry was involved and engaged in public matters. But Alexandria also had a unique public temperament. Throughout the demonstration, during the police intervention, and in the subsequent court hearings, Alexandria officials behaved with a civility not typically associated with racial confrontations or public civil rights protests. From their arrest, detention, and release, the activists were treated with courtesy and respect by police and court officers. In a later article about school desegregation issues, Jerry Kline described the city as one that "traditionally has de-emphasized racial problems." Armistead Boothe's daughter, Julie B. Perry, echoed that assessment: "Alexandrians were not enthusiastic in their acceptance of integration, but there wasn't as much hate in Alexandria as there was in other locales. Alexandrians were quiet and restrained about racial issues."[30]

This demeanor of gentility was rooted in tradition. The residents of Alexandria and surrounding areas of northern Virginia had long-standing associations with the aristocratic planter elite, who emphasized class over race and selfishly guarded the rights and privileges of property holders. Historians Jack M. Bloom and Armstead L. Robinson have argued that class-based discrimination preceded race-based discrimination, which they believe evolved as a way to perpetuate the South's political economy and manage the potential for class-based protest.[31] After the Civil War, the oligarchy reaffirmed its dominance in social, cultural, political, and economic affairs by withholding access to educational opportunities, disenfranchising the landless, and mandating registration certificates for voters. Each of these maneuvers reinforced their authority and minimized the opportunities for poor and rural citizens, regardless of their race, to affect legislative and economic decision making. Elite Whites consciously distanced themselves from working-class Whites, though they formed occasional alliances to safeguard racial supremacy and ensure Black subordination. Over time, these attitudes and traditions influenced the elites' inclination to guard against intrusions into the private and semi-private operations of the Alexandria Library.

Today, White and Black Alexandrians and a host of library and city officials celebrate the 1939 sit-in as a milestone in local history. Current circulation statistics, attendance figures at special events, and extensive usage of the library attest to the system's continued importance among the city's diverse citizens. Yet challenging and unpleasant issues remain, and simply focusing on the symbolism of the sit-in rather than its implications does not relieve us of responsibility for clarifying and addressing them.

During the seventy-fifth anniversary commemorations of the sit-in, for example, only one of the speakers, Patricia Timmons-Goodson, explicitly made a connection between the demonstration and the importance of reading and education in contemporary society, especially for Black citizens. She was also the only speaker to frame the protest as a struggle in the present for a better future and she described reading as a way to imagine alternative life opportunities. While former Robinson Library employee Gladys Howard Davis told me in her interview that she had encouraged Black children to read as a way to improve their lives and futures, that link was not on the minds of most of the dignitaries at the commemorations.[32] No one at the 2014 ceremonies spoke of the physical place, social space, or community role of libraries. No special events addressed key issues such as how and why libraries are important components of a city's educational infrastructure, how libraries, in their capacity as third spaces or public realms, can best serve diverse constituencies, how community and social activists can incorporate libraries into social-service programs, or how and why community involvement in the operation and management of libraries can enhance patron services. It would have been an opportune time to host a dialogue on the roles and responsibilities of libraries and their users, in the past, present, and future; or on access and engagement with libraries as a means of participating in the democratic process. It would have been an apt moment to initiate conversations about the symbolism of libraries, their responsibilities to communities, and communities' responsibilities to libraries. It would have been a propitious time to tackle challenging issues such as interest convergence and social constructions about race and racial categorizations, or to discuss the past, present, and future implications of activist initiatives such as the library sit-in. These efforts would have honored Samuel Tucker, the demonstrators, and the sit-in itself far more than a symbolic ceremony, which was virtually devoid of substantive meaning. As a result of these shortcomings, some aspects of the demonstration and its attendant implications remain isolated in the past, where they create no controversy in the present and trigger no repercussions for the future.

In short, commemorations of the sit-in have failed to address what Wiegand calls the "library in the life of the user" and the "user in the life of the library" or to address the "historical silences" associated with the protest that reflect the ambivalence and ambiguities associated with commemorations of past events.[33] Such ambiguities and ambivalences are heightened when race is a critical component in the interpretation of social history, especially in the South, where hierarchies of dominance, power, and control traditionally have been based on race. For every group celebrating an event, there may be another group for whom the occasion may have different symbolism. The sit-in and the presence of Blacks in the physical place and social space of the library posed a threat to White authority and power, and the progeny of those elite or nonelite Whites or of the White principals associated with the event may still feel a loss of privilege and prestige when they consider the demonstration and the resulting social upheaval. Some Whites may feel embarrassed, contrite, or ashamed about the injustices of the past, while others may feel no responsibility for past injustices and resent activities that call attention to their unearned privilege. Such individuals may not be willing to participate in discussions of the protest if they include discourse about shifting power dynamics in social, racial, and class contexts. For many Blacks, the sit-in was a civil rights milestone, but for others it may generate uneasiness about the potential repercussions of social and racial antagonisms or trigger feelings of ignominy or embarrassment associated with former conditions of subservience. Nonetheless, without the participation of a broad cross-section of citizens, it may be impossible to have a meaningful dialogue on the implications of the protest. The point of confronting the legacies of enslavement and Black subordination is not about assigning guilt or shame to Whites but about recognizing and acknowledging the imperative of long-overdue justice for Blacks. The question to be asked is, What can be done to compensate for generations of White advantages?

In an interview, Elsie Tucker Thomas remarked that the library sit-in spurred other protest activities in Alexandria, but she did not specify what other kinds of activities took place or who was involved. Nonetheless, the historian Theodore Carter DeLaney has emphasized that young sit-in demonstrators of the 1950s and 1960s benefited from the activism of young Blacks in the 1930s and 1940s. Florence Murray, a columnist for the *Washington Tribune*, noted in 1939 that reactions to the library sit-in reflected generational attitudes. She said that younger African Americans were heartened by the protest and the potential for change, while older Black citizens were concerned that "the 'agitation' . . . might . . . invite danger." Those concerns were understandable, given their memories of Whites' "retributive actions" in the years after Reconstruction. Yet today the sit-in may have little meaning or relevance for contemporary young people, who may have little knowledge of daily life during segregation.[34]

Socioeconomic stratification in Alexandria's Black community has also affected reactions to the sit-in, though such sociological and class differences are not limited to the city, to Virginia, or to the South. As Earl Lewis has shown in his study of twentieth-century Norfolk, there is more diversity among and between individuals of a particular race than there is between individuals of different races. Middle- and upper-middle-class Blacks, for example, have far more in common with Whites of a similar socioeconomic class than they do with the Black working class and underclass. The effect of economic stratification has simply been more pronounced in the Black community because of Whites' concerted efforts to foment divisiveness as a means of establishing and maintaining racial and social control. Middle-class Black Alexandrians such as the Tuckers could afford, materially and psychologically, to take risks in their public attitudes and actions because they were not as economically dependent on Whites as working-class Blacks were. As the scholar Kenneth Kusmer explains, "the increasingly frequent reliance of black professionals . . . upon a predominantly black clientele (thereby emancipating them from white influence to a degree) created the basis for a more militant leadership in fighting racism."[35] Unlike the Tuckers, some members of the Black working-class may have felt obliged to be more publicly deferential to Whites because their livelihoods frequently depended on White approval and acceptance. Yet, nationally, students and working-class Blacks were the backbone of local organized activism. This suggests that, although organized activism may not have typified the lives of some working-class Blacks, subtle acts of resistance at work and in public spaces, such as nonverbal communication and peer-to-peer interactions, sustained their personal dignity. In his study of Norfolk, Lewis identifies the nexus of race, class, and power dynamics in intra- and interracial relationships and notes that the interplay between race and class and the fluidity that characterized social relations helped to frame Blacks' interpretations of their own best interests.[36]

Documented events are often interpreted or imagined by those empowered to provide an "authorized" account. This often creates historical silences, and a case in point is the absence or minimization of the sit-in within existing histories of the Alexandria Library. Writing about Black memory in antebellum Virginia, Gregg D. Kimball notes that while some Blacks perceived themselves as "powerless to shape . . . the written, formal history privileged in a world dominated by elite and literate whites," others "envisioned another type of history, a hidden narrative of oppression and resistance that needed to be expressed publicly." His words continue to ring true. If Blacks were to insist on incorporating their local-history memories into the evolution of a larger narrative of collective memory, would Whites willingly acknowledge the validity of those memories? Or would Whites remain wedded to their own power and idealized past? If African American memories were acknowledged, how would differing Black and White recollections be reconciled? In their consideration of "historically significant silences and historically focused commemorations," Gerald Sider and Gavin Smith maintain that the distinction between history and histories is "deeply related to the further idea that power must be understood as engendering chaos and havoc—conceptual, cultural, and social-relational—as much as it does order."[37]

Historians investigate events from the inside out to understand and contextualize the past without imposing judgments. Yet judgements may nonetheless affect public history and collective memory. History consists of lived experiences, and cultural contexts influence the construction of individual and group memories. Societal memory is dynamic and organic, and changes in social, cultural, political, and economic milieus impact the interpretation of history and the evolution of collective memory. Therefore, there is no one history but a plurality of histories. There is no master narrative but rather a pluralistic one in which the components are not fully integrated.

In his "West India Emancipation" speech delivered on August 3, 1857, in Canandaigua, New York, Frederick Douglass remarked, "Power concedes nothing without a demand. It never did and it never will."[38] This has been especially true in the South, where hegemonic dominance and control have been based on Black subordination. But public protest in the form of sit-ins has been a powerful strategy to effect social change, and Tucker's valiant civil rights effort provided the initial impetus for the eventual desegregation of the library. As the architect of the sit-in, he deserves to be remembered not merely as the titular leader of a symbolic protest but as a proactive agent of social change imbued with meaning. The sit-in deserves to be remembered not simply as a symbolic past event but as a model and an intimation of future social activism. Two cases in point are the civil rights protests conducted in the wake of the 2020 murder of Black Minnesotan George Perry Floyd by White police officer Derek Chauvin and Alexandria's ongoing involvement in an Equal Justice Initiative Community Remembrance Project to memorialize the city's two lynching victims. The Alexandria Library sit-in warrants recognition and remembrance not only as a local civil rights event but also as a compelling part of American library history, American social and southern histories, and civil rights history. The library itself deserves acknowledgment as a community centerpiece, a centralized social and cultural agency, and a public-educational institution that now offers free access to organized knowledge resources and opportunities for individuals and groups to develop and advance intellectually, socially, and culturally. It is a site of voluntary and involuntary encounters among diverse patrons and between patrons and librarians, as well as a physical place and social space in which those interactions can be mediated, shaped, and reconciled.

Twenty-seven years after the 1939 sit-in demonstration to desegregate Alexandria's public library, two years after the passage of the Civil Rights Act of 1964, which, among other things, ended segregation in public places, and four years after the Alexandria Library had fully desegregated, the U.S. Supreme Court of the United States issued a ruling in the case of *Brown v. Louisiana*. The decision reversed a lower-court ruling concerning five Black men in Louisiana, who had been arrested and detained on the charge of breach of the peace for remaining in a Whites-only public library after one of them had requested a book from the collection.[39] There is no direct evidence to indicate that the justices were aware of the Alexandria sit-in case. However, the failure (or refusal) of Judge James Reese Duncan to issue a ruling in the Alexandria protesters' case likely had a bearing on subsequent legal implications. In the ruling, Chief Justice Earl Warren and Associate Justices William Orville Douglas and Abraham Fortas concluded:

1.  There is not the slightest evidence to sustain application of
    the breach of the peace statute to petitioners, since there was

nothing to indicate an intent by them to provoke a breach of the peace and there were no circumstances to indicate that such a breach might be occasioned, the demonstration having been peaceful, orderly, and unprovocative, and no patrons having been present in the library. Petitioners' conduct was considerably less disruptive than in any of the preceding three situations in which this Court invalidated convictions under the same Louisiana statute or its predecessor. . . .

2. The rights of peaceable and orderly protest which petitioners were exercising under the First and Fourteenth Amendments are not confined to verbal expression, but embrace other types of expression, including appropriate silent and reproachful presence, such as petitioners used here. Therefore, even if such action came within the statute, it would have to be held that the statute could not constitutionally reach petitioners' actions in the circumstances of this case. . . .

3. Regulation of libraries and other public facilities must be reasonable and nondiscriminatory, and may not be used as a pretext for punishing those who exercise their constitutional rights.[40]

The decisive ruling affirmed the constitutional right of all Americans, regardless of race, to access tax-supported public libraries and make use of information resources that confer knowledge and power. This right was assured even if those resources provided access and exposure to thoughts and ideas that potentially threatened hegemonic ideals and normative standards. The decision was reached after decades of local protests by Black civil rights activists such as Samuel Tucker, all of them working to secure the public library access that Whites took for granted. When interviewed shortly before his death, Tucker summarized the rationale for his lifetime of civil rights work with simple yet poignant eloquence: "You must understand that the struggle to be free is paramount. You cannot suppress it without it taking over your heart."[41]

# Turning the Page

To commemorate the eightieth anniversary of the Alexandria Library sit-in demonstration, the city issued a press release on October 19, 2019, announcing that on October 18 the city's circuit court had dismissed all of the technically extant charges against Otto L. Tucker, Edward Gaddis, Morris Murray, Clarence Strange, and William Evans—the five sit-in protesters. Bryan L. Porter, the Commonwealth's attorney for the city, served as petitioner in the dismissal request. Although the five men had been charged with disorderly conduct, there was no evidence that they had been disorderly or that their presence in the library had been aimed at disrupting its services or operations. In the court order, Porter noted that the demonstrators "were lawfully exercising their constitutional rights to free assembly, speech and to petition the government to alter the established policy of sanctioned segregation at the time of their arrest." He said that "sitting peacefully in a library reading books, was not in any fashion disorderly or likely to cause acts of violence" and established that "the defendants were, in fact, not breaking any law and no criminal charge was appropriate at the time of their arrest." He next remarked:

> In the time period since these charges were instituted the Supreme Court and Virginia Courts have held that government endorsed segregation and the policy of "separate but equal" are unconstitutional, diminish the dignity of American citizens and fail to ensure the lofty ideals contained in the Declaration of Independence, that all men are created equal and should enjoy the right to life, liberty and the pursuit of happiness.

Finally, Porter asked the court to order that "the disorderly conduct charges against the five defendants . . . should be and hereby are

DISMISSED with prejudice."[1] According to Barbara Ann Rowan, a local attorney, the phrase "with prejudice" in the dismissal order was intended to provide "historical clarity and forgiveness," though she emphasized that, "but for the sit-in protesters themselves, and their relatives, it has no current legal effect since every statute of limitations has expired and no charges could be brought against any living person at this point."[2] Nevertheless, the inclusion of the phrase represents a measure of conciliation and a gesture of apology and contrition that is a distinct departure from the discrimination with which the protesters were originally treated.

Alexandria's mayor, Justin M. Wilson, responded to the court order:

> I applaud the recent action by the Commonwealth's Attorney and the Circuit Court to right an important part of the wrong that occurred 80 years ago. . . . While the arc of the moral universe has just bent a little closer to justice, we know there remains much to be done to improve equality for all residents of Alexandria and our nation. Today's Alexandria Library is a thriving hub of learning and engagement for our diverse community, and I commend Library staff for commemorating our difficult history while working to create a bright future for all.[3]

On the following Monday, October 21, the staff at Alexandria's Charles E. Beatley, Jr., Central Library hosted a special ceremony that served as the climax of the year's worth of celebrations under the aegis of "We Are the Alexandria Library Sit-In." The ceremony included a panel discussion with Stephen A. Martin, the nephew of Morris Murray, and Joyce Angela Evans-Jackson and Kimberley Evans-Reed, descendants of sit-in protester William Evans. In the audience were Michael Strange, a descendant of Clarence and Robert Strange, and the Reverend Deborah Thomas-McSwain, the niece of Samuel and Otto Tucker. In the library's Story Time Room, a special-activity program was offered to children ages six and up. Rose T. Dawson, the executive director of Alexandria's Library System, facilitated the event, and library staff members helped to plan and execute it.

After Mayor Wilson read aloud the circuit court's order, library staff members presented each descendant with a personalized commemorative poster. Then Wilson read the city proclamation:

> NOW, THEREFORE, I, JUSTIN M. WILSON, Mayor of the City of Alexandria, Virginia, and on behalf of the Alexandria City Council, do hereby recognize and resolve that the Alexandria Library will annually celebrate: "THE ALEXANDRIA LIBRARY SIT-IN" [as] the first library sit-in to occur in the nation, and the Alexandria Library will continue the legacy of the peaceful protest ahead of its time by offering Library programs and collections that will center on civil rights, human rights, the African American diaspora, social freedoms and equity.[4]

In his subsequent remarks, Wilson emphasized the importance of discussing not only the events of the past but also the challenges and goals of the present and the future.

The panel discussion included a lively question-and-answer session. When an audience member asked how the sit-in had affected the descendants' lives, Kimberly Evans-Reed said that she had learned about the protest when she was nine or ten years old, but she was really too young to care about the event. Later, however, she remarked that she thought of her grandfather's courage when she decided to publish her first book. She recalled that, when she recounted the sit-in events to her own children, her older daughter immediately decided to work at a city shelter and her younger daughter became concerned about the injustices she was learning about in the media. Stephen Martin said that he had been unaware of the sit-in until 2015. In the meantime, however, he had become a civil rights pioneer in his own right, when he joined the Alexandria police force as the second Black man to serve in that capacity.

Deborah Thomas-McSwain told the audience that she had learned about the sit-in from her mother, not from her uncle Samuel, who would not speak of the protest in front of the children. When I later interviewed her, she recalled first visiting the Robinson Library as an elementary school student when she was about six years old. Beginning in 1957, she and her classmates were was taken there on regular school trips. Thomas-McSwain commented that her family had always been involved in civil rights initiatives. Her own parents often brought people to voter registration drives and polling places, Samuel spent much of the rest of his life working to integrate school systems in Virginia, and Otto and his wife Louise had been singled out for their beliefs during the McCarthy era. She also commented that Samuel's father-in-law, the Reverend William Thomas, had been president of the Alexandria chapter of the Congress of Racial Equality and recalled that her parents had marched on Washington, D.C., with the Reverend Dr. Martin Luther King, Jr.

When I asked if her family's example had inspired her to participate in civil rights initiatives, Thomas-McSwain described her professional work as an ordained minister practicing liberation theology. She said that she had been selected to be installed at the National Cathedral in Washington, D.C., as the first Black female chaplain for the Episcopal Caring Response to AIDS endeavor. She was the first Black female minister at Kennedy Heights Presbyterian Church in Cincinnati, Ohio, installed specifically to bring greater diversity to a changing church. And she was the first Black woman to provide family ministry to youth and families at Mount Olivette Church in Arlington, Virginia.[5]

When an audience member asked, "What are the civil rights issues for today's youth?" both Evans-Reed and Martin answered that adults and city officials should promote education programs about the city's history—even, as Evans-Reed added, "if the children appear disinterested." In response, a teacher in the city school system mentioned that the city already includes a curriculum component about the library sit-in demonstration, one centering around Nancy Noyes Silcox's biography of Samuel Tucker. Noyes Silcox served as librarian at the city's Samuel W. Tucker Elementary School from 2000, the year the school opened, until she retired in 2011. Her biography of Tucker is aimed at students in grades 4 through 8. Today it is a curriculum component in Alexandria's seventh-grade U.S. history classes and in middle schools around Virginia. In an interview with the author, Noyes Silcox remarked,

> From the day the school opened the students were taught about
> Tucker and the 1939 Alexandria Library sit-in. Cathy David,
> the principal, believed it was important for students to know
> why their school was named for a hometown hero. . . . I thought
> someone should write [Tucker's] biography to tell young readers
> about their civil rights trailblazer. When I retired, I decided to
> tell this important story myself.

Thomas-McSwain summed up the feelings of the descendants and the audience when she said, "The thing that moves me so much is it took eighty years. . . . To have this happen in my lifetime is just wonderful."[6]

On June 8, 2020, the Alexandria Library was honored with the ALA Excellence in Programming Award for "We Are the Alexandria Library Sit-In." The award, which is supported by ALA's Cultural Communities Fund, is presented to "a library that demonstrates excellence by providing programs that have community impact and respond to community needs." The award includes $5,000 and a citation of achievement. Then, in August, the library was honored with ALA's prestigious 2020 John Cotton Dana Award for the "We Are the Alexandria Library Sit-In" program. This coveted award, which is supported by the H. W. Wilson Foundation with a $10,000 grant, recognizes outstanding library public relations. EBSCO Information Services honored the Alexandria Library at a reception at the virtual 2021 ALA Annual Conference in Chicago.[7]

These important awards recognize the ongoing efforts of an essential city department to serve a community with programs and policies that eliminate disparities and inequities. While these efforts are conceived to serve all races, religions, nationalities, sexual orientations, ages, genders, abilities, and socioeconomic backgrounds, they especially focus on communities of color and others who have been underserved or marginalized. This commitment affirms the city council's ALL Alexandria Resolution to promote racial and social equity: "(1) Ensure that equity is incorporated in [strategic] planning . . . , (2) Implement and sustain structures and capabilities to advance equity . . . , (3) Advance and conclude policy efforts designed to advance equity goals . . . , and (4) Ensure accountability mechanisms." According to Mayor Wilson, "With the help of the community, we are renewing our pledge to advance policies that will create a future that is more inclusive, fair and equitable for all of Alexandria's residents."[8]

Library system director Rose Dawson has identified seven priorities to guide the library's efforts in the coming years: "Support for Learners of All Ages; Library Collections; Technology Management and Access; Library as a Community Hub; Community Relations, Marketing and Branding; Organizational Health and Development; [and] Fundraising and Advocacy":

> This direction will bolster our role as leaders in early literacy and lifelong learning, emphasize our collection of high-quality materials, and empower our staff to navigate an ever-changing digital world. We are anxious to increase our engagement efforts and offer improved services to our diverse community. We are confident that this work will position the Library as a recognized contributor to the City of Alexandria.[9]

Clearly, Dawson is focused on community service and support and the promotion of the Alexandria Library System as an essential component of the city's educational infrastructure. By emphasizing the branches' positions as community hubs that serve the needs and interests of all the city's constituencies, she hopes to ensure they will continue to prioritize users and thus be prioritized by these same users.

On August 18, 2021, in response to controversy surrounding consideration of critical race theory in curriculum instruction, the ALA released a statement that reinforced the association's "commitment to safeguarding intellectual freedom and social justice." Such a commitment "requires that libraries not only protect the truth from suppression but also prevent its distortion." Unfortunately, the statement concluded with this sentence: "For more than 140 years, ALA has been the trusted voice of libraries, advocating for the profession and the library's role in enhancing learning and ensuring access to information for all." Shortly after the release of the ALA statement, Wayne A. Wiegand—library historian, scholar, civil rights advocate, and member of the Library History Round Table—issued a forceful corrective to this sentence, noting the association's historical hesitation to address discrimination. As evidence of his contention, he offered multiple examples of ALA's refusal to support Black initiatives for access to White libraries, one of which was the sit-in at the Alexandria Library, which took place shortly after the passage of ALA's first "Library's [sic] Bill of Rights" (1939). He also notes that in the 1960s, "ALA filed several *amicus* briefs in censorship cases," though none were filed on behalf of Black students attempting to desegregate White libraries in the South. In her response to Wiegand's corrective, Bernadette Lear, a librarian at Pennsylvania State University and a member of the Library History Round Table, commented that the concluding statement "is probably boilerplate language that is widely used on many ALA statements" but she agreed that "it's not always appropriate." The truth is that the assertion is *never* appropriate. The ALA has a historical record of tacit complicity and denial regarding its role in the perpetuation of racism. While its acknowledgment of that history and its apology for past injustices and inequities are long awaited and most welcome, they are, in fact, relatively recent. Carol A. Leibiger, chair of the Library History Round Table and associate professor at the University of South Dakota, also concurred with Weigand and stated that "it's past time for ALA to engage with its past so as to better align with its present support of diversity, equity, and inclusion."[10]

# APPENDIX A

# "Library's [*sic*] Bill of Rights," Adopted June 19, 1939

Today indications in many parts of the world point to growing intolerance, suppression of free speech, and censorship affecting the rights of minorities and individuals. Mindful of this, the Council of the American Library Association publicly affirms its belief in the following basic policies which should govern the services of free public libraries.

I. Books and other reading matter selected for purchase from the public funds should be chosen because of value and interest to people of the community, and in no case should the selection be influenced by the race or nationality or the political or religious views of the writers.

II. As far as available material permits, all sides of questions on which differences of opinion exist should be represented fairly and adequately in the books and other reading matter purchased for public use.

III. The library as an institution to educate for democratic living should especially welcome the use of its meeting rooms for socially useful and cultural activities and the discussion of current public questions. Library meeting rooms should be available on equal terms to all groups in the community regardless of their beliefs or affiliations.

*Source:* Trina Magi and Martin Garnar, eds., *A History of ALA Policy on Intellectual Freedom: A Supplement to the Intellectual Freedom Manual,* 9th ed. (Chicago: ALA Editions, 2015), 45. Reprinted with permission of the American Library Association.

# APPENDIX B

# "Library Bill of Rights," Approved February 2, 1961

The Council of the American Library Association reaffirms its belief in the following basic policies which should govern the services of all libraries.

I.   As a responsibility of library service, books and other reading matter selected should be chosen for values of interest, information, and enlightenment of all the people of the community. In no case should any book be excluded because of the race or nationality or the political or religious views of the writer.

II.   There should be the fullest practicable provision of material presenting all points of view concerning the problems and issues of our times, international, national, and local; and books or other reading matter of sound factual authority should not be proscribed or removed from library shelves because of partisan or doctrinal disapproval.

III.   Censorship of books, urged or practiced by volunteer arbiters of morals or political opinion or by organizations that would establish a coercive concept of Americanism, must be challenged by libraries in maintenance of their responsibility to provide public information and enlightenment through the printed word.

IV.   Libraries should enlist the cooperation of allied groups in the fields of science, of education, and of book publishing in resisting all abridgment of the free access to ideas and full freedom of expression that are the tradition and heritage of Americans.

V.   The rights of an individual to the use of a library should not be denied or abridged because of his race, religion, national origins or political views.

VI. As an institution of education for democratic living, the library should welcome the use of its meeting rooms for socially useful and cultural activities and discussion of current public questions. Such meeting places should be available on equal terms to all groups in the community regardless of the beliefs and affiliations of their members.

By official action of the council on February 3, 1951, the "Library Bill of Rights" shall be interpreted to apply to all materials and media of communication used or collected by libraries.

*Source:* Trina Magi and Martin Garnar, eds., *A History of ALA Policy on Intellectual Freedom: A Supplement to the Intellectual Freedom Manual,* 9th ed. (Chicago: ALA Editions, 2015), 49. Reprinted with permission of the American Library Association.

# APPENDIX C

# "Statement on Individual Membership, Chapter Status, and Institutional Membership," Adopted June 19, 1962

In a free society, a library is one of the primary instruments through which citizens gain understanding and enlightenment. The institution, the people who work for it, and the professional associations with which they identify themselves should be worthy examples of the high principles which libraries endeavor to promote.

The American Library Association holds that so long as one librarian is unable to make his full contribution to the library profession by reason of racial, religious, or personal belief, and so long as one individual citizen cannot realize his full potential as a useful member of society because of such artificial barriers, the welfare of the nation is diminished. The Association cannot fulfill its obligations until it obtains the same rights and privileges for all its members and gains the same freedom of access to all libraries for all citizens. THEREFORE:

1. Concerning Individual Membership, the Council calls on each and every member of the American Library Association as a citizen and a librarian, by vigorous personal example, to work in libraries and in chapters so that discrimination for reasons of race, religion, or personal belief may cease and that all people may have equal access to the tools of learning. Thus the educational process will contribute in an increasing way to the national good and purpose, undiminished and unrestrained by the frictions of prejudice and misunderstanding.

2. Concerning Chapter Status, the Council shall—

   a. Inform the chapters of the basic rights and privileges of membership as stated here and request the chapters to make every immediate effort to secure and grant these rights to each member, with special emphasis on the requirements of Article III of the American Library Association Constitution. These rights are: 1) To receive notices. 2) To attend meetings. 3) To speak. 4) To vote. 5) To present motions, resolutions, or other business. 6) To nominate. 7) To be a candidate for office. 8) To resign, if all obligations to the organization have been fulfilled. 9) To have a hearing before expulsion or other penalties are applied. 10) To inspect official records of the organization. 11) To insist on the enforcement of the rules of the organization and the rules of parliamentary law. 12) To exercise any other rights given by the constitution or rules of the organization.

   b. Require chapters to certify that they are meeting these requirements. Chapters may request of the Council postponement of application of this provision for a period of time not to exceed three years. If they are unable to do so, or the Council is not satisfied that they are following the policies prescribed, such chapters shall be asked to withdraw until the provisions can be complied with.

3. Concerning Institutional Membership, the Council shall—

   a. Pursue with diligence the study of access to libraries so that factual data on this subject are collected.

   b. Make public promptly the results of this study.

   c. Urge libraries which are institutional members not to discriminate among users on the basis of race, religion, or personal belief, and if such discrimination now exists to bring it to an end as speedily as possible.

   d. Advise libraries applying henceforth for institutional membership of the Association's attitude toward and general policies relating to access to libraries and that in accepting institutional membership they are also accepting the responsibility for working toward free and ready access to libraries by all persons regardless of race, religion, or personal belief.

*Source:* "Statement on Individual Membership, Chapter Status, and Institutional Membership," *ALA Bulletin* 56, no. 7 (July–August 1962): 637. Used with permission of the American Library Association.

# NOTES

## PREFACE AND ACKNOWLEDGMENTS

1. August Meier and Elliott Rudwick, *Along the Color Line: Explorations in the Black Experience* (Urbana: University of Illinois Press, 2002), 341, 342.

2. While freely acknowledging the concepts of race and racial categorizations as social constructs, I prefer to use the term *Black* when referring to people of Black African descent because it evinces and affirms the continuum and unity of diasporic populations. On occasion, however, the appellation *African American* is used for linguistic variation.

3. Richard Wright, *Black Boy: A Record of Childhood and Youth* (New York: Harper and Brothers, 1945); Francis Edward Kearns, *The Black Experience: An Anthology of American Literature for the 1970s* (New York: Viking, 1970).

## INTRODUCTION: ALEXANDRIA AS MICROCOSM

1. City of Alexandria is the official name of the politically and administratively independent Virginia municipality profiled in this book. Throughout, I often refer to the community as Alexandria, as do its citizens. However, it should not be confused with the section of Fairfax County, Virginia, known as Alexandria. That is not the place featured in this study. For more on the history of Virginia's city structure, see "Cities of Virginia," in *Encyclopedia Virginia*, December 7, 2020, https://www.encyclopediavirginia.org.

   The city's library was incorporated as The Alexandria Library, but in 2000, following the construction of the Charles E. Beatley, Jr., Central Library, much of the system's holdings moved to the new building. The original structure, now known as the Kate Waller Barrett Branch Library, continues to house the local history/special collections division and (as of 2019) a circulating collection of 46,046 items. In this book, I refer to the original building as the Alexandria Library and to the aggregate of library branches as the Alexandria Library System.

2. In this book, *racial segregation* refers to a system of de jure enforced separation of racial groups by discriminatory means, such as barriers to social interaction, exclusion from educational institutions or public meeting places, and segregated seating on public transportation or in places of worship or entertainment. *De facto segregation*, in contrast, refers to racial separation based on local or regional customs or mores or, on occasion, on personal preference, as when Blacks consciously and intentionally choose to live in environments occupied primarily by other Blacks.

3. I have derived my use of the term *public library* from Carleton B. Joeckel's *The Government of the American Public Library* (Chicago: University of Chicago Press, 1935) for its timeliness relative to the library protest: "The only really essential requirement in the definition of a public library is that its use should be free to all residents of the community on equal terms" (x). In contrast, Lloyd Vernor Ballard's *Social Institutions* (New York: Appleton-Century, 1936) defines it as *"an institution for the continuous communication of knowledge and ideas"* that enables individuals to be more effective in

their daily lives (231, emphasis in original). Although he succinctly describes the function of a public library, Ballard makes no mention of the scope of users.

4. In the initial newspaper accounts of the 1939 Alexandria Library demonstration, the protest was referred to as a sit-down. A *sit-down* is "a cessation of work by employees while maintaining continuous occupation of their place of employment as a protest and means toward forcing compliance with demands." Use of the term originated during 1930s labor strikes. In contrast, a *sit-in* is "an act of occupying seats in a racially segregated establishment in organized protest against discrimination" and "a tactic of nonviolent civil disobedience." I use both applications in this book. See *Merriam-Webster's Collegiate Dictionary*, 11th ed. (Springfield: Merriam-Webster, 2007), 1166; Rachel Meyer, "The Rise and Fall of the Sit-Down Strike," in *The Encyclopedia of Strikes in American History*, ed. Aaron Brenner, Immanuel Ness, and Benjamin Day (Armonk, NY: Sharpe, 2009), 204–15; Todd Michney, "Civil Rights Strikes," in ibid., 118–23; Joel Seidman, *Sit-Down* (New York: League for Industrial Democracy, 1937); *Merriam-Webster's Collegiate Dictionary*, 1166; and *Encyclopædia Britannica*, http://www.britannica.com.

5. A writ of mandamus is "an order from a court to an inferior government official ordering the government official to properly fulfill their official duties or correct an abuse of discretion" (Legal Information Institute [hereafter cited as LII], Cornell Law School, n.d., https://www.law.cornell.edu).

6. A continuance refers to "the suspension or postponement of a trial or court proceeding. Continuance is made on a case-by-case basis at the court's discretion." Courts balance giving enough time to the party that requests a continuance, the need to proceed quickly though a trial, and the interests of justice (LII), https://www.law.cornell.edu.

7. "For each city of the state [of Virginia], there shall be a court called a 'corporation court,' to be held by a judge, with like qualifications and elected in the same manner as judges of the county court" (Code Va. 1SS7, in *Black's Law Dictionary Online*, n.d., http://thelawdictionary.org).

8. Unless otherwise specified, in this book, *South* and *southern* refer to Alabama, Arkansas, Florida, Georgia, Kentucky, Louisiana, Mississippi, North Carolina, Oklahoma, South Carolina, Tennessee, Texas, and Virginia.

9. Brent Tarter, "First Military District," *Encyclopedia Virginia*, August 11, 2015, https://www.encyclopediavirginia.org; Richard L. Hume, "Negro Delegates to the State Constitutional Conventions of 1867–69," in *Southern Black Leaders of the Reconstruction Era*, ed. Howard N. Rabinowitz (Urbana: University of Illinois Press, 1982), 129–53; Richard L. Hume, "The Membership of the Virginia Constitutional Convention of 1867–1868: A Study of the Beginnings of Congressional Reconstruction in the Upper South," *Virginia Magazine of History and Biography* 86, no. 4 (1978): 461–84; "Constitutional Convention," and "Remaking Virginia: Transformation through Emancipation," *Virginia Memory*, http://www.virginiamemory.com.

10. "Constitution of Virginia 1902," *For Virginians: Government Matters*, http://vagovernmentmatters.org; John J. Dinan, *The Virginia State Constitution: A Reference Guide* (New York: Greenwood, 2006); Wythe W. Holt, *Virginia's Constitutional Convention of 1902* (New York: Garland, 1990); Ralph Clipman McDanel, *The Virginia Constitutional*

*Convention of 1901–1902* (Baltimore: Johns Hopkins University Press, 1928); "1901–1902 Constitutional Convention," *Virginia Constitutional Convention*, http://www2.vcdh.virginia.edu; Charles E. Wynes, *Race Relations in Virginia, 1870–1902* (Charlottesville: University of Virginia Press, 1961).

11. "Racial Integrity Laws (1924–1930)," *Encyclopedia Virginia*, February 17, 2009, https://www.encyclopediavirginia.org; "Separation of Races (1926)," *Encyclopedia Virginia*, September 22, 2015, https://www.encyclopediavirginia.org; General Assembly of Virginia, *1926 Supplement to the Virginia Code of 1924; Containing All the General Laws of 1926 With Full Annotations* (Charlottesville: Michie, 1926), 42–43; General Assembly of Virginia, *Acts of Assembly, 1926, Public Assemblages Act* (Charlottesville, VA: Michie, 1926), 945–46; Richard B. Sherman, "'The Last Stand': The Fight for Racial Integrity in Virginia in the 1920s," *Journal of Southern History* 54, no. 1 (1988): 69–92; J. Douglas Smith, *Managing White Supremacy: Race, Politics, and Citizenship in Jim Crow Virginia* (Chapel Hill: University of North Carolina Press, 2002), 117; Charles E. Wynes, "The Evolution of Jim Crow Laws in Twentieth Century Virginia," *Phylon* 28, no. 4 (1967): 421.

12. Jim McClellan, "1619: Race, Gender, and the State," lecture for the Dr. Joseph Windham Lecture Series on Race Relations and the Office of Historic Alexandria, Alexandria History Museum, Alexandria, Virginia, October 8, 2019. A note on usage: I prefer to use an adjectival modifier rather than a demeaning and dehumanizing noun as a human description. Thus, I refer to bonded servants as "enslaved people," "enslaved Blacks," or "the enslaved" rather than "slaves."

13. Exceptions included Ruth Brown of Oklahoma's Bartlesville Public Library; Juliette Hampton Morgan and Emily Wheelock Reed of Alabama's Montgomery Public Library; and Tommie Dora Barker, at various times the president of the Georgia Library Association and the Southeastern Library Association and the southern regional field agent for the ALA.

14. Patterson Toby Graham, "Public Librarians and the Civil Rights Movement: Alabama, 1955–1965," *Library Quarterly* 71, no. 1 (2001): 1; Rosemary Ruhig Du Mont, "Race in American Librarianship: Attitudes of the Library Profession," *Journal of Library History (1974–1987)* 21, no. 3 (1986): 504. See also LaTesha Velez and Melissa Villa-Nicholas, "Mapping Race and Racism in U.S. Library History Literature, 1997–2015," *Library Trends* 65, no. 4 (2017): 540–54; and Eino Sierpe, "Confronting Librarianship and Its Function in the Structure of White Supremacy and the Ethno State," *Journal of Radical Librarianship* 5 (May 2019), 84–102.

15. These individuals included Stanley Jasspon Kunitz, the editor of the *Wilson Bulletin for Librarians*; Eric Edward Moon, the editor of *Library Journal*; Rice Estes and E. J. Josey, activist southern librarians; Spencer G. Shaw, a children's consultant and activist librarian in New York's Nassau Library System; Eli M. Oboler, a librarian at Idaho State College; Archie L. McNeal, chair of the Intellectual Freedom Committee; and James E. Bryan and Rutherford Rogers, members of the Intellectual Freedom Committee. A note on usage: *Racial integration* is a broad social term that refers to the process of reducing or eliminating barriers to social interaction; creating equal opportunities, regardless of race; and developing a diverse society of equal citizens

that values and respects various cultures. Oscar Handlin, on the other hand, offers two distinct definitions, each with its own objective ("The Goals of Integration," special issue, "The Negro American—2," *Daedalus* 95, no. 1 [1966]: 270):

> Integration sometimes refers to the openness of society, to a con-
> dition in which every individual can make the maximum number
> of voluntary contacts with others without regard to qualifications
> of ancestry. In that sense, the objective is a leveling of all barriers
> to association other than those based on ability, taste, and personal
> preference.
>
> [It] sometimes also refers to a condition in which individuals
> of each racial or ethnic group are randomly distributed through the
> society so that every realm of activity contains a representative cross
> section of the population. In that sense, the object is the attainment,
> in every occupational, educational, and residential distribution, of
> a balance among the constituent elements in the society.

16.  The statement was endorsed by the American Book Publishers Council on June 18, 1953, and by the ALA's council on June 25, 1953.

17.  Trina Magi, ed., *A History of ALA Policy on Intellectual Freedom: A Supplement to the Intellectual Freedom Manual*, 9th ed. (Chicago: ALA Editions, 2015), 48; Louise S. Robbins, *Censorship and the American Library: The American Library Association's Response to Threats to Intellectual Freedom, 1939–1969* (Westport: Greenwood, 1996), 107–21, 153; "ALA Adopts Integration Statement," *Wilson Library Bulletin* 35 (March 1961): 486; "Integration, an Interim Report," *Wilson Library Bulletin* 35 (April 1961): 632; John Wakeman, "Talking Points: Segregation and Censorship," *Wilson Library Bulletin* 35 (September 1960): 63–64; "Segregation in Libraries: Negro Librarians Give their Views," *Wilson Library Bulletin* 35 (May 1961): 707–10; E[ric] M[oon], "The Silent Subject," *Library Journal* 85, no. 22 (1960): 4436–37; Wayne A. Wiegand, "'Any Ideas?' The American Library Association and the Desegregation of Public Libraries in the American South," *Libraries* 1, no. 1 (2017): 1–22. See also William F. Yust, "What of the Black and Yellow Races?" *Bulletin of the American Library Association* 7, no. 4 (1913): 158–67. For the complete text of the "Freedom to Read" statement and the names of its creators, see Robbins, *Censorship and the American Library*, 188–95. For a history of the statement, see Magi, *A History of ALA Policy on Intellectual Freedom*, 79–100. Also see Robbins, *Censorship and the American Library*, 117; Archie McNeal, "A New Statement and Its Significance," *ALA Bulletin* 56, no. 7 (1962): 623, 665; Evelyn Levy and Jerome Cushman, "ALA Membership and Segregation," *Wilson Library Bulletin* 36 (April 1962): 668; E[ric] M[oon], "A Concern for Users: ALA Highlights from Miami Beach," *Library Journal* 87, no. 13 (1962): 2494–97; E[ric] M[oon], "Integration and Censorship," *Library Journal* 87, no. 5 (1962): 904–8, 937; "Legislation Urged against Segregated Libraries," *Wilson Library Bulletin* 36 (November 1961): 202; E[ric] M[oon], "Two Stars from Georgia: Reflections on the ALA Conference in St. Louis," *Library Journal* 89, no. 14 (1964): 2919–28; John Wakeman, "Segregated Libraries and Executive Action," *Wilson Library Bulletin* 36

(October 1961): 165; "Segregation and ALA," *Wilson Library Bulletin* 37 (September 1962): 12; "Segregation in Libraries," "Looking and Listening," *The Crisis* 68, no. 6 (1961): 342–43; "Segregation in Libraries: Negro Librarians Give their Views," *Wilson Library Bulletin* 35 (May 1961): 707–10; Eli M. Oboler, "What Are the Responsibilities of a Professional Organization?," *ALA Bulletin* 55, no. 7 (1961): 608; and John Wakeman, "Time to Act," *Wilson Library Bulletin* 36 (April 1962): 677.

18. "ALA Takes Responsibility for Past Racism, Pledges a More Equitable Association," *ALAnews*, June 26, 2020, http://www.ala.org.

19. George Lipsitz, *The Possessive Investment in Whiteness: How White People Profit from Identity Politics*, 20th anniversary ed. (Philadelphia: Temple University Press, 2018), vii; Richard Dyer, "White," *Screen* 29, no. 4 (1988): 44; Charles W. Mills, *The Racial Contract* (Ithaca, NY: Cornell University Press, 1997), 19; Richard Dyer, *White*, 20th anniversary ed. (London: Routledge, 2017), xxxv; Lipsitz, *The Possessive Investment in Whiteness*, 1. A note on terminology: "Authority is the official permission or right to act, often on behalf of another. Authority may also be a person or institution that has power over another person" (LII, https://www.law.cornell.edu).

20. *Physical place* and *library as space* refer to a community-focused, constructed edifice or dedicated locale situated in a geographical space or setting. *Physical place* and *library as place* also refer to the interior of such a community edifice or locale and to the functions, services, activities, and resources involved therein. Included are multimedia-based sources of, and means for, individual, group, and community informational or experiential sharing, such as information retrieval and processing; group or community classes, meetings, and special events; cultural and civic engagement; quiet, private contemplation and active social interaction; and recreational pursuits. *Social space* refers to "the social factors within which [libraries as physical places are] embedded." In Alexandria, these social factors include racialized community attitudes and mores as well as discriminatory library and lifeways policies. In the microcosm of Alexandria during the period under study, the impact of systemic racism and segregation was all-pervasive. The Black community was, effectively, a separate microcosm within the larger microcosm of the White community as African Americans bonded for safety and security and for emotional and psychological support and personal investment. See Loretta Lees, "Ageographia, Heterotopia and Vancouver's New Public Library," *Environment and Planning D* 15, no. 3 (1997): 321–47; John E. Buschman and Gloria J. Leckie, "Space, Place, and Libraries: An Introduction," in *The Library as Place: History, Community, and Culture*, eds. John E. Buschman and Gloria J. Leckie (Westport: Libraries Unlimited, 2007), 12; and Julia A. Hersberger, Lou Sua, and Adam L. Murray, "The Fruit and Root of the Community: The Greensboro Carnegie Library, 1904–1964," in ibid., 80.

21. Richard Delgado and Jean Stefancic, *Critical Race Theory: An Introduction*, 2nd ed. (New York: New York University Press, 2012), 3. See also Richard Delgado and Jean Stefancic, eds., *The Derrick Bell Reader* (New York: New York University Press, 2005).

22. Kimberlé Crenshaw, Neil Gotanda, Gary Peller, and Kendall Thomas, eds., *Critical Race Theory: The Key Writings That Formed the Movement* (New York: New Press, 1995); Derrick A. Bell, "Who's Afraid of Critical Race Theory?," *University of Illinois Law*

*Review* 893 (1995), http://lawdawghall.blogspot.com; H. Timothy Lovelace, Jr., "Critical Race Theory and the Political Uses of Legal History," in *The Oxford Handbook of Legal History*, ed. Markus Dirk Dubber and Christopher Tomlins (Oxford: Oxford University Press, 2018), 621–39; Delgado and Stefancic, *Critical Race Theory*, 7–9.

23. David Sibley, *Geographies of Exclusion: Society and Difference in the West* (New York: Routledge, 1995), xv, xvi, x.

24. W. E. B. Du Bois, *The Philadelphia Negro: A Social Study* (Philadelphia: University of Pennsylvania Press, 1996). See also W. E. B. Du Bois, "The Souls of White Folk," in *Darkwater: Voices from within the Veil* (Mineola, NY: Dover, 1999), 17–31; and Sibley, *Geographies of Exclusion*, xvi, 148–54, 153.

25. Buschman and Leckie, "Space, Place, and Libraries," 3.

26. Gill Valentine, *Social Geographies: Space and Society* (Essex, England: Prentice Hall, 2001); Sibley, *Geographies of Exclusion*, xiii.

27. Martha Howell and Walter Prevenier, *From Reliable Sources: An Introduction to Historical Methods* (Ithaca, NY: Cornell University Press, 2001), 135–36.

28. Krystyn R. Moon, "Navigating Everyday Life in Jim Crow Alexandria," lecture for the Equal Justice Initiative on behalf of the Office of Historic Alexandria, Alexandria, Virginia, November 16, 2019; *Plessy v. Ferguson*, 163 U.S. 537 (1896), no. 210, argued April 18, 1896, decided May 18, 1896, U.S. Supreme Court, https://supreme.justia.com; *Williams v. Mississippi*, 170 U.S. 213 (1898), no. 531, argued and submitted March 18, 1898, decided April 25, 1898, U.S. Supreme Court, https://supreme.justia.com; *Equal Justice Initiative*, https://eji.org; "Alexandria's Community Remembrance Project, Equal Justice Initiative," flier, 2020; "A History of Racial Injustice, 2020 Calendar," Montgomery, AL: Equal Justice Initiative, 2019, [24]; "NAACP History: Dyer Anti-Lynching Bill," NAACP, https://naacp.org. See also Philip Dray, *At the Hands of Persons Unknown: The Lynching of Black America* (New York: Random House, 2002); W. Fitzhugh Brundage, *Lynching in the New South: Georgia and Virginia, 1880–1930* (Urbana: University of Illinois Press, 1993); Inter-Fraternal Council, Committee on Public Affairs, "A Terrible Blot on American Civilization: 3,424 Lynchings in 33 Years" (Washington, D.C.: Northeastern Federation of Colored Women, District of Columbia Anti-Lynching Committee, 1922), archived in Printed Ephemera Collection, portfolio 208, folder 36, Library of Congress, https://www.loc.gov; Jamelle Bouie, "It Took a Century to Get an Anti-Lynching Bill," *New York Times*, April 3, 2022, SR9.

29. Notable works on microhistory include Clifford Geertz, *The Interpretation of Cultures: Selected Essays* (New York: Basic Books, 1973); Clifford Geertz, *Local Knowledge: Further Essays in Interpretive Anthropology* (New York: Basic Books, 1983); Carlo Ginzburg, "Microhistory: Two or Three Things That I Know about It," trans. John Tedeschi and Anne C. Tedeschi, *Critical Inquiry* 20, no. 1 (1993): 10–35; Brad S. Gregory, "Is Small Beautiful? Microhistory and the History of Everyday Life," *History and Theory* 38, no. 1 (February 1999): 100–10; Georg G. Iggers, *Historiography in the Twentieth Century: From Scientific Objectivity to the Postmodern Challenge* (Middletown: Wesleyan University Press, 2005), 101–17; Giovanni Levy, "On Microhistory," in *New Perspectives on Historical Writing*, 2nd ed., ed. Peter Burke (University Park: Pennsylvania State University Press, 2001), 97–119; Alf Lüdtke, *The History of*

*Everyday Life: Reconstructing Historical Experiences and Ways of Life,* trans. William Templer (Princeton, NJ: Princeton University Press, 1995); and István Szijártó, "Four Arguments for Microhistory," *Rethinking History* 6, no. 2 (2002): 209–15. Also see Charles Joyner, *Shared Traditions: Southern History and Folk Culture* (Urbana: University of Illinois Press, 1999), 1; Iggers, *Historiography in the Twentieth Century,* 103; and Joseph A. Amato, "Local History: A Way to Place and Home," in *Why Place Matters: Geography, Identity, and Civic Life in Modern America,* ed. Wilfred M. McClay and Ted V. McAllister (New York: Encounter, 2014), 217.

30. Iggers, *Historiography in the Twentieth Century,* 112.

31. Joyner, *Shared Traditions,* 2; Eliza Atkins Gleason, *The Southern Negro and the Public Library: A Study of the Government and Administration of Public Library Service to Negroes in the South* (Chicago: University of Chicago Press, 1941), 10–11 (Gleason's book includes the first scholarly account of the 1939 Alexandria Library sit-in); Yust, "What of the Black and Yellow Races?," 160.

32. Nancy Noyes Silcox, *Samuel Wilbert Tucker: The Story of a Civil Rights Trailblazer and the 1939 Alexandria Library Sit-in* (Fairfax, VA: History4All, 2013; Arlington, VA: Noysil, 2014); Beverly Seehorn Brandt, "The Alexandria, Virginia, Library: Its History, Present Facilities, and Future Programs" (master's thesis, Catholic University of America, April 1950); Jeanne G. Plitt and Marjorie D. Tallichet, "A History of the Alexandria Library," *Fireside Sentinel* (July 1988): 61–68; William Seale, *The Alexandria Library Company* (Alexandria, VA: Alexandria Library Company, 2007); Wayne A. Wiegand and Shirley A. Wiegand, *The Desegregation of Public Libraries in the Jim Crow South: Civil Rights and Local Activism* (Baton Rouge: Louisiana State University Press, 2018); Smith, *Managing White Supremacy.*

33. Samuel Wilbert Tucker, letter to Carl Budwesky, February 13, 1940, box 98, Special Collections Clipping File, Lloyd House, Alexandria Library.

## CHAPTER ONE: BLACK ACCESS TO PUBLIC LIBRARIES

1. U.S. Supreme Court, *Brown v. Louisiana,* 383 U.S. 131 (1966), no. 41, argued December 6, 1965, decided February 23, 1966, https://supreme.justia.com; Abigail A. Van Slyck, *Free to All: Carnegie Libraries & American Culture, 1890–1920* (Chicago: University of Chicago Press, 1995), 158–59.

2. "Segregation in Libraries: Negro Librarians Give their Views," *Wilson Library Bulletin* 35, no. 9 (1961): 707–10.

3. See, for instance, James P. Danky and Wayne A. Wiegand, eds., *Print Culture in a Diverse America* (Urbana: University of Illinois Press, 1998); Wayne A. Wiegand, "American Library History Literature, 1947–1997: Theoretical Perspectives?," *Libraries and Culture* 35, no. 1 (2000): 4–34; LaTesha Velez and Melissa Villa-Nicholas, "Mapping Race and Racism in U.S. Library History Literature, 1997–2015," *Library Trends* 65, no. 4 (2017): 540; Karla J. Strand, "Disrupting Whiteness in Libraries and Librarianship: A Reading List," Bibliographies in Gender and Women's Studies, no. 89 (Madison: University of Wisconsin System, 2019), https://www.library.wisc.edu; Brigitte Fielder and Jonathan Senchyne, eds., *Against a Sharp White Background: Infrastructures of African American Print* (Madison: University of Wisconsin Press, 2019); Cheryl Knott, *Not Free,*

*Not for All: Public Libraries in the Age of Jim Crow* (Amherst: University of Massachusetts Press, 2015); Michael Fultz, "Black Public Libraries in the South in the Era of De Jure Segregation," *Libraries and the Cultural Record* 41, no. 3 (2006): 337–59; Wayne A. Wiegand and Shirley A. Wiegand, *The Desegregation of Public Libraries in the Jim Crow South: Civil Rights and Local Activism* (Baton Rouge: Louisiana State University Press, 2018); Aisha M. Johnson-Jones, *The African American Struggle for Library Equality: The Untold Story of the Julius Rosenwald Fund Library Program* (Lanham, MD: Rowman and Littlefield, 2019); Wayne A. Wiegand, "'Any Ideas?': The American Library Association and the Desegregation of Public Libraries in the American South," *Libraries* 1, no. 1 (2017): 1–22; Gina Schlesselman-Tarango, "The Legacy of Lady Bountiful: White Women in the Library," *Library Trends* 64, no. 4 (2016): 667–86; and Eino Sierpe, "Confronting Librarianship and Its Function in the Structure of White Supremacy and the Ethno State," *Journal of Radical Librarianship* 5 (May 2019): 84–102.

4. Shannon Mattern, "Fugitive Libraries," *Places Journal* (October 2019), https://placesjournal.org; Jennifer Monaghan, "Reading for the Enslaved, Writing for the Free: Reflections on Liberty and Literacy," in *Proceedings of the American Antiquarian Society* 108 (2000): 309–10.

5. E. J. Josey, "Libraries, Reading, and the Liberation of Black People," *Library Scene* 1, no. 1 (1972): 4–7; Renate L. Chancellor, *E. J. Josey: Transformational Leader of the Modern Library Profession* (Lanham, MD: Rowman and Littlefield, 2020; Marya Annette McQuirter, "A Brief History of African Americans in Washington, DC," *African American Heritage Trail*, https://www.culturaltourismdc.org; Lillian S. Patterson, interview with the author, May 16, 2021; Lovell A. Lee, interview with the author, May 24, 2021; "Literary Societies and Middlebrow Reading," *Encyclopedia.com*, https://www.encyclopedia.com; Michelle N. Garfield, "Literary Societies: The Work of Self-Improvement and Racial Uplift," in *Black Women's Intellectual Traditions: Speaking Their Minds*, ed. Kristin Waters and Carol B. Conaway (Burlington: University of Vermont Press, 2007), 113–28; Caitlin M. J. Pollack and Shelley P. Haley, "'When I Enter': Black Women and Disruption of the White, Heteronormative Narrative of Librarianship," in *Pushing the Margins: Women of Color and Intersectionality in LIS*, ed. Rose L. Chou and Annie Pho (Sacramento: Library Juice Press, 2019), 15–59.

6. Magnus and his brother, the Reverend Robert B. Robinson, were the sons of the Reverend Robert H. Robinson, for whom Alexandria's segregated Black library was later named.

7. "The Colored Reading Room Opened," *Alexandria Gazette*, March 25, 1890, image 2, Library of Congress, Chronicling America, https://chroniclingamerica.loc.gov.

8. H. B. F. MacFarland, address at the dedication of the public library, Washington, D.C., January 7, 1903, recorded in the trustees' annual report (Washington, D.C., 1902), reprinted in "D.C. Public Library Survey, Traceries (1997)," 33.

9. Andrew Carnegie, address at the dedication of the public library, Washington, D.C., January 7, 1903, in ibid.

10. "The Colored Reading Room Opened."

11. Dorothy B. Porter, "The Organized Educational Activities of Negro Literary Societies, 1828–1846," *Journal of Negro Education* 5, no. 4 (1936): 557.

12. "The Colored Reading Room Opened"; "Harrison's Colored Friends: The President-Elect Sends Them Words of Good Cheer," *Duluth Daily News*, January 2, 1889, 1; "Anniversary," *Tombstone Daily Prospector*, January 4, 1889, 2; "Negro Emancipation," *Dallas Morning News*, January 4, 1889, 1; Porter, "The Organized Educational Activities of Negro Literary Societies," 557–58; Char Adams, "Black-Owned Bookstores Have Always Been at the Center of the Resistance," *Mic*, https://www.mic.com.

13. Porter, "The Organized Educational Activities of Negro Literary Societies," 556–58; Knott, *Not Free, Not for All*, 2; Circular, *Colored American*, June 16, 1838, 69; Porter, "The Organized Educational Activities of Negro Literary Societies," 568; Wiegand and Wiegand, *The Desegregation of Public Libraries in the South*, 18; Porter, "The Organized Educational Activities of Negro Literary Societies," 568–69; Adams, "Black-Owned Bookstores"; Porter, "The Organized Educational Activities of Negro Literary Societies," 575–76.

14. "Alexandria's Own: Magnus Robinson," *Alexandria Times*, February 8, 2018, reprinted at https://www.alexandriava.gov; Irvine Garland Penn, "Magnus L. Robinson, Editor, *National Leader*," in *Afro-American Press and Its Editors* (New York: Wiley, 1891), https://en.wikisource.org; "News of City Told in Brief," *Alexandria Gazette*, April 10, 1919, 1.

15. Ebony Vanessa Bowden, "'We Seek What We Find; We See What We Look For': Looking for Literary Production in Washington, D.C., 1921–1928" (master's thesis, University of Maryland, College Park, 2006); Adams, "Black-Owned Bookstores"; "Literary Societies and Middlebrow Reading"; "NAACP: A Century of Freedom, 1909–2009" and "The New Negro Movement," online exhibits, Library of Congress, https://www.loc.gov; William L. Andrews, "The Advent of Urban Realism" and "African American Literature," *Encyclopedia Britannica*, https://www.britannica.com.

16. "A Whole Library for Twelve Dollars," advertisement, *Colored American*, June 9, 1838, 64; advertisement for a complete library, Sears, Roebuck stationery catalogue, c. 1903, in Thomas Augst, "Introduction," in *Institutions of Reading: The Social Life of Libraries in the United States*, ed. Thomas Augst and Kenneth Carpenter (Amherst: University of Massachusetts Press, 2007), 13; Augst, "Introduction," 12.

17. Eliza Atkins Gleason, *The Southern Negro and the Public Library: A Study of the Government and Administration of Public Library Service to Negroes in the South* (Chicago: University of Chicago Press, 1941), 90.

18. *Desegregation* refers specifically to the process of ending systemic racial segregation through legal means.

19. Alexandra Zukas, "'A Power So Compelling': Services for African Americans and Steps Toward Integration at the Richmond Public Library, 1925–1964," *Libraries* 5, no. 1 (2021): 49–50; Wiegand, "Any Ideas?," 3; Wiegand and Wiegand, *The Desegregation of Public Libraries in the Jim Crow South*, 15.

20. George S. Bobinski, "So, Stop Already!," letter to the editor, *ALA Bulletin* 63, no. 11 (1969): 1514; George S. Bobinski, *Carnegie Libraries: Their History and Impact on American Public Library Development* (Chicago: American Library Association, 1969); Robert Sidney Martin, *Carnegie Denied: Communities Rejecting Library Construction Grants, 1898–1925* (Westport: Greenwood, 1993); Carolyn Hall Leatherman, "Richmond Rejects a Library: The Carnegie Library Movement in Richmond, Virginia, in the

Early Twentieth Century" (PhD diss., Commonwealth University, 1992); Zukas, "'A Power So Compelling,'" 50–51, 64–65; "RPL History," *Richmond Public Library*, https://rvalibrary.org.

21. Wiegand and Wiegand, *The Desegregation of Public Libraries in the Jim Crow South*, 82–90; Matt Schudel, "Wyatt Tee Walker, Civil Rights Leader and Top Assistant to Martin Luther King, Jr., Dies at 89," *Washington Post*, January 23, 2018; Stephen Cresswell, "The Last Days of Jim Crow in Southern Libraries," *Libraries and Culture* 31, no. 3/4 (1996): 558–60; Howard G. Cooley, conversation with Nancy Noyes Silcox, February 8, 2020; Markus Schmidt, "The 50th Anniversary of the Petersburg Library Sit-In, the First of the Civil Rights Era," *Progress-Index*, February 26, 2010, https://www.progress-index.com; Knott, *Not Free, Not for All*, 261.

22. Wiegand and Wiegand, *The Desegregation of Public Libraries in the Jim Crow South*, 90–100; U.S. Congress, *Library Services Act: Hearings Before the Select Subcommittee on Education of the Committee on Education and Labor, House of Representatives, Eighty-Eighth Congress, First Session, on H.R. 4879, and Similar Bills to Amend the Library Services Act . . .* (Washington, D.C.: U.S. Government Printing Office, 1963), 88.

23. Wiegand and Wiegand, *The Desegregation of Public Libraries in the Jim Crow South*, 90–100; U.S. Congress, *Library Services Act*, 88; Cresswell, "The Last Days of Jim Crow in Southern Libraries," 559; "The Danville, Virginia, Public Library," *Wilson Library Bulletin* 36 (June 1962): 798; "Library Closing Voted: Referendum in Danville, Va., Opposes Integration Step," *New York Times*, June 15, 1960, 28; Gerard Tetley, "A Library Closes in Danville," *Wilson Library Bulletin* 35 (September 1960): 52, 54; Gerard Tetley, "Danville Reopens—with a Difference," *Wilson Library Bulletin* 35 (November 1960): 224; "The Danville Story, Open Again but Not an Open Library," *Library Journal*, November 1, 1960, 3942–43; Rosemary Neiswender and R. Neiswender, "Danville and Russia," letter to the editor, *Wilson Library Bulletin* 36 (November 1961): 218; Knott, *Not Free, Not for All*, 261–62; U.S. Congress, *Library Services Act*, 89.

24. *Monthly Meeting* is a divisional unit of the Society of Friends that is entitled to conduct business. In 1849, the AMM recognized its new members as a separately organized branch known as the "Woodland Meeting." Martha Claire Catlin, personal communication with author, August 11, 2021, and December 30, 2021.

25. Roger Hansen, "'The Blessed Community': The Mutual Influences of Friends General Conference and the New Meetings Movement, 1915–1945," *Quaker History* 97, no. 2 (2008): 44; Martha Claire Catlin, "Alexandria Friends Meeting at Woodlawn," *Woodlawn Friends*, https://woodlawnfriends.org; Martha Claire Catlin, personal communication with author, August 11, 2021; "History," *Sidwell Friends*, https://www.sidwell.edu; Dorothy G. Harris, "History of the Friends' Meeting Libraries," *Bulletin of Friends Historical Association* 31, no. 2 (1942): 52–62; Catlin, personal communication; Beverly Seehorn Brandt, "The Alexandria, Virginia, Library: Its History, Present Facilities, and Future Programs" (master's thesis, Catholic University of America, 1950); Harris, "History of the Friends' Meeting Libraries," 62; Martha Claire Catlin, personal communication with author, August 18, 2021; Lovell A. Lee, personal communication with author, August 16, 2021. See also V. G. Gray, "The

Friend's [sic] Free Library, 1848–1948: Some Notes in Retrospect," *The Friend* 122 (1948): 6–9.

26. Cephas Brainerd, "Libraries of Young Men's Christian Associations," in *Public Libraries in the United States of America: Their History, Condition, and Management*, compiled by U.S. Department of the Interior, Bureau of Education (Washington, D.C.: Government Printing Office, 1876), 386–88; "African Americans and the YMCA" *University of Minnesota Libraries*, https://libguides.umn.edu; "History of Washington, D.C. YMCA," *YMCA of Metropolitan DC*, https://www.ymcadc.org; Lovell A. Lee, personal communication.

27. Patterson, interview; Lovell A. Lee, interviews with the author, May 24, 2021, August 16, 2021; Gladys Howard Davis, interview with the author, January 17, 2014; Carol Hymowitz, "Black Lives Matter Creates a Boom for Black-Owned Bookstores," *Bloomberg Businessweek*, October 22, 2020, https://www.bloomberg.com; Troy D. Johnson, blog entry, March 31, 2014, https://aalbc.com; Shirley M. Lee, interview with the author, May 24, 2021; Lovell A. Lee, interview, May 24, 2021; Gladys Howard Davis, interview.

### CHAPTER TWO: BOLD BEGINNINGS

1. Raymond Arsenault, *Freedom Riders: 1961 and the Struggle for Social Justice* (Oxford: Oxford University Press, 2006), 6; J. Douglas Smith, *Managing White Supremacy: Race, Politics, and Citizenship in Jim Crow Virginia* (Chapel Hill: University of North Carolina Press, 2002), 257–59; Earl Lewis, *In Their Own Interests: Race, Class, and Power in Twentieth-Century Norfolk, Virginia* (Berkeley: University of California Press, 1991), 156.

2. Smith, *Managing White Supremacy*, 259; Commission on Interracial Cooperation, *The New Georgia Encyclopedia*, http://www.georgiaencyclopedia.org. "The Commission on Interracial Cooperation, founded in Atlanta in 1919, worked until its 1944 merger with the Southern Regional Council to oppose lynching, mob violence, and peonage and to educate white southerners concerning the worst aspects of racial abuse. The commission remained based in Atlanta but had state-level committees throughout the South and, in the 1920s, some 800 local interracial committees" (Smith, *Managing White Supremacy*, 259, 250–51). On southern paternalism toward Blacks, see Guion Griffis Johnson, "Southern Paternalism toward Negroes after Emancipation," *Journal of Southern History* 23, no. 4 (1957): 483–509.

3. Thurgood Marshall, letter to Walter White, November 29, 1937, Legal Files, Box I-D-91, NAACP Records, Manuscript Division, Library of Congress (hereafter cited as NAACP Records); Mark V. Tushnet, *The NAACP's Legal Strategy against Segregated Education, 1925–1950* (Chapel Hill: University of North Carolina Press, 1987), 77–81; Nathan R. Margold, *Preliminary Report to the Joint Committee Supervising the Expenditure of the 1930 Appropriation by the American Fund for Public Service* [1931], typescript, NAACP Records; Patricia Sullivan, *Lift Every Voice: The NAACP and the Making of the Civil Rights Movement* (New York: New Press, 2009); Minnie Finch, *The NAACP: Its Fight for Justice* (Metuchen, NJ: Scarecrow, 1981), 84; "The Civil Rights Act of 1964: A Long Struggle for Freedom—The Segregation Era (1900–1939),"

exhibition, Library of Congress, https://www.loc.gov. On Garland's American Fund for Public Service, see Gloria Garrett Samson, *The American Fund for Public Service: Charles Garland and Radical Philanthropy, 1922–1941* (Westport, CT: Greenwood, 1996). Margold had been recruited for the NAACP position by his mentor, Felix Frankfurter, and another former student of Frankfurter's, Charles Hamilton Houston. Frankfurter was a member of the NAACP's National Legal Committee and later became an associate justice of the U.S. Supreme Court. Houston served as vice dean of Howard University's Law School (1929–35) and was a litigation director for the NAACP. On Houston, see Genna Rae McNeil, *Groundwork: Charles Hamilton Houston and the Struggle for Civil Rights* (Philadelphia: University of Pennsylvania Press, 1983); and Genna Rae McNeil, "Before *Brown*: Reflections on Historical Context and Vision," *American University Law Review* 52 (2002): 1431–60. On the NAACP's efforts to end segregated education, see Tushnet, *The NAACP's Legal Strategy against Segregated Education*; and Richard Kluger, *Simple Justice: The History of "Brown v. Board of Education" and Black America's Struggle for Equality* (New York: Vintage, 2004). On the Supreme Court's involvement in desegregation initiatives before *Brown*, see Michael J. Klarman, *From Jim Crow to Civil Rights: The Supreme Court and the Struggle for Racial Equality* (Oxford: Oxford University Press, 2004). On the Court's subversion of equal rights, see Lawrence Goldstone, *Inherently Unequal: The Betrayal of Equal Rights by the Supreme Court, 1865–1903* (New York: Walker, 2011).

4. *Raymond A. Pearson and Others, Officers and Members of the University of Maryland v. Donald G. Murray,* no. 53, October term, 1935, https://www2.law.umaryland.edu; "Editorial Comment: The University of Maryland versus Donald Gaines Murray," *Journal of Negro Education* 5, no. 2 (1936): 166–74; John Egerton, *Speak Now against the Day: The Generation before the Civil Rights Movement in the South* (Chapel Hill: University of North Carolina Press, 1995), 152–53; McNeil, "Before *Brown*," 1445–46; McNeil, *Groundwork*, 114–17; Gerald N. Rosenberg, *The Hollow Hope: Can Courts Bring about Social Change?*, 2nd ed. (Chicago: University of Chicago Press, 2008), 72–73; Mark V. Tushnet, *Making Civil Rights Law: Thurgood Marshall and the Supreme Court, 1956–1961* (New York: Oxford University Press, 1987), 11–15; Tushnet, *The NAACP's Legal Strategy against Segregated Education,* 51–58; *Yick Wo v. Hopkins, Sheriff,* 118 U.S. 356 (1886), U.S. Supreme Court, submitted April 14, 1886, decided May 10, 1886, https://supreme.justia.com and https://caselaw.findlaw.com. See also Christopher W. Schmidt, "Divided by Law: The Sit-ins and the Role of the Courts in the Civil Rights Movement," *Law and History Review* 33, no. 1 (2015): 93–149. Marshall served as attorney for the Baltimore office of the NAACP and, in 1967, became an associate justice of the Supreme Court.

5. "Along the NAACP Battlefront. 30th Annual Conference in Richmond, Va.," "Resolution V.: Civil Rights," and "Resolution VI.: Education," *The Crisis* 46, no. 9 (1939): 281; William H. Hastie, "A Look at the NAACP," ibid., 264.

6. *Plessy v. Ferguson,* 163 U.S. 537 (1896), no. 210, argued April 18, 1896, decided May 18, 1896, U.S. Supreme Court, https://supreme.justia.com. In 1890, the state of Louisiana passed the Separate Car Act, which required state railways to provide separate cars for Black and White riders. Plessy, a Black man of primarily White ancestry, argued in his orchestrated 1892 test case, *Homer Adolph Plessy v. the State of*

*Louisiana*, that the state law denied him his rights under the Thirteenth and Fourteenth amendments to the U.S. Constitution. A Louisiana judge, John Howard Ferguson, ruled that the state had the right to regulate the policies of rail companies operating within its jurisdiction. The 1896 decision in the subsequent Supreme Court case upheld state laws that mandated segregation of the races in public accommodations, transportation, and educational systems. *Plessy v. Ferguson* thereby instituted a de jure Supreme Court decision that legalized the de facto segregation imposed by the Black Codes established in the South after the Civil War. Although *Plessy v. Ferguson* is commonly cited as the first of this Jim Crow legislation, state-level legal decisions mandating separation of the races had been issued in Mississippi in 1865 and in Tennessee in 1881. See Stanley J. Folmsbee, "The Origin of the First 'Jim Crow' Law," *Journal of Southern History* 15, no. 2 (1949): 235–47. In a prelude to the *Plessy* decision, the Supreme Court struck down portions of the Civil Rights Act of 1875 in its 1888 *Civil Rights Cases* ruling. That act prohibited the denial of equal accommodations in hotels and theaters and on railroads and other forms of public conveyance. See *Civil Rights Cases*, 109 U.S. 3 (1883), submitted October term, 1882, decided October 16, 1888, U.S. Supreme Court, https://supreme.justia.com.

7.  Charles M. Payne and Adam Green, eds., *Time Longer Than Rope: A Century of African American Activism, 1850–1950* (New York: New York University Press, 2003), 1–2.

8.  James Clyde Sellman, "Great Depression," in *Africana: The Encyclopedia of the African and African American Experience*, ed. Kwame Anthony Appiah and Henry Louis Gates, Jr. (New York: Basic Civitas Books, 1999), 868.

9.  Nancy Noyes Silcox, *Samuel Wilbert Tucker: The Story of a Civil Rights Trailblazer and the 1939 Alexandria Library Sit-in* (Fairfax, VA: History4All, 2013; Arlington, VA: Noysil, 2014), 20.

10. In 1882, the delegate Alfred W. Harris, an African American attorney, sponsored a bill in Virginia's general assembly to charter the Virginia Normal and Collegiate Institute as a historically Black college. In 1902, amid sweeping legislative changes to Virginia's constitution, opposition to the collegiate elements of the program led to legislative revision of the charter, and the institution became known as Virginia Normal and Industrial Institute. The collegiate program was restored in 1923, and in 1930 the school was renamed Virginia State College for Negroes. A third name change in 1946, this time to Virginia State College, was followed in 1979 by a legislative act resulting in a final name change: to Virginia State University (Virginia State University, "History of VSU," http://www.vsu.edu). See also "Sit Down and Take a Stand," exhibition notes, February 8, 2014, Alexandria Black History Museum, Alexandria, Virginia; and Matthew Dull, remarks during the annual Samuel Wilbert Tucker Walk, summer 2012.

11. William A. Elwood, "Interview with Samuel Wilbert Tucker and Otto L. Tucker, January 18, 1985," conducted for the Civil Rights Lawyers Project (Charlottesville: University of Virginia, 2006), DVD; Julia Spaulding Tucker, interview by Matt Spangler, summer 1999.

12. "Criminal Warrant" of complainant [Lottie May] Jernigan against Louis Tucker [*sic*] and George Tucker, June 21, 1927, box 1, folder 2, no. B2010.001, Samuel Wilbert Tucker Collection, Alexandria Black History Museum, Alexandria, Virginia

(hereafter cited as Tucker Collection); Smith, *Managing White Supremacy*, 261; Elsie Tucker Thomas, interview by Matt Spangler, September 30, 1998.

13. Elsie Tucker Thomas, interview; "Parker-Gray School, 1920–2020," https://www.alexandriava.gov; S. J. Ackerman, "S. W. Tucker Chronology," vertical file, unpublished document, August 15, 2000, [1], ALSCAV.

14. Zachery R. Williams, *In Search of the Talented Tenth: Howard University Public Intellectuals and the Dilemmas of Race, 1926–1970* (Columbia: University of Missouri Press, 2009), 80–81, 114, 54–58; Julia Spaulding Tucker, interview; Martha Claire Catlin, personal communication, August 18, 2021. See also Stephen W. Angell, "Howard Thurman and Quakers," *Quaker Theology*, https://quakertheology.org; and Fellowship of Reconciliation, "Committed to Overcoming Social Injustices," https://forusa.org/.

15. Noyes Silcox, *Samuel Wilbert Tucker*, 28, 72. Issues of *The Crisis* between September 1939 and May 1949 do not contain news of Tucker or the sit-in. The Virginia Bar Association, which does not require lawyers to possess a degree to practice law, invites voluntary membership from all licensed Virginia lawyers in good standing as well as from law students. It is often confused with the Virginia State Bar, which is the state regulatory agency with mandatory membership.

16. Philip S. Foner, *History of Black Americans: From Africa to the Emergence of the Cotton Kingdom* (New York: Greenwood, 1975), 577–78. Community law practices, also known as community-embedded law practices, are small businesses operated by solo practitioners or small firms that serve the legal education and service needs of citizens with modest incomes. The attorneys in these practices address needs such as divorce settlements, the creation of wills, evictions, representation of victims and perpetrators of domestic violence, representation of small-business owners, and struggles with civil justice and criminal charges. See Luz E. Herrera, "Community Law Practice," *Daedalus* 148, no. 1 (2019): 106–12.

17. "Alice Jackson—U. Va. Desegregation Case," microfilm 1568, part 3A, reel 6, group 1, box C–203, Library Special Collections, University of Virginia, Charlottesville; "Application of Negro Student Rejected by University Board," *Richmond Times-Dispatch*, September 20, 1935, 1; Walker McKusick, "First Post for a First," *Historian News*, November 28, 2010; Terrell L. Strayhorn, "Alice Carlotta Jackson: She Was the First Black Applicant to the University of Virginia," *Journal of Blacks in Higher Education* 51 (Spring 2006): 19; "University of Virginia Case before NAACP," NAACP press release, September 20, 1935; Peter Wallerstein, "Segregation, Desegregation, and Higher Education in Virginia," paper delivered at the Policy History Conference, Charlottesville, Virginia, June 3, 2006, https://fliphtml5.com/; "Women at the University of Virginia: Breaking and Making Tradition. An Exhibition in Special Collections, Alderman Library, May 16–November 3, 2003," University of Virginia, Charlottesville.

18. Wayne State University, Walter P. Reuther Library, "(11434) Bendix Strike, South Bend, Indiana, 1936" and "(11444) Chrysler Strike, Cadillac Square, Detroit, Michigan, March 24, 1937," October 2009, http://www.reuther.wayne.edu; Sidney Fine, *Sit-Down: The General Motors Strike of 1936–1937* (Ann Arbor: University of Michigan Press, 1969); Rachel Meyer, "The Rise and Fall of the Sit-Down Strike,"

in *The Encyclopedia of Strikes in American History*, ed. Aaron Brenner, Immanuel Ness, and Benjamin Day (Armonk, NY: Sharpe, 2009), 204–15; Daniel Nelson, "Origins of the Sit-Down Era: Worker Militancy and Innovation in the Rubber Industry, 1934–38," *Labor History* 23, no. 2 (1982): 198–225; Joel Seidman, *Sit-Down* (New York: League for Industrial Democracy, 1937). See also Mike Smith, "'Let's Make Detroit a Union Town': The History of Labor and the Working Class in the Motor City," *Michigan Historical Review* (Fall 2001): 157–73; and Stephen Meyer, "The Degradation of Work Revisited: Workers and Technology in the American Auto Industry, 1900–2000," http://www.autolife.umd.umich.edu.

19. Eric W. Rise, *The Martinsville Seven: Race, Rape, and Capital Punishment* (Charlottesville: University Press of Virginia, 1995).

20. "African-American Biographies—20th Century" and "Tucker, Samuel," Vertical File, Special Collections, Alexandria Library, Alexandria, VA; Ackerman, "S. W. Tucker Chronology," [5]; Noyes Silcox, *Samuel Wilbert Tucker*, 61.

21. *Brown v. Board of Education of Topeka*, 347 U.S. 483 (1954), argued December 9, 1952, reargued December 8, 1953, decided May 17, 1954, U.S. Supreme Court, https://supreme.justia.com. See also Kluger, *Simple Justice*; and *Green v. County School Board of New Kent County, Charles C. Green et al. v. County School Board of New Kent County, Virginia et al.* 391 U.S. 430 (1968), no. 695, argued April 3, 1968, decided May 27, 1968, U.S. Supreme Court, https://www.law.cornell.edu; David Bradley and Shelley Fisher Fishkin, eds., *The Encyclopedia of Civil Rights in America* (Armonk, NY: Sharp Reference, 1998), 2, 411; "African-American Biographies—20th Century," "Tucker, Samuel"; Ackerman, "S. W. Tucker Chronology," [1–14]. The Ming Advocacy Award was established by the NAACP's national board of directors in April 1974 "and is awarded annually to a lawyer who exemplifies the spirit of financial and personal sacrifice that Mr. Ming displayed in his legal work for the NAACP" (https://naacp.org).

22. Deborah Thomas-McSwain, interview with the author, January 19, 2020.

## CHAPTER THREE: PRELUDE TO THE SIT-IN, PART ONE

1. U.S. Census Bureau, *Twenty-fourth Decennial Census* (Washington, D.C.: Government Printing Office, 2020), https://www.census.gov.

2. City of Alexandria, "Archaeology and Alexandria's Prehistory" and "Alexandria History," https://www.alexandriava.gov; "Cities of Virginia," *Encyclopedia Virginia*, https://www.encyclopediavirginia.org.

3. City of Alexandria, "Archaeology and Alexandria's Prehistory"; City of Alexandria, "Alexandria History"; "Cities of Virginia"; William Seale, *A Guide to Historic Alexandria*, 2nd ed. (Alexandria, VA: Office of Historic Alexandria, 2000), 16–18; Michael Lee Pope, *Hidden History of Alexandria, D.C.*, 2nd ed. (Charleston, SC: History Press, 2011), 9–11. See also Donald M. Sweig, "The Importation of African Slaves to the Potomac River, 1732–1772," *William and Mary Quarterly*, 3rd ser., 42, no. 4 (1985): 507–24.

4. Diane Riker, "Alexandria and Belhaven: A Case of Dual Identity," https://www.alexandriava.gov.

5. City of Alexandria, "Alexandria History"; "Cities of Virginia"; "History of Alexandria," box 21, folder "Annual Reports 1961–62," Office of Historic Alexandria.

6. "The History of Washington, DC," https://washington.org; Chris Myers Asch, "How a Debt Deal Made DC a Slave Capital," *Washington Post*, July 24, 2011, B5.

7. "The History of Washington, DC"; "Cities of Virginia"; "Dumbarton Oaks Conference" and "Georgetown, District, Washington, District of Columbia, United States," *Encyclopædia Britannica*, http://www.britannica.com. George Town, now the Georgetown section of Washington, D.C., was merged into the District of Columbia in 1871 and annexed to the city in 1878.

8. In 2014, the *Alexandria Gazette Packet* ran a series of articles by Ted Pulliam about Alexandria and the War of 1812: see "The United States Declares War—1812," July 10, 2014, 12–13; "Alexandria in 1812," July 17, 2014, 14; "Blockade and Raids—1813," July 24, 2014, 21; "Alexandrians vs. British Raiders—June 1814," July 31, 2014, 20–21; "The British and the Slaves—July 1814," August 7, 2014, 12, 23; "Alexandria Prepares Its Defense—August 1814," August 14, 2014, 12–13; "Battle of Bladensburg—August 1814," August 21, 2014, 21; "Alexandria Surrenders—August 1814," August 28, 2014, 20; and "Alexandria Looted—August and September 1814," September 4, 2014, 12, 19.

9. On enslavement before and during the Revolutionary War and the War of 1812, see David Brion Davis, *The Problem of Slavery in the Age of Revolution, 1770–1823* (Ithaca, NY: Cornell University Press, 1975); Paul Finkelman, *Slavery and the Founders: Race and Liberty in the Age of Jefferson*, 3rd ed. (New York: Routledge, 2015); Gene Allen Smith, *The Slaves' Gamble: Choosing Sides in the War of 1812* (New York: Palgrave Macmillan, 2013); and Alan Taylor, *American Revolutions: A Continental History, 1750–1804* (New York: Norton, 2016). On enslavement in Virginia before and during the Revolutionary War, in the War of 1812, and in the years before the Civil War, see Edmund S. Morgan, *American Slavery, American Freedom: The Ordeal of Colonial Virginia* (New York: Norton, 1995); Alan Taylor, *The Internal Enemy: Slavery and War in Virginia, 1772–1832* (New York: Norton, 2013); Donald M. Sweig, "Northern Virginia Slavery: A Statistical and Demographic Investigation" (PhD diss., College of William and Mary, 1982); and Eva Sheppard Wolf, *Race and Liberty in the New Nation: Emancipation in Virginia from the Revolution to Nat Turner's Rebellion* (Baton Rouge: Louisiana State University Press, 2006). On the United States after the War of 1812 and before the Civil War, see Paul Finkelman and Donald R. Kennon, eds., *In the Shadow of Freedom: The Politics of Slavery in the National Capital* (Athens: Ohio University Press, 2011); Daniel Walker Howe, *What God Hath Wrought: The Transformation of America, 1815–1848* (Oxford: Oxford University Press, 2007); and Manisha Sinha, *The Slave's Cause: A History of Abolition* (New Haven, CT: Yale University Press, 2016). Howe's in-depth treatise is particularly pertinent to Virginia, especially on the dramatic impact of Nat Turner's 1831 Southampton rebellion.

10. Kevin M. Levin, "'Until Every Negro Has Been Slaughtered,'" *Civil War Times* 49, no. 5 (2010), 32–37; "Alexandria Surrenders—August 1814," 20.

11. Department of Planning and Community Development and Alexandria Archaeology, "Alexandria Canal" and "History of the Alexandria Canal," n.d., both in unpaginated brochure, Office of Historic Alexandria, https://www.alexandriava.gov.

12. John Kelly, "Slave Trade and Alexandria's 'Retrocession,'" *Washington Post*, September 19, 2010, C3. On the influence of Black enslavement on White Alexandrians' interest in retrocession, see A. Glenn Crothers, "The 1846 Retrocession of Alexandria: Protecting Slavery and the Slave Trade in the District of Columbia," in *In the Shadow of Freedom: The Politics of Slavery in the National Capital*, ed. Paul Finkelman and Donald R. Kennon (Athens: Ohio University Press, 2011), 141–68. On the constitutionality of retrocession, see Hannis Taylor, *Retrocession Act of 1846 . . . Letter from Hannis Taylor to Thomas H. Carter . . . Rendering an Opinion as to the Constitutionality of the Act . . .*, 61st Congress, 2nd session, doc. 286 (Washington, D.C.: Government Printing Office, 1910).

13. City of Alexandria, "Alexandria History"; Bruce Levine, *The Fall of the House of Dixie: The Civil War and the Social Revolution that Transformed the South* (New York: Random House, 2013), 23; Michael P. Johnson and James L. Roark, *Black Masters: A Free Family of Color in the Old South* (New York: Norton, 1984), 36–37; and Ira Berlin, *Slaves without Masters: The Free Negro in the Antebellum South* (New York: New Press, 1992), 270–73. On how Virginia statutes affected free Blacks, see Ellen Eslinger, "Free Black Residency in Two Antebellum Virginia Counties: How the Laws Functioned," *Journal of Southern History* 79, no. 2 (2013): 261–98.

14. City of Alexandria, "History of Alexandria's African American Community," https://www.alexandriava.gov; Seale, *A Guide to Historic Alexandria*, 39; U.S. Census Bureau, "Population Division, Historical Census Statistics on Population Totals by Race, 1790 to 1990, and by Hispanic Origin, 1970 to 1990, for the United States, Regions, Divisions, and States," working paper no. 56, September 2002, https://census.gov; "1850 Census Index—Alexandria & Alexandria County, Virginia," in *Alexandria, Virginia, City and County, 1850 Census*, transcribed by Marjorie D. Tallichet (Bowie, MD: Heritage Books, 1986), https://alexandria.libnet.info. The free Black population is listed in the 1850 census as "col'd" males and females.

15. "Neighborhoods: Alexandria's Free Black Neighborhoods," in *Courageous Journey: A Guide to Alexandria's African American History*, unpaginated brochure, n.d.; City of Alexandria, "History of Alexandria's African American Community." On other free Black communities in Virginia, see Eslinger, "Free Black Residency in Two Antebellum Virginia Counties," 261–98.

16. Philip S. Foner, *History of Black Americans: From Africa to the Emergence of the Cotton Kingdom* (New York: Greenwood, 1975), 569, 562.

17. Krystyn R. Moon, "Navigating Everyday Life in Jim Crow Alexandria," lecture for the Equal Justice Initiative Community Remembrance Project, November 16, 2019, Alexandria, VA.

18. Davis, *The Problem of Slavery in the Age of Revolution*; David Brion Davis, *The Problem of Slavery in Western Culture* (Ithaca, NY: Cornell University Press, 1966); and Ira Berlin, Marc Faureau, and Steven F. Miller, eds., *Remembering Slavery: African Americans Talk about their Personal Experiences of Slavery and Emancipation* (New York: New Press; Washington, D.C.: Library of Congress, 1998); anonymous (a Marylander), "The Law of Slavery in the State of Louisiana," *National Era*, September 2, 1847, n.p.; "The Black Code of Louisiana, 1806," law of June 7, 1806, part 3, sec. 9, https://www.accessible-archives.com; Joshua D. Rothman, *The Ledger and the Chain: How*

*Domestic Slave Traders Shaped America* (New York: Basic Books, 2021), 134–135, 136. Rothman's treatise is the definitive work on the business operation of Franklin and Armfield and its impact on the American economy.

19. Sweig, "Northern Virginia Slavery: A Statistical and Demographic Investigation." See Donald M. Sweig's series of articles, "Alexandria to New Orleans: The Human Tragedy of the Interstate Slave Trade," in the *Alexandria Gazette Packet*: part 1, October 2, 2014, 18–19; part 2, October 9, 2014, 14; part 3, October 16, 2014, 12; part 4, October 23, 2014, 34–35. Also see Sweig, "The Importation of African Slaves to the Potomac River, 1732–1772," 507–24; and James Donald Munson, "From Empire to Commonwealth: Alexandria, Virginia, 1749–1780" (PhD diss., University of Maryland, 1984), esp. chap. 7.

20. Rothman, *The Ledger and the Chain*, 150–55.

21. Hannah Natanson, "They Were Once America's Cruelest, Richest Slave Traders. Why Does No One Know Their Names?," *Washington Post*, September 9, 2014, https://www.washingtonpost.com.

22. Joshua D. Rothman, personal communication, June 11, 2019.

23. David J. Libby, "Franklin and Armfield," in *Slavery in the United States: A Social, Political, and Historical Encyclopedia*, ed. Junius P. Rodriguez (Santa Barbara, CA: ABC-CLIO, 2007), 1:293–94; City of Alexandria, "History of Alexandria's African American Community," https://www.alexandriava.gov; City of Alexandria, "The Slave Trade," https://www.alexandriava.gov; Seale, *A Guide to Historic Alexandria*, 39, 41; City of Alexandria, "Freedom House Museum," https://www.alexandriava.gov. Pope describes the interior of the Franklin and Armfield compound and the firm's operation in *Hidden History of Alexandria, D.C.*, 73–86.

24. On enslavement in the nation's capital, see Crothers, "The 1846 Retrocession of Alexandria," 141–68; Don E. Fehrenbacher, *The Slaveholding Republic: An Account of the United States Government's Relations to Slavery*, comp. and ed. Ward M. McAfee (New York: Oxford University Press, 2001); and Paul Finkelman, "Slavery in the Shadow of Liberty," in Finkelman and Kennon, *In the Shadow of Freedom*, 3–15.

25. Ernest B. Furgurson, "Mr. Lincoln's Slaves," *Washingtonian* 47, no. 7 (2012): 55; Ernest B. Furgurson, "Compromise of 1850," https://www.ourdocuments.gov/; Crothers, "The 1846 Retrocession of Alexandria," 141–68; U.S. Census Bureau, "Census of Population and Housing," 1940, https://www.census.gov.

26. Furgurson, "Mr. Lincoln's Slaves," 56; American Battlefield Trust, "Shiloh: Pittsburg Landing," https://www.civilwar.org; "Ending Slavery in the District of Columbia" and "DC Emancipation Day," https://emancipation.dc.gov.

27. Seale, *A Guide to Historic Alexandria*, 47, 50–57; Michael Lee Pope, "Alexandria Is Ours," *Alexandria Gazette Packet*, May 5, 2011, 6; Michael Lee Pope, "Hostile Takeover," *Alexandria Gazette Packet*, November 17, 2011, 7; James M. McPherson, *Battle Cry of Freedom: The Civil War Era* (New York: Oxford University Press, 1988), 306. On collective memory and southern identity, see W. Fitzhugh Brundage, ed., *Where These Memories Grow: History, Memory, and Southern Identity* (Chapel Hill: University of North Carolina Press, 2000). For international perspectives on distinctions between analytically abstracted memories and real-world experiences as well as the connections

between power, order, and chaos, see Gerald Sider and Gavin Smith, eds., *Between History and Histories: The Making of Silences and Commemorations* (Toronto: University of Toronto Press, 1997).

28. Plaque on the base of the monument *Appomattox*, Alexandria, VA; "Walking Tours of Historic Alexandria," n.d., unpaginated document, Alexandria, VA. In 1889, the Virginia House of Delegates was petitioned to protect Confederate monuments throughout the Commonwealth and prohibit their removal. In 2016, however, Alexandria's city council unanimously recommended that *Appomattox* be moved. Legislation to initiate the move was never introduced because of expectations that it would fail in the Republican-controlled general assembly. Citizens made subsequent efforts in 2018 and 2019 to remove *Appomattox* or at least grant local communities the authorization to make decisions about statue removals but were thwarted by Republicans. In 2020, when both houses of the general assembly were controlled by Democrats for the first time since 1994, legislation was introduced to authorize local control over the Commonwealth's Confederate memorials. The legislation was passed, and Governor Ralph S. Northam signed it into law. The United Daughters of the Confederacy, the owners of the statue, decided to remove the monument on June 2, 2020, a month before the legislation's official date of enactment. They did not inform the city of the statue's new location. See Jeanne Theismann, "Historic Moment in Alexandria: Statue Relocated to an Undisclosed Location," *Alexandria Gazette Packet*, June 4, 2020, 1, 14; Austen Bundy, "A Controversial Confederate Statue with Its Back to the North Was Removed in Historic Old Town Alexandria," CNN, June 2, 2020, https://www.cnn.com; Cody Mello-Klein, "State Legislation to Allow City to Remove Controversial Statue," *Alexandria Times*, April 17, 2020.

29. Levine, *The Fall of the House of Dixie*, 105; James M. McPherson, *The Negro's Civil War: How American Blacks Felt and Acted during the War for the Union* (New York: Vintage, 1993), 28; McPherson, *Battle Cry of Freedom*, 355.

30. Seale, *A Guide to Historic Alexandria*, 53; City of Alexandria, "History of Alexandria's African American Community"; City of Alexandria, "Contrabands and Freedmen Cemetery," http://www.alexandriava.gov; Michael Lee Pope, "'Healthy Resistance': Historic Structure on Duke Street Takes on New Life," *Alexandria Gazette Packet*, July 28, 2011, 1, 3; Robert Samuels, "In Alexandria, Honoring Slaves' Flight to Freedom," *Washington Post*, September 7, 2014, C1, C6; "Memorial Cemetery Dedicated," *Alexandria Gazette Packet*, September 11, 2014, 1. On the history of the Freedmen's Cemetery, see Michael Lee Pope, "Mystery Endures: As Dedication Approaches, Full Story of Freedman's [sic] Cemetery May Never Be Known," *Alexandria Gazette Packet*, August 28, 2014, 1, 18.

31. Edward A. Miller, Jr., "Volunteers for Freedom: Black Civil War Soldiers in Alexandria National Cemetery, Part I," *Historic Alexandria Quarterly* (Fall 1998): 1–16; City of Alexandria, "Contrabands and Freedmen Cemetery Memorial." On September 6, 2014, a memorial to the approximately 1,800 deceased buried at Freedmen's Cemetery was unveiled at what is now known as Contrabands and Freedmen's Cemetery in Alexandria.

32. Levine, *The Fall of the House of Dixie*, 259, 177–81; W. E. B. Du Bois, *Black Reconstruction in America, 1860–1880* (New York: Free Press, 1998), 623. See also William J. F. Meredith, "The Black Codes," *Negro History Bulletin* 3, no. 5 (1940): 76–77; Daniel A. Novak, "The Black Codes," in *The Wheel of Servitude: Black Forced Labor after Slavery* (Lexington: University Press of Kentucky, 1978): 1–8; Peter Wallenstein, *Blue Laws and Black Codes: Conflict, Courts, and Change in Twentieth-Century Virginia* (Charlottesville: University of Virginia Press, 2004); Theodore Brantner Wilson, *The Black Codes of the South* (Tuscaloosa: University of Alabama Press, 1965); and B. BlackPast, "(1866) Mississippi Black Codes," December 15, 2010, http://www.blackpast.org. On race relations and the emergence of the New South, see Howard N. Rabinowitz, *Race Relations in the Urban South, 1865–1890* (New York: Oxford University Press, 1978); Howard N. Rabinowitz, *The First New South, 1865–1920* (Arlington Heights, IL: Harlan Davidson, 1992). On the New South after Reconstruction, see C. Vann Woodward, *Origins of the New South, 1877–1913* (Baton Rouge: Louisiana State University Press, 1951).

33. Eric Foner and John A. Garraty, eds. *The Reader's Companion to American History* (Boston: Houghton Mifflin, 1991), 922–23; W. E. B. Du Bois, *Black Reconstruction in America, 1860–1880* (New York: Free Press, 1998), 219–30; Eric Foner, *Reconstruction: America's Unfinished Revolution, 1863–1877* (New York: Perennial Classics, 1989), 68–70, 97–99, 144.

34. Du Bois, *Black Reconstruction in America*, 220–31, 648–67; Foner, *Reconstruction*, 142–48.

35. Amy Bertsch and Lance Mallamo, "The Desire for Streetcars in Alexandria," *Alexandria Times*, October 8, 2015, n.p., http://www.alexandria.gov.

36. "The Ford Plant: A Reflection of Alexandria," *Zebra Press*, April 2021, 17.

37. Daniel Lee, personal communication, July 26, 2019; Seale, *A Guide to Historic Alexandria*, 66; U.S. Census Bureau, *Sixteenth Census of the United States: 1940. Population*, vol. 2, *Characteristics of the Population* (Washington, D.C.: Government Printing Office, 1943), 169.

38. Stanley J. Folmsbee, "The Origin of the First 'Jim Crow' Law," *Journal of Southern History* 15, no. 2 (1949): 235–47. On Black life during Jim Crow, see Litwack, *Trouble in Mind*. On Black life and agency in a Virginia city during the same era, see Earl Lewis, *In their Own Interests: Race, Class, and Power in Twentieth-Century Norfolk, Virginia* (Berkeley: University of California Press, 1991). The most influential book on Jim Crow is C. Vann Woodward, *The Strange Career of Jim Crow*, rev. ed. (New York: Galaxy [Oxford University Press], 1957). The best counter-argument to Woodward's thesis is in Howard N. Rabinowitz, "More than the Woodward Thesis: Assessing *The Strange Career of Jim Crow*," *Journal of American History* 75, no. 3 (1988): 842–56. Also see Blair L. M. Kelley, *Right to Ride: Streetcar Boycotts and African American Citizenship in the Era of "Plessy v. Ferguson"* (Chapel Hill: University of North Carolina Press, 2010). On the impact of Jim Crow legislation in Virginia, see J. Douglas Smith, *Managing White Supremacy: Race, Politics, and Citizenship in Jim Crow Virginia* (Chapel Hill: University of North Carolina Press, 2002); Wallenstein, *Blue Laws and Black Codes*; and Charles E. Wynes, "The Evolution of Jim Crow Laws in Twentieth Century Virginia," *Phylon* 28, no. 4 (1967): 416–25.

39. Seale, *A Guide to Historic Alexandria*, 70.

## CHAPTER FOUR: HISTORY AS CONTEXT

1. In minstrel shows, which date back to the early 1830s, Whites blackened their faces with burnt cork, greasepaint, or coal and danced and sang in ways that caricatured Black life, characters, and aspirations. They were popular throughout the nation, continuing even in the North until the 1960s. Some Blacks exploited the profitability of minstrelsy by performing for their own benefit. See "Blackface! Origins of Jump Jim Crow," http://black-face.com/jim-crow.htm; Leon F. Litwack, *Trouble in Mind: Black Southerners in the Age of Jim Crow* (New York: Knopf, 1998), xiv–xv; Steve Luxenberg, *Separate: The Story of "Plessy v. Ferguson" and America's Journey from Slavery to Segregation* (New York: Norton, 2019); and Vicky Gan, "The Story Behind the Failed Minstrel Show at the 1964 World's Fair," *Smithsonian Magazine*, April 28, 2014, https://www.smithsonianmag.com.

2. James Hugo Johnston, *Race Relations in Virginia and Miscegenation in the South, 1776–1860* (Amherst: University of Massachusetts Press, 1970); Joel Williamson, *New People: Miscegenation and Mulattoes in the United States* (Baton Rouge: Louisiana State University Press, 1995); Stanley J. Folmsbee, "The Origin of the First 'Jim Crow' Law," *Journal of Southern History* 15, no. 2 (1949): 235–47; Joel Williamson, comp., *The Origins of Segregation* (Boston: Heath, 1968); Joel Williamson, *A Rage for Order: Black-White Relations in the American South Since Emancipation* (New York: Oxford University Press, 1986); William H. Chafe, Raymond Gavins, and Robert Korstad, eds., *Remembering Jim Crow: African Americans Tell about Life in the Segregated South* (New York: New Press; Raleigh, NC: Duke University, Center for Documentary Studies, 2001); Litwack, *Trouble in Mind*; Howard N. Rabinowitz, "More than the Woodward Thesis: Assessing *The Strange Career of Jim Crow*," *Journal of American History* 75, no. 3 (1988): 842–56; Howard N. Rabinowitz, *Race Relations in the Urban South, 1865–1890* (Athens: University of Georgia Press, 1996); Howard N. Rabinowitz, *The First New South, 1865–1920* (Arlington Heights, IL: Harlan Davidson, 1992); Peter Wallenstein, *Blue Laws and Black Codes: Conflict, Courts, and Change in Twentieth-Century Virginia* (Charlottesville: University of Virginia Press, 2004); C. Vann Woodward, *The Strange Career of Jim Crow*, rev. ed. (New York: Oxford University Press, 1957); Richard Wormser, *The Rise and Fall of Jim Crow* (New York: St. Martin's, 2003); Charles E. Wynes, "The Evolution of Jim Crow Laws in Twentieth Century [sic] Virginia," *Phylon* 28, no. 4 (1967): 416–25.

3. Gregory Michael Dorr, *Segregation's Science: Eugenics and Society in Virginia* (Charlottesville: University of Virginia Press, 2008); "Tried to Lynch Negro: Mob Attempted to Enter Alexandria County Jail," *Washington Post*, July 15, 1899, 2.

4. Susan Breitzer, "Virginia Constitutional Convention (1901–1902)," *Encyclopedia Virginia*, https://www.encyclopediavirginia.org; "Constitution of Virginia, 1902," http://vagovernmentmatters.org; Folmsbee, "The Origin of the First 'Jim Crow' Law," 235–47; Wynes, "The Evolution of Jim Crow Laws in Twentieth Century Virginia," 416–25. See also John J. Dinan, *The Virginia State Constitution: A Reference Guide* (New York: Greenwood, 2006); Wythe W. Holt, *Virginia's Constitutional Convention of 1902* (New York: Garland, 1990); and Ralph Clipman McDanel, *The Virginia Constitutional Convention of 1901–1902* (Baltimore: Johns Hopkins University Press, 1928). The Black franchise was not restored until passage of the Voting Rights Act of 1965. Even

then, pockets of resistance remained, and the discriminatory mandates implemented by the 1902 constitution were not officially revoked in Virginia until 1971.

5. Commonwealth of Virginia, General Assembly, *Acts and Joint Resolutions Passed by the General Assembly of the State of Virginia, During the Session of 1901–2* (Richmond, VA: J. H. O'Bannon, Superintendent of Public Printing, 1902), 639–40; Commonwealth of Virginia, General Assembly, *Acts and Joint Resolutions Passed by the General Assembly of the State of Virginia, During the Extra Session of 1902–3–4* (Richmond, VA: J. H. O'Bannon, Superintendent of Public Printing, 1902 i.e. 1902–04 [*sic*]), 987–88, 990–91; Commonwealth of Virginia, General Assembly, *Acts and Joint Resolutions Passed by the General Assembly of the State of Virginia, During the Session of 1906* (Richmond, VA: J. H. O'Bannon, Superintendent of Public Printing, 1906), 92–94; "'Separate the Races': Passenger and Power Company Will Put New Law into Operation Wednesday," *Richmond Times-Dispatch*, April 17, 1904, 17; "'Jim Crow' Street-Car Law Set to Catch Negroes. Only White Folks in the Trap," *Richmond Planet*, April 20, 1904, 1; "The Negroes Will Walk," *Richmond Times-Dispatch*, April 20, 1904, 1; "Citizens Protest," *Richmond Planet*, April 23, 1904, 1; "Negroes and Street-Cars," *Richmond Planet*, April 30, 1904, 4; "A Voice from Roanoke," *Richmond Planet*, May 7, 1904, 4; "Must Keep Together," *Richmond Planet*, May 21, 1904, 1; "That Street-Car Discrimination," *Richmond Planet*, May 21, 1904, 1; "Street-Car Situation Here," *Richmond Planet*, May 21, 1904, 1; untitled article about Jim Crow streetcar boycotts, *Richmond Planet*, May 28, 1904, 4; untitled article about Jim Crow streetcar laws, *Alexandria Gazette*, November 4, 1904, 2; Ann Field Alexander, *Race Man: The Rise and Fall of the "Fighting Editor" John Mitchell Jr.* (Charlottesville: University of Virginia Press, 2002); James H. Brewer, "The War against Jim Crow in the Land of Goshen," *Negro History Bulletin* 24, no. 3 (1960): 53–57; Blair L. M. Kelley, *Right to Ride: Streetcar Boycotts and African American Citizenship in the Era of "Plessy v. Ferguson"* (Chapel Hill: University of North Carolina Press, 2010), 139–63; August Meier and Elliott Rudwick, "The Boycott Movement against Jim Crow Streetcars in the South, 1900–1906," *Journal of American History* 55, no. 4 (1969): 756–75; "'Stay Off the Cars'—The Boycott of the Virginia Passenger and Power Company," *The Uncommonwealth: Voices from the Library of Virginia*, https://uncommonwealth.virginiamemory.com. In 1946, the U.S. Supreme Court struck down the Virginia statute mandating segregation on interstate public transit carriers, calling it a violation of the Constitution's commerce clause. William H. Hastie and Thurgood Marshall argued the case for the NAACP on behalf of Irene Morgan, a Black woman who had refused to move to the Jim Crow seats on a Greyhound bus traveling from Virginia to Maryland. The victory foreshadowed Rosa Parks's 1955–56 protest campaign against segregated seating on the Montgomery, Alabama, public transit system. See Augustus M. Burns III, "*Morgan v. Virginia*," in *The Oxford Guide to United States Supreme Court Decisions*, https://www.oxfordreference.com; *Morgan v. Virginia*, 328 U.S. 373 (1946), no. 704, U.S. Supreme Court, argued March 27, 1946, decided June 3, 1946, https://supreme.justia.com; and Derek C. Catsam and Brendan Wolfe, "*Morgan v. Virginia* (1946)," *Encyclopedia Virginia*, http://www.encyclopediavirginia.org.

6. James C. Scott, *Domination and the Arts of Resistance: Hidden Transcripts* (New Haven, CT: Yale University Press, 1990), 2–6; Robin D. G. Kelley, "'We Are Not What We Seem': Rethinking Black Working-Class Opposition in the Jim Crow South," *Journal of American History* 80, no. 1 (1993): 78; Scott, *Domination and the Arts of Resistance*, 5. See also Jane Dailey, *Before Jim Crow: The Politics of Race in Postemancipation Virginia* (Chapel Hill: University of North Carolina Press, 2000), 103–4.

7. Litwack, *Trouble in Mind*, xiii.

8. See Leon Fink, *Workingmen's Democracy: The Knights of Labor and American Politics* (Urbana: University of Illinois Press, 1985); Erik S. Gellman, *Death Blow to Jim Crow: The National Negro Congress and the Rise of Militant Civil Rights* (Chapel Hill: University of North Carolina Press, 2012); Jason Kaufman, "Rise and Fall of a Nation of Joiners: The Knights of Labor Revisited," *Journal of Interdisciplinary History* 31, no. 4 (2001): 553–79; Nicholas Lemann, *The Promised Land: The Great Black Migration and How It Changed America* (New York: Knopf, 1991), 6; August Meier and John H. Bracey, Jr., "The NAACP as a Reform Movement, 1909–1965: 'To Reach the Conscience of America,'" *Journal of Southern History* 59, no. 1 (1993): 3–30; Rabinowitz, *The First New South, 1865–1920*; and Isabel Wilkerson, *The Warmth of Other Suns: The Epic Story of America's Great Migration* (New York: Random House, 2010).

9. Gunnar Myrdal, *An American Dilemma: The Negro Problem and Modern Democracy*, 2 vols. (reprint, New Brunswick, NJ: Transaction, 1996); *Sweatt v. Painter*, 339 U.S. 629 (1950), no. 44, argued April 4, 1950, decided June 5, 1950, U.S. Supreme Court, https://supreme.justia.com; *George W. McLaurin v. Oklahoma State Regents for Higher Education, et al.*, 339 U.S. 637 (1950), no. 34, argued April 3–4, 1950, decided June 5, 1950, https://www.law.cornell.edu; Andrea Hsu, "'Sweatt v. Painter': Nearly Forgotten, but Landmark Texas Integration Case," *The Two-Way*, National Public Radio, October 10, 2012, https://www.npr.org; "Massive Resistance" and "The Closing of Prince Edward County Schools," exhibits at the Virginia Museum of History and Culture, https://www.virginiahistory.org.

10. "Integrating Alexandria: Remembering the Struggle to Desegregate the City's Schools," *Alexandria Gazette Packet*, February 22, 2006, http://www.connectionnewspapers.com; Scott Schraff, "Reliving History: Panelists Remember Path to Integration," *Alexandria Journal*, February 25, 1994, n.p.

11. "African American Hall of Fame," https://www.alexandriaafricanamericanhalloffame.org, 4; Lillian S. Patterson, interview with the author, May 16, 2021.

12. Lovell A. Lee, interview with the author, May 24, 2021; Shirley M. Lee, interview with the author, May 24, 2021.

13. Patterson, interview; Lovell A. Lee, interview.

14. Krystyn R. Moon, "Finding a Place to Call Home: Race and Place in Alexandria, Virginia, 1860s–1960s," webinar for the Alexandria Community Remembrance Project, Alexandria, VA, May 20, 2021; Krystyn R. Moon, "The African American Housing Crisis in Alexandria, Virginia, 1930s–1960s," *Virginia Magazine of History and Biography* 124, no. 1 (2016): 28–68; Shirley M. Lee, interview; *J. D. Shelley and Ethel Lee Shelley v. Louis Kraemer and Fern Kraemer*, 334 U.S. 1 (1948), argued

January 15–16, 1948, decided May 3, 1948, U.S. Supreme Court, https://supreme
.justia.com; Moon, "Finding a Place to Call Home."

15. "African American Hall of Fame," 10; Shirley M. Lee, interview; "African American
Hall of Fame," 5, 4; "Courageous Journey: A Guide to Alexandria's African American
History," brochure, 2019, 12, https://assets.simpleviewinc.com; "African American
Hall of Fame," 4; "Courageous Journey," 11–12; "African American Hall of Fame," 4,
5; "This Week in Alexandria's History," Alexandria eNews article, March 29, 2021.

16. Daniel Lee, personal communication, July 26, 2019; "Courageous Journey," 17.

17. Krystyn R. Moon, "Navigating Everyday Life in Jim Crow Alexandria," lecture
sponsored by the Equal Justice Initiative for the Office of Historic Alexandria, Alexandria, VA, November 16, 2019.

18. Amy Bertsch and Lance Mallamo, "The Desire for Streetcars in Alexandria," Alexandria
Times, October 8, 2015, https://www.alexandriava.gov.

19. Ariel Veroske, "Mary Custis Lee Challenges Streetcar Segregation," Boundary Stones,
June 13, 2013, https://blogs.weta.org; untitled article about Mary Custis Lee's vio-
lation of the Jim Crow streetcar ordinance, Alexandria Gazette, June 14, 1902, 2; "Sat
in Negroes' Seat: Daughter of Robert E. Lee Arrested on Electric Car," Washington
Post, June 14, 1902, 2; "Miss Mary Custis Lee Arrested by Police: Charged with
Violating the Jim Crow Car Law," The Times, June 14, 1902, 1; "Alexandria Affairs:
Miss Lee's Misunderstanding of State Law," Evening Star, June 14, 1902, 6; "Miss Lee
Was Fined: Failed to Appear in Court and Forfeited Collateral," Richmond Dispatch,
June 15, 1902, 1; "Miss Mary Custis Lee Pays Small Fine: She Did Not Appear, but
Forfeited Her Collateral," The Times, June 15, 1902, 2; "Sequel to an Episode: Soldiers of
South Want Jim Crow Measure Repealed," Washington Post, June 16, 1902, 4; "Alex-
andria Affairs: Aftermath of Arrest," Evening Star, June 16, 1902, 3; "Miss Mary Lee
Arrested," Lexington Gazette, June 20, 1902, 1; "An Odious Car Law," Colored American,
June 21, 1902, 8; Scott E. Casper, Sarah Johnson's Mount Vernon: The Forgotten History
of an American Shrine (New York: Hill and Wang, 2008), 201; Mary P. Coulling, The
Lee Girls (Winston-Salem, NC: Blair, 1987), 190; untitled article about Mary Custis
Lee's violation of the Jim Crow streetcar ordinance, Colored American, July 5, 1902, 8.

20. "The Lynching of Joseph H. McCoy, April 23, 1897," Alexandria Community Remembrance Project, https://www.alexandriava.gov; "Hanged by a Mob," Alexandria
Gazette and Virginia Advertiser, April 23, 1897, n.p.; "On a Lamp-Post," Washington
Post, April 23, 1897, 1; "Lynched at Alexandria," Staunton Spectator and Vindicator,
April 29, 1897, n.p.; "The Lynching at Alexandria," Richmond Planet, May 1, 1897,
n.p.; "Murdered Him: A Disgraceful Proceeding," Richmond Planet, May 1, 1897,
1. See also W. Fitzhugh Brundage, Lynching in the New South: Georgia and Virginia,
1880–1930 (Urbana: University of Illinois Press, 1993).

21. "The Lynching of Benjamin Thomas, August 8, 1899," Alexandria Community
Remembrance Project, https://www.alexandriava.gov; "Lynching of a Negro,"
Alexandria Gazette, August 9, 1899, n.p.; "A Negro Lynched at Alexandria: Little
Girl Was Assaulted," Free Lance, August 10, 1899, n.p.; "A Lynching in Alexandria,"
Richmond Planet, August 12, 1899, 1; "The Lynching at Alexandria," Richmond Planet,
August 12, 1899, 4; "Favored a Boycott," Alexandria Gazette, August 29, 1899, n.p.;

Audrey [P.] Davis, "My View: Lynchings in Alexandria," *Alexandria Times*, August 8, 2019, 18, https://alextimes.com; Audrey P. Davis, "Commentary: A Man Was Lynched in Alexandria: 120 Years Ago Today," *Alexandria Gazette Packet*, August 12, 2019, http://www.connectionnewspapers.com.

22. "Tried to Lynch Negro: Mob Attempted to Enter Alexandria County Jail," *Washington Post*, July 15, 1899, 2; "Negro's Jail Changed: Alexandria Officials Feared Attempt at Lynching," *Washington Post*, May 13, 1904, 5; "Hurried Away to Jail: Alexandria Police Feared that Negro Might Be Lynched," *Washington Post*, October 29, 1904, 5; "Fears for Negro in Alexandria Jail," *New York Times*, May 24, 1920, 16; "Soldiers Guard Jail: Negro Who Killed T. M. Moore Fears Mob Violence," *Washington Post*, May 24, 1920, 1; "Troops Guard Alexandria, Va.," *Washington Post*, May 27, 1920, 1; "Alexandria in Arms: City in Terror, Fearing Negro Rioters from Washington," *Washington Post*, May 27, 1920, 1; "Turner Due to Arrive in Richmond, Va., Last Night," *Washington Post*, May 27, 1920, 1; "Denies Riot Was Planned: Interracial Congress Says Alexandria Raid Report Was False," *Washington Post*, June 1, 1920, 10. Alexandria is participating in the Equal Justice Initiative's Community Remembrance Project to honor the city's two lynching victims. On April 23, 2021, a memorial service was held to commemorate the life of Joseph McCoy; on August 8, 2021, a similar service was held for Benjamin Thomas. A duplicate steel pillar engraved with McCoy's and Thomas's names will be retrieved from the Equal Justice Initiative's National Memorial for Peace and Justice and positioned in Market Square.

23. Douglas Smith, "Anti-Lynching Law of 1928," *Encyclopedia Virginia*, https://www.encyclopediavirginia.org. See also James Allen, Hilton Als, John Lewis, and Leon F. Litwack, *Without Sanctuary: Lynching Photography in America* (Santa Fe, NM: Twin Palms, 2018); Brundage, *Lynching in the New South*; Holland Cotter, "Remembering Lynching's Toll," *New York Times*, June 3, 2018, AR1, AR14; Juanita W. Crudele, "A Lynching Bee: Butler-County Style," *Alabama Historical Quarterly* 42, no. 1/2 (1980): 59–71; Philip Dray, *At the Hands of Persons Unknown: The Lynching of Black America* (New York: Random House, 2002); Crystal N. Feimster, "Lynching's Hidden Victims," *New York Times*, April 29, 2018, SR11 (especially valuable for its inclusion of Black women as lynching victims); Trudier Harris, "White Men as Performers in the Lynching Ritual," in *Black on White: Black Writers on What It Means to Be White*, ed. David R. Roediger (New York: Schocken, 1998), 299–304; Sherrilyn A. Ifill, *On the Courthouse Lawn: Confronting the Legacy of Lynching in the Twenty-First Century* (Boston: Beacon, 2007); James R. McGovern, *Anatomy of a Lynching: The Killing of Claude Neal* (Baton Rouge: Louisiana State University Press, 1982); Arthur F. Raper, *The Tragedy of Lynching* (Mineola, NY: Dover, 2003); Jacqueline Jones Royster, ed., *"Southern Horrors" and Other Writings: The Anti-Lynching Campaign of Ida B. Wells, 1892–1900*, 2nd ed. (Boston: Bedford/St. Martin's, 2016); J. Douglas Smith, *Managing White Supremacy: Race, Politics, and Citizenship in Jim Crow Virginia* (Chapel Hill: University of North Carolina Press, 2002); Brent Staples, "When Newspapers Justified Lynching," *New York Times*, May 6, 2018, SR8; David M. Tucker, "Miss Ida B. Wells and Memphis Lynching," *Phylon* 32, no. 2 (1971): 112–22; and Robyn Wiegman, "The Anatomy of Lynching," in *American Sexual Politics: Sex, Gender, and Race Since the Civil War*,

ed. John C. Fout and Maura Shaw Tantillo (Chicago: University of Chicago Press, 1993), 223–45. On lynching in southern collective memory, see Bruce E. Baker, "Under the Rope: Lynching and Memory in Laurens County, South Carolina," in *Where These Memories Grow: History, Memory, and Southern Identity*, ed. W. Fitzhugh Brundage (Chapel Hill: University of North Carolina Press, 2000), 319–45.

### CHAPTER FIVE: PRELUDE TO THE SIT-IN, PART TWO

1. Doris Hargrett Clack, "Segregation and the Library," in *Encyclopedia of Library and Information Science*, vol. 27, ed. Allen Kent, Harold Lancour, and Jay E. Daily (New York: Dekker, 1968), 184–204; U.S. Bureau of Education, *Statistics of Libraries and Library Legislation in the United States* (Washington, D.C.: Government Printing Office, 1897), 523; Carleton B. Joeckel, *The Government of the American Public Library* (Chicago: University of Chicago Press, 1935), 2–8. The Charleston Library Association was formed in South Carolina in 1741 but was not formally incorporated until 1755.

2. U.S. Bureau of Education, *Statistics of Libraries and Library Legislation in the United States*, 524; George S. Bobinski, *Carnegie Libraries: Their History and Impact on American Public Library Development* (Chicago: American Library Association, 1969), 4–5.

3. U.S. Bureau of Education, *Statistics of Libraries and Library Legislation in the United States*, 524; Moses Coit Tyler, "The Historic Evolution of the Free Public Library in America and Its True Function in the Community," in *Contributions to American Library History*, ed. Thelma Eaton (Champaign, IL: Illini Bookstore, 1961), 26–27.

4. U.S. Bureau of Education, *Statistics of Libraries and Library Legislation in the United States*, 524.

5. Joeckel, *The Government of the American Public Library*, 8–14.

6. Two classic works provide background on American public library development: Jesse H. Shera, *Foundations of the Public Library: The Origins of the Public Library Movement in New England, 1629–1855* (Chicago: University of Chicago Press, 1949); and Sidney Ditzion, *Arsenals of a Democratic Culture: A Social History of the American Public Library Movement in New England and the Middle States from 1850 to 1900* (Chicago: American Library Association, 1947). See also Bobinski, *Carnegie Libraries*, 5–7. On public libraries in the southeast, see Mary Edna Anders, "The Development of Public Library Service in the Southeastern States, 1895–1950" (PhD diss., University of Michigan, Ann Arbor, 1958).

7. U.S. Bureau of Education, *Statistics of Libraries and Library Legislation in the United States*, 524–26; Bobinski, *Carnegie Libraries*, 4–5.

8. U.S. Bureau of Education, *Statistics of Libraries and Library Legislation in the United States*, 524–26; Commonwealth of Virginia, General Assembly, "Joint Legislative Audit and Review Commission, the Virginia General Assembly, Commission Draft, Review of State Aid to Public Libraries," 2000, http://jlarc.virginia.gov; Anders, "The Development of Public Library Service in the Southeastern States, 1895–1950"; Sue Quinn, "Old Dominion Lagging in Development of Public Libraries: More than One-Half [of] Rural Virginia Lacks Access to Books," *Richmond Times-Dispatch*, May 12, 1946, 6D.

9. William Seale, *The Alexandria Library Company* (Alexandria, VA: Alexandria Library Company, 2007), 5–9, 23. A history of the Alexandria Library, written in 1968,

mentions neither the 1939 sit-in, the partial desegregation of the library in 1959, nor its total desegregation in 1962. The years 1938–58 are only cursorily addressed, which suggests that the document relied at least in part on Beverly Seehorn Brandt's "The Alexandria, Virginia, Library: Its History, Present Facilities, and Future Programs" (master's thesis, Catholic University of America, April 1950). The document is available in Alexandria Library Company, records, 1794–1990, box 2B, folder 17, Alexandria Library Special Collections, Alexandria, VA (hereafter cited as ALSCAV). For other primary-source materials on the history of the Alexandria Library Company see box 2M, folder 17C, ALSCAV. In her thesis, Brandt merely notes that a few Blacks applied for library privileges at the Alexandria Library after it opened (24–26). Jeanne G. Plitt, a former director of the library, does mention a library integration or desegregation initiative in the 1940s, though no primary-source documentation attests to such an effort. Plitt is likely referring to the 1940 hiring of Evelyn Roper Beam as librarian of the Black branch, which did not constitute either integration or desegregation, because the Alexandria Library remained all-White. See Jeanne G. Plitt, memo to Douglas Harman, October 26, 1981, Vertical File: "Alexandria Library—Sit-in, 1939," ALSCAV. Research indicates, however, that Black library professionals began working directly with their White colleagues at the Alexandria Library in 1958, Black high school students and adults were allowed to use the library in 1959, and full desegregation that included Black children occurred in 1962. See Alexandria Library Company, annual reports, Robert Robinson Library, 1958–63, records, 1937– , box 98C, folder 14, ALSCAV.

10. "History of Alexandria Library," https://alexlibraryva.org.

11. Seale, *The Alexandria Library Company*, 11, 17–19, 22–23, 56; "Alexandria Library Company: A Brief Historical Sketch," https://alxndria.ent.sirsi.net.

12. Seale, *The Alexandria Library Company*, 37–38.

13. Ibid., 39, 41–42.

14. Benjamin Hallowell, *Autobiography of Benjamin Hallowell, Written at the Request of His Daughter, Caroline H. Miller, for His Children and Grandchildren, in the Seventy-Sixth Year of His Age* (Philadelphia: Friends' Book Association, 1884), 95–110.

15. Seale, *The Alexandria Library Company*, 45–46.

16. Ibid., 48.

17. Ibid., 49, 51–52.

18. Ibid., 92.

19. Ibid., 89.

20. Ibid., 91.

21. Ibid., 92–93.

22. Alexandria Library Company, meeting minutes, October 14, 1930, 191–92, and November 12, 1930, 194–95, records, 1794–1990, box 2M, folder "1911–1930," ALSCAV; Brandt, "The Alexandria, Virginia, Library," 21.

23. Alexandria Library Company, meeting minutes, January 11, 1937, 131–34, January 28, 1937, 135–36, and February 8, 1937, 138, records, 1794–1990, box 2M, folder "1931–1947," ALSCAV; Bertha S. Buckman and Charles M. Pidgeon, meeting notes of the Alexandria Monthly Meeting of the Religious Society of Friends, January 10, 1937, in Alexandria Library Company, records, 1937– , box 98J, folder 2, ALSCAV;

Bertha S. Buckman, letter to Mary Powell Scott, January 11, 1937, in ibid.; Alexandria Library Company, records, 1794–1990, box 2B, folder 17B: "Quaker Contract with Library," ALSCAV; Agreement for the establishment of a public library, "Alex. Lib.—By Laws, Charter, Agreements 1937–1950s," box 98A, folder 1, March 6, 1937, 1–3, ALSCAV. Also see "By–Laws [sic] of the Alexandria Library," "Alex. Lib.—By Laws, Charter, Agreements 1937–1950s," box 98A, folder 1, n.d., 1–4, ALSCAV.

24. Alexandria Library Company, meeting minutes, April 19, 1939, 28, records, 1937– , box 98B, folder 16, ALSCAV; Seale, *The Alexandria Library Company*, 97; City of Alexandria, "America's First Sit-Down Strike," "History of Alexandria's African American Community," "Alexandria's African American History," and "Civil Rights: Samuel Tucker and America's First Sit-Down Strike," http://alexandriava.gov; "Council to Study Library Branch," *Washington Post*, August 8, 1939, 13.

25. Alexandria Library Company, meeting minutes, June 10, 1940, 55–56, February 10, 1941, 67–68, box 98B, folder 16, ALSCAV.

26. Seale, *The Alexandria Library Company*, 99.

27. "History of Alexandria Library."

28. Ibid.

## CHAPTER SIX: PRELUDE TO THE SIT-IN, PART THREE

1. Robert Jones Shafer, ed., *A Guide to Historical Method*, 3rd ed. (Homewood, IL: Dorsey, 1980), 30.

2. "City Library Board Outlines Position on Colored Branch: Statement Is Issued Today through Mrs. A. A. Smoot, President," *Alexandria Gazette*, August 28, 1939, 1, 9. Although the statement is credited to Smoot, Armistead Lloyd Boothe, Alexandria's city attorney, vice president of the library board, and the prosecutor in the trial against the sit-in protesters, had primary responsibility for drafting the text. See also "Alexandria's Library Backs Restrictions: Explains Situation That Led to Arrest of 5 Boys There," *Washington Times-Herald*, August 29, 1939, 7; and Eliza Atkins Gleason, *The Southern Negro and the Public Library: A Study of the Government and Administration of Public Library Service to Negroes in the South* (Chicago: University of Chicago Press, 1941), 90.

3. William A. Elwood, "Interview with Samuel Wilbert Tucker and Otto L. Tucker, January 18, 1985," conducted for the Civil Rights Lawyers Project (Charlottesville: University of Virginia, 2006), DVD.

4. August Meier and Elliott Rudwick, *Along the Color Line: Explorations in the Black Experience* (Urbana: University of Illinois Press, 2002), 282–83. On the "Don't-Buy-Where-You-Can't-Work" campaign, see ibid., 314–32.

5. John A. Davis, "We Win the Right to Fight for Jobs," *Opportunity* 16, no. 8 (1938): 230–37; Michele Francine Pacifico, "A History of the New Negro Alliance of Washington, D.C., 1933–1941" (PhD diss., George Washington University, 1983); Gilbert Ware, "The New Negro Alliance: 'Don't Buy Where You Can't Work,'" *Negro History Bulletin* 49, no. 3 (1986): 3–8; August Meier, Elliott Rudwick, and Francis L. Broderick, eds., *Black Protest Thought in the Twentieth Century*, 2nd ed. (Indianapolis:

Bobbs-Merrill, 1971); Susan Cianci Salvatore, "Civil Rights in America: Racial Desegregation of Public Accommodations," 2009, https://www.nps.gov.

6. Bayard Rustin, *Down the Line: The Collected Writings of Bayard Rustin* (Chicago: Quadrangle, 1971), 111–22; Jacquelyn Dowd Hall, "The Long Civil Rights Movement and the Political Uses of the Past," *Journal of American History* 91, no. 4 (2005): 1235; Jacquelyn Dowd Hall, "Mobilizing Memory: Broadening Our View of the Civil Rights Movement," *Chronicle of Higher Education*, July 27, 2001, B7, B11; Theodore Carter DeLaney, "The Sit-in Demonstrations in Historical Perspective," *North Carolina Historical Review* 87, no. 4 (2010): esp. 431–32; Evelyn Brooks Higginbotham, "Foreword," in *Freedom North: Black Freedom Struggles outside the South, 1940–1980*, ed. Jeanne Theoharis and Komozi Woodard (New York: Palgrave Macmillan, 2003), viii–xvi; Thomas J. Sugrue, *Sweet Land of Liberty: The Forgotten Struggle for Civil Rights in the North* (New York: Random House, 2008).

7. Sarajanee Davis, "Black Student Activism in the 1920s and 1930s" and "Sparking a Century of Challenges and Change," *NCpedia*, https://www.ncpedia.org; Edward K. Graham and Margaret Mead, "The Hampton Institute Strike of 1927: A Case Study in Student Protest," *American Scholar* 38, no. 4 (1969): 668–83.

8. "Washington Area Spark: D.C. Anti-lynching Demonstration (3): 1934," photograph, December 13, 1934, https://www.flickr.com; "Howard University Students Picket the National Crime Conference in Washington, D.C. 1934 When the Leaders of the Conference Refuse to Discuss Lynching as a National Crime," photograph, International News Photo Company, 1934, NAACP Records, Prints and Photographs Division, Library of Congress, https://www.loc.gov; Lyonel Florant, "Youth Exhibits a New Spirit," *The Crisis* 43, no. 8 (1936): 237–38, 253–54; Maurice Gates, "Negro Students Challenge Social Forces," *The Crisis* 42, no. 8 (1935): 232–33, 251; Joel Rosenthal, "Black Student Activism: Assimilation vs. Nationalism," *Journal of Negro Education* 44, no. 2 (1975): 115–17; Rayford W. Logan, *Howard University: The First Hundred Years, 1867–1967* (New York: New York University Press, 1968), 120–22.

9. Jim Pope, "Worker Lawmaking, Sit-Down Strikes, and the Shaping of American Industrial Relations, 1935–1958," *Law and History Review* 24, no. 1 (2006): 45–113; John Tully, "Sisters, Brothers, Unite!: The Rubber Workers' Union in Akron," in *The Devils Milk: A Social History of Rubber*, ed. John Tully (New York: New York University Press, 2011), 159–82; John L. Woods, "Rubber Workers' Strikes," in *The Encyclopedia of Strikes in American History*, ed. Aaron Brenner, Benjamin Day, and Immanuel Ness (Armonk, NY: Sharpe, 2009), 398–409; "UAW History: Bendix Sit-Down Strike," November 17, 2020, https://uaw.org; Mike Smith, "'Let's Make Detroit a Union Town': The History of Labor and the Working Class in the Motor City," *Michigan Historical Review* 27, no. 2 (2001): 157–73; Steve Babson, *Working Detroit: The Making of a Union Town* (New York: Adama, 1984); Sidney Fine, *Sit-Down: The General Motors Strike of 1936–1937* (Ann Arbor: University of Michigan Press, 1969); "National Negro Congress Which Met in Chicago Acclaimed a Success," *New York Age*, February 22, 1936, 1, 2; "Red Scare at Race Congress Proves to Be a Colossal Joke," *Chicago Defender*, February 22, 1936, 1, 2; "'Jim Crow Practices' Assailed by Miners," *Chicago Defender*, February 22, 1936, 4; "Universal Unrest among Black People

Revealed at National Negro Congress Here: Delegates Make Cry for New Deal in America," *Chicago Defender*, February 22, 1936, 1, 4; Robert B. Hill, "Philly Sends Delegation to Race Congress," *Chicago Defender*, February 22, 1936, 9; "'Forward!' Exhortation of A. Phillip [sic] Randolph to Congress," *Chicago Defender*, February 22, 1936, 2, 10; "Resolutions Adopted by the National Congress," *Chicago Defender*, February 22, 1936, 10; "Negro Youth to Meet Here This Morning," *Richmond Times-Dispatch*, February 13, 1937, 2; "Richmond Inquiring Reporter," *New Journal and Guide*, April 24, 1937, 11; Augusta V. Jackson, "A New Deal for Tobacco Workers," *The Crisis* 45, no. 10 (1938): 322–24, 330; Lester B. Granger, "The National Negro Congress: An Interpretation," *Opportunity* 14, no. 5 (1936): 151–53; Erik S. Gellman, *Death Blow to Jim Crow: The National Negro Congress and the Rise of Militant Civil Rights* (Chapel Hill: University of North Carolina Press, 2012).

10.  Alexandra Zukas, "'A Power So Compelling': Services for African Americans and Steps toward Integration at the Richmond Public Library, 1925–1964," *Libraries* 5, no. 1 (2021): 49–50; "R[ichmond] P[ublic] L[ibrary] History," https://rvalibrary.org.

11.  "The Death of John Mitchell, Jr., and the On-Going Life of the *Planet*," *Richmond Planet*, December 7, 1929, https://www.lva.virginia.gov; Jean L. Preer, "'This Year—Richmond!' The 1936 Meeting of the American Library Association," *Libraries and Culture* 39, no. 2 (2004): esp. 153.

12.  Sugrue, *Sweet Land of Liberty*, xviii–xix.

13.  "Modern History Sourcebook: The Molotov-Ribbentrop Pact, 1939," January 20, 2021, http://www.fordham.edu; Frank Ellis et al., "Dance of the Snakes: Soviet and German Diplomacy, August 1939–June 1941," in *Barbarossa 1941: Reframing Hitler's Invasion of Stalin's Soviet Empire*, ed. Frank Ellis (Lawrence: University Press of Kansas, 2015), 121–63; Gabriel Gorodetsky, "The Impact of the Ribbentrop-Molotov Pact on the Course of Soviet Foreign Policy," *Cahiers du Monde Russe et Soviétique* 31, no. 1 (1990): 27–41; David Kirby, "Incorporation: The Molotov-Ribbentrop Pact," in *The Baltic States: The National Self-Determination of Estonia, Latvia and Lithuania*, ed. Graham Smith (London: Palgrave Macmillan, 1996), 69–85; Geoffrey Roberts, "The Soviet Decision for a Pact with Nazi Germany," *Soviet Studies* 44, no. 1 (1992): 57–78; Joseph I. Vizulis, *The Molotov-Ribbentrop Pact of 1939: The Baltic Case* (Westport, CT: Greenwood, 1990); "German-Soviet Pact," in *Holocaust Encyclopedia*, August 20, 2021, https://encyclopedia.ushmm.org; Glenda Elizabeth Gilmore, *Defying Dixie: The Radical Roots of Civil Rights, 1919–1950* (New York: Norton, 2009), 299.

14.  Elsie Tucker Thomas, interview with Matt Spangler, September 30, 1998; Clifford L. Muse, Jr., interview with the author, spring 2015; Elwood "Interview with Samuel Wilbert Tucker and Otto L. Tucker."

15.  On the history of sit-in demonstrations as a civil rights strategy, see DeLaney, "The Sit-in Demonstrations in Historical Perspective," 431–38. On the bases of contestation among lawyers and the courts and the demonstrators whose activism inspired and challenged them, see Christopher W. Schmidt, "Divided by Law: The Sit-Ins and the Role of the Courts in the Civil Rights Movement," *Law and History Review* 33, no. 1 (2015): 93–149.

16.  Schmidt, "Divided by Law," 149.

## CHAPTER SEVEN: A SEAT AT THE READING TABLE

1. Alexandria Library Company, Board—Minutes 1938–Oct. 1947, meeting minutes January 11, 1940, 44–45, box 98B, folder 16, ALSCAV. Many of the library board meeting minutes cited in this chapter are archived in Alexandria Library Company, Board—Minutes 1938–Oct. 1947, box 98B, folder 16, ALSCAV. When box and folder numbers for meeting minutes differ, those numbers are included in the citation. Also see, "Rules and Regulations of the Alexandria Library for 1937," Alexandria Library, Rules, Regulations, Review Articles—Early 1937–1955, n.d., box 98III, folder 8, 1, ALSCAV; "Proposed Rules and Regulations for the Alexandria Library," Alexandria Library, Rules, Regulations, Review Articles—Early 1937–1955, n.d., box 98III, folder 8, 1, ALSCAV.

2. Alexandria Library Company, meeting minutes, June 14, 1937, 162, records 1794–1990, box 2M, folder "1931–1947," ALSCAV.

3. Alexandria Library Company, meeting minutes, April 10, 1939, 28–29.

4. "Librarian Faces Jim Crow Suit," *Chicago Defender*, May 20, 1939, 1; "Fight Negro Ban in Virginia Library," *New York Age*, June 3, 1939, 5; "5 Arrested at City Library: Colored Youths Ignore Request to Leave," *Alexandria Gazette*, August 21, 1939, 1; "Five Colored Youths Stage Alexandria Library 'Sit-Down': All to Face Court Today on Charge of Disorderly Conduct for Efforts to Compel Extension of Book Privileges," *Washington Post*, August 22, 1939, 3; "Suit Filed to Secure Use of City Library: Alexandria Denies Use of Public Library to Race," *New Journal and Guide*, May 13, 1939, 10; "Use of Library in Alexandria Denied," *New Journal and Guide*, May 20, 1939, 8; Florence Murray, ed., *The Negro Handbook: A Manual of Current Facts, Statistics and General Information Concerning the Negro in the United States*, "Alexandria Library Case: 1939–40" (New York: Wendell Malliet, 1942), 45–46.

5. Alexandria Library Company, meeting minutes April 10, 1939, 28; Alexandria City Public Schools, "A History of ACPS," https://www.acps.k12.va.

6. Alexandria Library Company, meeting minutes, April 10, 1939, 28.

7. Ibid.

8. Ibid., 28–29.

9. Alexandria Library Company, meeting minutes, May 8, 1939, 30. Sources do not reveal Lowrie's given name or his relationship to the library board.

10. Ibid., 30–31.

11. Alexandria Library Company, meeting minutes, June 12, 1939, 32–33.

12. Samuel Wilbert Tucker, interview, in "The Road to Brown," directed by Mykola Kulish (California Newsreel, 1989), videocassette; Samuel Wilbert Tucker, interview, in "Out of Obscurity: The Story of the 1939 Alexandria Library Sit-In," directed by Matt Spangler (River Road Productions, 1999), DVD; Ted Poston, "Alexandria Library Opens This Month," *Pittsburgh Courier*, March 16, 1940, 12.

13. Dorothy Evans Turner, interview with the author, April 29, 2014. Also see William Evans, interview by Matt Spangler, summer 1998.

14. Ben Prendergast, "Was the Nation's First Sit-In Demonstration in Alexandria?," *Alexandria Life*, February 18, 1999, 20.

15. Ibid. Evans's sister Dorothy said that, before his death, he relayed "information about the sit-in to [her] because he wanted to ensure that the history of the event would continue to be known" (interview, April 29, 2014). Also see August Meier, Elliott Rudwick, and Francis L. Broderick, eds. *Black Protest Thought in the Twentieth Century,* 2nd ed. (Indianapolis: Bobbs-Merrill, 1971), 246.

16. "5 Arrested for Using City Library in Virginia," *Chicago Defender,* September 2, 1939, 1–2.

17. Audrey P. Davis, interview by the author, winter 2015; Evans, interview by Spangler; William A. Elwood, "Interview with Samuel Wilbert Tucker and Otto L. Tucker, January 18, 1985," conducted for the Civil Rights Lawyers Project (Charlottesville: University of Virginia), 2006, DVD; Virginia Mansfield, "'39 Library Protest: Alexandria's Page in History," *Washington Post,* May 17, 1990, V1, V8.

18. Elwood, "Interview with Samuel Wilbert Tucker and Otto L. Tucker"; Mansfield, "'39 Library Protest," V1, V8.

19. Newspaper accounts of the protest initially cited Evans's age as sixteen, but he later stated that he was eighteen at the time (Evans, interview by Spangler). This assertion is improbable, not only because Evans was born in 1919 but also because it is highly unlikely that Tucker would have involved a sixteen-year-old in a direct-action protest in which arrests were likely. His correct age at the time of the protest was nineteen.

20. "5 Arrested at City Library," 1; "5 Youths Face Strike Charge: Denied Use of Library in Virginia, Boys Stage Sit-Down," *New York Amsterdam News,* September 9, 1939, 3; "Five Colored Boys, Refusing to Leave Library, Arrested," *Washington Times-Herald,* August 22, 1939, 4; "Denied Library Use, Youths Face Trial in Sit-Down Strike," *Pittsburgh Courier,* September 7, 1939, 2; "Five Colored Youths Stage Alexandria Library 'Sit-Down,'" 3; "5 Arrested for Using City Library in Virginia," *Chicago Defender,* September 2, 1939, 1–2; "It's a Crime to Use This Library," *Chicago Defender,* September 2, 1939, 1; "Quintet Arrested for Library 'Sit-Down,'" *Washington Tribune,* August 26, 1939, 1–2; "Boys Wanted to Read, but Librarians Had Them Jailed: Judge Continues Case for Week to Study Charges," *New Journal and Guide,* September 2, 1939, 1; "Did the First Sit-In Take Place Here?" *Alexandria Life/Alexandria Gazette,* February 18, 1993, 19–20, 26. Lovell A. Lee, interview by the author, May 24, 2021. The *Washington Tribune,* a Black newspaper, was published between 1921 and 1946. Unfortunately, the institutions with *Tribune* microform holdings have issues only through 1935. The exception is the New York Public Library, which has a few issues from 1940. The *Tribune* articles I cite in this book were found in various archives, but all were acquired from donors who inconsistently noted newspaper names, dates of publication, and page numbers on the clippings.

21. Elwood, "Interview with Samuel Wilbert Tucker and Otto L. Tucker."

22. Ibid.; "5 Arrested for Using City Library in Virginia," 1–2; "Quintet Arrested for Library 'Sit-Down,'" 1–2.

23. "Decision Is Deferred on Library Case," *Alexandria Gazette,* August 22, 1939, 1.

24. "5 Arrested for Using City Library in Virginia," 1–2; "Five Colored Boys, Refusing to Leave Library, Arrested," 4; "Five Colored Youths Stage Alexandria Library

'Sit-Down,'" 3; "Arrest Five for Using Library in Virginia: It's a Crime to Use This Library," *Chicago Defender*, September 2, 1939, 1; "Quintet Arrested for Library 'Sit-Down,'" 1–2.

25. Curtis Kopf, "Pioneer Sit-In Is Recalled," *Alexandria Journal*, December 6, 1990, A4. In this article, Bobby Strange implied that he, too, entered the library. There is no evidence, however, that he ventured any farther than the library vestibule.

26. "5 Arrested for Using City Library in Virginia," 1–2; "Quintet Arrested for Library 'Sit-Down,'" 1–2; "Five Colored Youths Stage Alexandria Library 'Sit-Down,'" 3; "Boys Wanted to Read, but Librarians Had Them Jailed," 1.

27. "Five Colored Boys, Refusing to Leave Library, Arrested," 4; "Five Colored Youths Stage Alexandria Library 'Sit-Down,'" 3; "Arrest Five for Using Library in Virginia," 1; "Quintet Arrested for Library 'Sit-Down,'" 1–2.

28. Elwood, "Interview with Samuel Wilbert Tucker and Otto L. Tucker"; Florence Murray, "Claims Cops Broke Law in Library Case: Says Race Is No Crime Under Ordinance of Trespassing," *Chicago Defender*, September 23, 1939, 4.

29. "Decision Is Deferred on Library Case," 1; "Heroic Conduct," 8. According to the latter article, under the terms of an Alexandria ordinance, "a Negro who dares to enter and use the facilities of the City Library which white employees have come to regard as No-Colored Man's Land is liable to [the] charge [of disorderly conduct]." Also see "Five Colored Youths Stage Alexandria Library 'Sit-Down,'" 3.

30. "Opinions Are Asked in Use of Library: Cases of Five Colored Men Again Go Over Following Hearing of Two Today; Crowd at Hearing; Authorities to Be Submitted by Friday to Judge James Reece Duncan," *Alexandria Gazette*, August 29, 1939, 1; "5 Arrested for Using City Library in Virginia," 1–2. A news photographer and printer, Murray was not the first civil rights pioneer in his family. His forebear Freeman Henry Morris Murray had been a community and church leader in Alexandria, a member of the Black intellectual elite, a staunch proponent of civil rights and racial justice for African Americans, an early Black federal employee who worked as a clerk in the War Department's Office of Records and Pensions, and an industrious entrepreneur. He was also one of the twenty-nine individuals to attend the 1905 meeting organized by W. E. B. Du Bois to address racial discrimination and Black disenfranchisement. That first meeting of the Niagara Movement led to the establishment of the NAACP in 1909 (Anita Hackley-Lambert, *F. H. M. Murray: First Biography of a Forgotten Pioneer for Civil Justice* [Fort Washington, MD: HLE, 2006], 47–56, 111–28).

31. "Quintet Arrested for Library 'Sit-Down,'" 1–2; "5 Arrested for Using City Library in Virginia," 1–2; "Library 'Sitters' in Alexandria Win Court Delay," *Washington Tribune*, August 22 [29?], 1939, n.p.

32. "Quintet Arrested for Library 'Sit-Down,'" 1–2; "Va. Library War in Court Again: Five Youths Arrested for Using Public Institution," *Washington Afro-American*, August 26, 1939, 1–2.

33. "Denied Library Use, Youths Face Trial in Sit-Down Strike," 2.

34. Ibid.

35. "Five Colored Boys, Refusing to Leave Library, Arrested," 4.

36. Tucker, interview, in "Out of Obscurity."
37. "Quintet Arrested for Library 'Sit-Down,'" 1–2; Prendergast, "Was the Nation's First Sit-In Demonstration in Alexandria?," 20, 26, 32; "Decision in Alexandria Library Case Delayed: Prosecutor Raps 14th, 15th Amendments," *Washington Tribune*, September 2, 1939, 1–2.
38. "5 Arrested for Using City Library in Virginia," 1–2; "Va. Library War in Court Again: Five Youths Arrested for Using Public Institution," 1–2.
39. "5 Arrested for Using City Library in Virginia; Case Puzzles Judge," 1–2; and "Va. Library War in Court Again: Five Youths Arrested for Using Public Institution," 1–2.
40. "Denied Library Use, Youths Face Trial in Sit-Down Strike," 2; "Five Colored Youths Stage Alexandria Library 'Sit-Down,'" 3.
41. "Decision Is Deferred on Library Case," 1.
42. Ibid.
43. Alexandria Library Company, meeting minutes, August 27, 1939, 34.
44. Ibid.
45. At the December 11, 1939, meeting of the library board, the secretary read a letter from Armistead Boothe announcing his resignation from the board. The reason is not included in the board minutes. Boothe had previously submitted correspondence announcing his resignation from the board during the April 10, 1939, board meeting, but the board would not accept his resignation at that time. That letter is also unavailable. Alexandria Library Company, meeting minutes, December 11, 1939, 40, and April 10, 1939, 28–29.
46. "City Library Board Outlines Position on Colored Branch: Statement Is Issued Today Through Mrs. A. A. Smoot, President," *Alexandria Gazette*, August 28, 1939, 1, 9; "Alexandria's Library Backs Restrictions: Explains Situation that Led to Arrest of 5 Boys There," *Washington Times-Herald*, August 29, 1939, 7; J. Douglas Smith, *Managing White Supremacy: Race, Politics, and Citizenship in Jim Crow Virginia* (Chapel Hill: University of North Carolina Press, 2002), 266.
47. "City Library Board Outlines Position on Colored Branch," 1, 9; "Alexandria's Library Backs Restrictions," 7; Smith, *Managing White Supremacy*, 266.
48. "City Library Board Outlines Position on Colored Branch," 1, 9; "Alexandria's Library Backs Restrictions," 7; Smith, *Managing White Supremacy*, 266.
49. Alexandria Library Company, meeting minutes, April 10, 1939, 28.
50. In the summer of 1963, City of Danville was the site of the most violent incident of the civil rights movement in the Commonwealth of Virginia. On May 31, 1963, a coalition of Black leaders affiliated with the Danville Christian Progressive Association marched to the municipal building to demand "desegregated facilities, equal employment opportunities, representation in city government, and creation of a biracial commission to monitor racial progress" (Virginia Museum of History and Culture, "Danville," https://www.virginiahistory.org). The city rebuffed their demands and implemented a systematic program of intimidation. On June 10, the leaders of a group of sixty high school students who had marched to the municipal building were arrested. The remaining students were beaten with nightsticks and sprayed with high-pressure water hoses. Parents who tried

to retrieve their children were arrested. Although protests continued throughout the summer of 1963, the demands made by the demonstrators were ignored until passage of the Civil Rights Act of 1964 and the Voting Rights Act of 1965.

51. "Five Colored Boys, Refusing to Leave Library, Arrested," 4.

52. "City Library Board Outlines Position on Colored Branch," 1, 9.

53. "Hearing on Sitdown at Library Scheduled," *Washington Tribune*, August 28, 1939, [?]; "Arguments Tomorrow in Cases of Five Colored Men Taken at Library," *Alexandria Gazette*, August 28, 1939, 1.

54. "Hearing on Sitdown at Library Scheduled"; "Arguments Tomorrow in Cases of Five Colored Men Taken at Library," 1.

55. "Opinions Are Asked in Use of Library," 1; Smith, *Managing White Supremacy,* 267.

56. "Opinions Are Asked in Use of Library," 1; "Hearing Is Set In Alexandria Library Case: 5 Youths Who Staged 'Sitdown Strike' Will Face Court Tuesday," *Washington Tribune*, August 21[?], 1939, [?].

57. "Opinions Are Asked in Use of Library," 1; "Hearing Is Set In Alexandria Library Case"; "5 Arrested for Using City Library in Virginia," 1–2; "Five to Face Trial for Sit Strike," *Atlantic Daily World*, August 28, 1939, 1; "5 Youths Face Strike Charge," 3; "Denied Library Use, Youths Face Trial in Sit-Down Strike," 2; "Judicial Red Tape Delays Library Case: Question Validity of the 14th and 15th Amendments," *Chicago Defender*, September 9, 1939, 6.

58. "City Library Board Outlines Position on Colored Branch," 1, 9.

59. "Va. Library War in Court Again: Five Youths Arrested for Using Public Institution," 1–2; "Judicial Red Tape Delays Library Case," 6; "Decision in Alexandria Library Case Delayed," 1–2.

60. Julius Newman, "In and Around Alexandria," *Chicago Defender*, November 11, 1939, 11.

61. "Opinions Are Asked in Use of Library," 1; "Authorities to Be Submitted in Library Case Tomorrow Morning," *Alexandria Gazette*, September 1, 1939, 1; "Library 'Sit-In' Strike Still Puzzle to Virginia Courts: Can't Find Law to Fit Case of Negro Boys Who Went into 'White' Library to Read," *Pittsburgh Courier*, September 16, 1939, 6; Newman, "In and Around Alexandria," 11; "Judicial Red Tape Delays Library Case," 6.

62. "Court Awaits Written Arguments in Library Case Which Is Pending," *Alexandria Gazette*, September 2, 1939, 9.

63. "Judicial Red Tape Delays Library Case," 6; "5 Arrested for Using City Library in Virginia," 1, 2; "Arrest Five for Using Library in Virginia," 1; "Library 'Sit-In' Strike Still Puzzle to Virginia Courts," 6; "Denied Library Use, Youths Face Trial in Sit-Down Strike," 2. A *stay of proceedings* is a "ruling by a court to stop or suspend a proceeding or trial temporarily or indefinitely. A court may later lift the stay and continue the proceeding. Some stays are automatic, but others are up to judicial discretion. Usually, the pendency of an appeal . . . stays proceedings in the court below" (LII).

64. "Judicial Red Tape Delays Library Case," 6; "Library 'Sit-In' Strike Still Puzzle to Virginia Courts," 6.

65. Murray, "Claims Cops Broke Law in Library Case," 4; *The People of the State of New York, Respondent, v. I. Silvan Galpern, Appellant,* 259 N.Y. 279, 281, Court of Appeals

of the State of New York, argued January 11, 1932, decided June 1, 1932, appeal from the Court of Special Sessions of the City of New York, https://cite.case.law; "5 Arrested for Using City Library in Virginia," 1–2.

66.  Murray, "Claims Cops Broke Law in Library Case," 4.

67.  Ibid.

68.  Ibid.

69.  Ibid.

70.  Ibid.

71.  Barbara Ann Rowan, personal communication, June 17, 2015.

72.  "Library Case on Calendar for December: Alexandria Citizen Sues for Right to Borrow Literature," *Chicago Defender*, December 2, 1939, 1.

73.  "Attorneys File Briefs in Virginia Library Case," *Chicago Defender*, September 23, 1939, 3; "Alexandria City Council to Meet Tonight: Library Branch, Loan for Housing Project on Heavy Docket," *Washington Post*, September 12, 1939, 17; "Electric Inspector's Salary Is Approved: Will Have an Assistant," 1, 9. The *Chicago Defender* reported the facility's cost as $3,900.

74.  "Attorneys File Briefs in Virginia Library Case," 3; "Alexandria City Council to Meet Tonight," 17; "Electric Inspector's Salary Is Approved," 1, 9.

75.  "Alexandria City Council to Meet Tonight," 17; "Va. Library Case Gets Continuance," *Chicago Defender*, December 16, 1939, 8; Alexandria City Council, meeting minutes, September 26, 1939, ACC# A2003–016, City Clerk's Department, Alexandra, VA.

76.  "Deny Petition for Writ in Library Case: Decision Handed Down This Afternoon by Judge William P. Woolls," *Alexandria Gazette*, September 12, 1939, 1; "Attorneys File Briefs in Virginia Library Case," 3; Murray, *The Negro Handbook*, 45–46. "Argument to Use Library Is Before Court: Final Arguments in Mandamus Proceedings to Be Made Next Monday," *Alexandria Gazette*, July 10, 1939, 1.

77.  "Attorneys File Briefs in Virginia Library Case," 3. A *demurrer* is "a written response to a complaint filed in a lawsuit which, in effect, pleads for dismissal on the point that even if the facts alleged in the complaint were true, there is no legal basis for a lawsuit. A hearing before a judge . . . will then be held to determine the validity of the demurrer" ("Services and Resources Dictionary," *Law.com*, 2021, http://dictionary.law.com).

78.  Ibid.

79.  Ibid.

80.  "Hearing on Library Case Is Continued: Trial Held Over Due to Absence of Attorney for Petitioner," *Alexandria Gazette*, December 4 [14?], 1939, 1; "Va. Library Case Gets Continuance," *Chicago Defender*, December 16, 1939, 8; "Lawyer's Tardiness in Court Delays Va. Public Library Case," *Washington Tribune*, December 9 [19?], 1939, 1.

81.  Elwood, "Interview with Samuel Wilbert Tucker and Otto L. Tucker."

82.  "Colored Resident Denied Writ to Force Library Privileges: Mandamus Denied George Wilson by Court on Technicality," *Alexandria Gazette*, January 11, 1940, 1.

83.  Ibid.; "Way Paved to Open Alexandria Library to Colored: Judge Finds No Legal Bar against Them but Jurist Denies Petition, However, on Technicality," *New Journal and Guide*, January 20, 1940, 4; "Attorneys File Briefs in Virginia Library Case," 3;

"Judge's Decision Opens Library in Alexandria," *Washington Tribune*, January 13, 1940, 1. Library rules explicitly limit use of the facility to Whites.

84. Murray, *The Negro Handbook*, 45–46.

85. Ibid.; "Colored Resident Denied Writ to Force Library Privileges," 1; "Earmark $2,500 for Va. Library as Aftermath of Alexandria Court Tilt," *Chicago Defender*, January 27, 1940, 1; Murray, *The Negro Handbook*, 46.

86. "Earmark $2,500 for Va. Library as Aftermath of Alexandria Court Tilt," 1; Alexandria Library Company, meeting minutes, January 11, 1940, 44–45.

87. Ibid.

88. Ibid.

89. "Fund for Colored Library Is Passed on First Reading," *Alexandria Gazette*, January 13, 1940, 1.

90. Ibid.; "Earmark $2,500 for Va. Library as Aftermath of Alexandria Court Tilt," 1.

91. "Fund for Colored Library Is Passed on First Reading," 1.

92. Alexandria Library Company, meeting minutes, January 22, 1940, 46.

93. Ibid.

94. Ibid.

95. Ibid. The excerpts from the city council minutes (from January 23 and February 27, 1940) were inserted into these meeting notes.

96. Samuel Wilbert Tucker, letter to Carl Budwesky, February 13, 1940, Alexandria Library Company, records 1937– , box 98J, folder 2, ALSCAV; "Alexandria Officials Welsh in Library Case: Applicants Still Denied Right to Use Facilities," *Washington Tribune*, February 3, 1940, 9.

97. Tucker, letter to Budwesky.

98. Elsie Tucker Thomas, interview by Matt Spangler, September 30, 1998.

99. Alexandria Library Company, meeting minutes, February 12, 1940, 48; Murray, *The Negro Handbook*, 45–46.

100. Alexandria Library Company, meeting minutes, February 12, 1940, 47.

101. Alexandria Library Company, meeting minutes, December 11, 1939, 40.

102. "Library Branch Work to Start," *Alexandria Gazette*, February 5, 1940, 1.

103. "Colored Library Addition Rapidly Nearing Completion," *Alexandria Gazette*, March 4, 1940, 1; "New Library Construction Is Under Way: Expect Colored Library Building Will Be Completed Before April 1," *Alexandria Gazette*, March 6, 1940, 1, 9; "Library Branch Near Completion," *Alexandria Gazette*, March 20, 1940, 1. Also see Agreement between the parties for the construction of a public library, "Alex. Lib.—By Laws, Charter, Agreements 1937–1950s," box 98A, folder 1, March 6, 1937, 2, ALSCAV.

104. "City Library Circulation on Increase: February Report Shows Gain in Circulation over 1939," *Alexandria Gazette*, March 20, 1940, 1.

105. "Earmark $2,500 for Va. Library as Aftermath of Alexandria Court Tilt," 1; "Fund for Colored Library Is Passed on First Reading," 1; Murray, *The Negro Handbook*, 46; Poston, "Alexandria Library Opens This Month," 12; "Electric Inspector's Salary Is Approved," 1, 9; "Alexandria Bans Realty Fees for City Attorney," *Washington Times-Herald*, September 14, 1939, 7.

106. Poston, "Alexandria Library Opens This Month," 12; Alexandria Library Company, meeting minutes, January 22, 1940, 46.

107. Poston, "Alexandria Library Opens This Month," 12.

108. Katharine Scoggin Martyn, interview by Matt Spangler, summer 1999.

109. Alexandria Library Company, meeting minutes, March 11, 1940, 49–50.

110. Alexandria Library Company, meeting minutes, April 8, 1940, 51–52.

111. Alexandria Library Company, meeting minutes, May 13, 1940, 53–54.

112. "Colored Library Opens," *Alexandria Gazette*, April 23, 1940, 1; Poston, "Alexandria Library Opens This Month," 12; "New Colored Library Branch to Open to Public Tomorrow: Extension of Present City Library Open at 9 a.m. for Inspection," *Alexandria Gazette*, April 22, 1940, 1.

113. "New Colored Library Branch to Open to Public Tomorrow," 1.

114. "Colored Library Opens," 1; Poston, "Alexandria Library Opens This Month," 12; Sarah Becker, "Residents Recall the Days of Jim Crow," *Alexandria Life*, February 18, 1999, 32; Lovell A. Lee, interview.

115. Cheryl Knott, *Not Free, Not for All: Public Libraries in the Age of Jim Crow* (Amherst: University of Massachusetts Press, 2015), 169.

116. Lillian S. Patterson, interview by the author, March 4, 2021.

117. Lovell A. Lee, interview.

118. Murray, *The Negro Handbook*, 46; letter to the Alexandria mayor and members of the city council proposing the establishment of a public library, Alexandria Library—Rules, Regulations, Review Articles—Early 1937–1955, box 98III, folder 8, n.d., 1, ALSCAV.

119. Gladys Howard Davis, interview by the author, January 17, 2014; Ferdinand T. Day, interview by the author, September 25, 2014; Patterson, interview.

120. Becker, "Residents Recall the Days of Jim Crow," 32.

121. Alexandria Library Company, meeting minutes, November 6, 1944, 192–93, box 2M, folder: "1931–47," ALSCAV.

122. Alexandria Library Company, meeting minutes, June 14, 1937, 164, box 2M, folder "1931–47," ALSCAV.

123. Alexandria Library Company, meeting minutes, June 10, 1940, 55–56; September 18, 1940, 57–58.

124. Alexandria Library Company, meeting minutes, September 18, 1940, 57–58; October 14, 1940, 59–60; and November 18, 1940, 61–62.

125. Alexandria Library Company, meeting minutes, December 9, 1940, 63–64.

126. Alexandria Library Company, meeting minutes, January 13, 1941, 65–66.

127. Ibid.

128. Alexandria Library Company, meeting minutes, March 10, 1941, 69–70.

129. Alexandria Library Company, meeting minutes, April 14, 1941, 71–72.

130. Alexandria Library Company, meeting minutes, November 2, 1942, box 2M, folder "1931–47," ALSCAV. (This is an unpaginated document inserted into meeting minutes, 1942, 182–83.) According to Beverly Seehorn Brandt, Beam was the Robinson librarian from 1940 to 1943, but the November 2, 1942, library board meeting minutes refute this. See Beverly Seehorn Brandt, "The Alexandria,

Virginia, Library: Its History, Present Facilities, and Future Programs" (master's thesis, Catholic University of America, April 1950), 26.

131.  Alexandria Library Company, meeting minutes, June 14, 1937, 160–65, box 2M, folder "1931–47," ALSCAV.

132.  Alexandria Library Company, meeting minutes, November 6, 1944, 192, box 2M, folder "1931–47," ALSCAV.

133.  "Negro Library Observes First Anniversary Year Tomorrow: Harmon Foundation Art Will Be Exhibited in Open House," *Alexandria Gazette*, April 23, 1941, 8. "The William E. Harmon Foundation, a nonprofit, private organization active from 1922 to 1967, helped foster an awareness [and appreciation] of African [and African American] art." When the foundation ceased operation in 1967, works in the collection were distributed to multiple repositories, including the National Archives, Fisk University, the Smithsonian's American Art Museum, the National Portrait Gallery, the San Francisco Museum of Modern Art, and other institutions (see http://www.archives.gov).

134.  Alexandria Library Company, meeting minutes, May 12, 1941, 74.

135.  Gordon Lubold, "50 Years, Her Life's an Open Book: Library's Davis Is a City Treasure," *Alexandria Journal*, February 13, 1997, A1, A8.

136.  Gladys Howard Davis, interview; Lovell A. Lee, interview.

137.  Lovell A. Lee, interview; Gladys Howard Davis, interview.

138.  Alexandria Library Company, monthly report of the Robert Robinson Memorial Library, in meeting minutes, May 11, 1950, n.p., records 1937– , box 98II–1, folder 7, ALSCAV.

139.  Alexandria Library Company, monthly report of the Robert Robinson Memorial Library, in meeting minutes, July 2, 1956, n.p., records 1937– , box 98II–1, folder 11, ALSCAV.

140.  Alexandria Library Company, monthly report of the Robert Robinson Memorial Library, in meeting minutes, June 4, 1956, n.p., records 1937– , box 98II–1, folder 11, ALSCAV.

141.  Shirley M. Lee, interview by the author, May 24, 2021; Lovell A. Lee, interview.

142.  Alexandria Library Company, monthly reports of the Robert Robinson Memorial Library, in meeting minutes, December 11, 1958, n.p., March 13, 1959, n.p., records 1937– , box 98II–1, folder 12, ALSCAV.

143.  Alexandria Library Company, annual report of the Robert Robinson Memorial Library, 1959–60, 12–14, records 1937– , box 98C, folder 14, ALSCAV.

144.  Ibid.; Alexandria Library Company, monthly report of the Robert Robinson Memorial Library, in meeting minutes, March 13, 1959, n.p., records 1937– , box 98C, folder 14, ALSCAV.

145.  Southern Regional Council, http://www.southerncouncil.org; Ellen Coolidge Burke, letter to Staige D. Blackford, May 13, 1963, Alexandria Library Company, records 1937– , box 98J, folder 10, ALSCAV.

146.  "Schools' Racial History Traced: Alexandria Began Compliance in 1959," *Alexandria Gazette*, May 17, 1971, 1; "Brown v. Board and the Desegregation of Alexandria City Public Schools," Alexandria City Public Schools, https://www.acps.k12.va.us.

147.  Gladys Howard Davis, interview.

148. Ibid.
149. Ibid.
150. Day, interview.
151. Ibid.
152. Patterson, interview.
153. Turner, interview.
154. Elsie Tucker Thomas, interview by Spangler.
155. Jeanne G. Plitt, memo to Douglas Harman, October 26, 1981, Vertical file: "Alexandria Library Sit-In, 1939," ALSCAV.
156. Alexandria Library Company, meeting minutes May 8, 1944, 111, and September 11, 1944, 112, file 1931–47, microfilm reel 37.
157. Alexandria Library Company, meeting minutes, April 9, 1948, 2, box 98B1–1, folder 1, ALSCAV.
158. Alexandria Library Company, monthly reports of the Robert Robinson Memorial Library, in meeting minutes, April 9, 1948, 3, and June 23, 1948, 5–6, records 1937– , box 98B–1, folder 1, ALSCAV.
159. Curtis Kopf, "Pioneer Sit-In Is Recalled," *Alexandria Journal*, December 6, 1990, A4.
160. Alexandria Library Company, monthly report of the Robert Robinson Memorial Library, in meeting minutes, February 15, 1960, 109–10, records 1937– , box 98B–1, folder 1, ALSCAV; Alexandria Library Company, monthly report of the Robert Robinson Memorial Library, in meeting minutes, February 13, 1959, n.p., records 1937– , box 98II–1, folder 12, ALSCAV; Alexandria Library Company, annual report of the Robert Robinson Library, 1958–59, records 1937– , box 98C, folder 13, n.p., ALSCAV; Alexandria Library Company, annual report, 1958–59," 9, records 1937– , box 98C, folder 13, n.p., ALSCAV; Alexandria Library Company, "The Alexandria Library: 1794–1968," April 1968, n.p., records 1794–1990, box 2B, folder 17, ALSCAV.
161. Alexandria Library Company, annual report, 1962–63, n.p., records 1937– , box 98C, folder 14, ALSCAV; Audrey P. Davis, interview by the author, February 4, 2015.
162. Alexandria Library Company, annual report of the Robert Robinson Memorial Library, 1960–61," n.p., records 1937– , box 98C, folder 14, ALSCAV; Alexandria Library Company, "Annual and Special Meetings, Minutes and Other Documents, 1961–1977," annual report, 1962–63, box 2–2, series 4, folder 7, 83, 84–85, ALSCAV.
163. "Historic Alexandria Mission Statement," City of Alexandria, https://www.alexandriava.gov.
164. "Alexandria Black History Museum" and "History of the Alexandria Black History Museum," City of Alexandria, https://www.alexandriava.gov.
165. James P. Moran, Jr., letter to Harry S. Burke, May 12, 1990, Alexandria Black History Museum, Alexandria, VA.
166. Mansfield, "'39 Library Protest," V1, V8; Annie Gowen, "Overdue at the Library: 60 Years Ago in Alexandria, Five Men Staged a Sit-In for the Books," *Washington Post*, August 23, 1999, C1, C2; Zoe Epstein, "Sit-In at the Alexandria Library: 60 Years Later," *Alexandria Gazette Packet*, August 5, 1999, 23, 32; "History Repeats Itself:

Re-enactment Commemorates 6oth Anniversary of Library Sit-Down Strike," *Alexandria Life*, August 26, 1999, 34; "Annals of the Civil Rights Movement: 60 Years Ago," *Journal of Blacks in Higher Education* (Autumn 1999): 29; Michael Lee Pope, "Shhh! History Being Made: Remembering Segregation and Defiance on 70th Anniversary of Alexandria's Civil-Rights Protest at Library," *Alexandria Gazette Packet*, August 27, 2009, 1, 4; "A History Lesson at the Library," *Washington Post*, August 27, 2009, 1.

167.  "Library Sit-In: 75 Years Later," *Alexandria Gazette Packet*, August 28, 2014, 1; Derrick Perkins, "Remembering a Key Civil Rights Event: Alexandria Library Sit-In's 75th Anniversary Commemorated," *Alexandria Times*, August 28, 2014, 1, 6, 7; Derrick Perkins, "Ahead of His Time: City Celebrates Samuel W. Tucker, a Homegrown Champion of Civil Rights," *Alexandria Times*, August 21, 2014, 1, 9, 13; "The 1939 Civil Rights Sit-In at Alexandria Library Reaches Its 75th Anniversary and We Kick Off Our Year-Long Celebration," *AlexandriaNews.org*, January 15, 2014, https://alex libraryva.org; Derrick Perkins, "Sitting Down to Stand Up: MLK Observance Focuses on Homegrown Civil Rights Leader," *Alexandria Times*, January 23, 2014, 9–10.

168.  Deborah Thomas-McSwain, interview by author, January 19, 2020, summer 2021; Otto Tucker's obituary, *Washington Post*, August 7, 1988, 60.

169.  Kopf, "Pioneer Sit-In Is Recalled," A4.

170.  Ibid.

171.  *Hill's Alexandria, Virginia, City Directory*, vols. 37–40 (Richmond, VA: Hill Directory Company, 1940, 1942, 1945, 1947–48).

172.  Lovell A. Lee, interview.

### CHAPTER EIGHT: WHAT HAPPENED? WHAT CHANGED?

1.  Margaret Edds, *We Face the Dawn: Oliver Hill, Spottswood Robinson, and the Legal Team That Dismantled Jim Crow* (Charlottesville: University of Virginia Press, 2018); Charles Flint Kellogg, *NAACP: A History of the National Association for the Advancement of Colored People*, vol. 1, *1909–1920* (Baltimore: Johns Hopkins University Press, 1967); Patricia Sullivan, *Lift Every Voice: The NAACP and the Making of the Civil Rights Movement* (New York: New Press, 2009); Mark V. Tushnet, *The NAACP's Legal Strategy Against Segregated Education, 1925–1950* (Chapel Hill: University of North Carolina Press, 1987).

2.  August Meier and Elliott Rudwick, *Along the Color Line: Explorations in the Black Experience* (Urbana: University of Illinois Press, 2002), 342.

3.  Julie B. Perry, interview by the author, November 17, 2014; Julius Newman, "In and Around Alexandria," *Chicago Defender*, November 11, 1939, 11; George Rutherglen, "A Tribute to Earl C. Dudley, Jr.," *Virginia Law Review* 94, no. 6 (2008): 1281–87; Perry, interview.

4.  Meier and Rudwick, *Along the Color Line*, 341, 342.

5.  Elsie Tucker Thomas, interview by Matt Spangler, September 30, 1998.

6.  Aldous Huxley, "Pathway to Profitable Living," *Black World/Negro Digest* 11, no. 10 (1962): 65; W. E. B. Du Bois, "Of the Training of Black Men," *Atlantic Monthly* 90 (September 1902): 291.

7.  "Council to Study Library Branch," *Washington Post*, August 8, 1939, 13; David Sibley, *Geographies of Exclusion: Society and Difference in the West* (London: Routledge, 1995), xi.

8. Alexandria Library Company, meeting minutes, February 12, 1940, 47–48, records 1937– , box 98B, folder 16, ALSCAV.

9. "Alexandria, Virginia," in *Encyclopedia of Southern Jewish Communities*, https://www.isjl .org. Catherine Weinraub also provided information on Rabbi Schiff and Congregation Beth El, from the archives of Beth El Hebrew Congregation, Alexandria, VA.

10. Jürgen Habermas, *The Structural Transformation of the Public Sphere: An Inquiry into a Category of Bourgeois Society* (Cambridge, MA: MIT Press, 1991); Jürgen Habermas, Sara Lennox, and Frank Lennox, "The Public Sphere: An Encyclopedia Article (1964)," *New German Critique* 3 (Autumn 1974): 49–55; Wayne A. Wiegand, "Library as Place," *North Carolina Libraries* 63, no. 3 (2005): 76–81; Jane Mansbridge, "Conflict and Commonality in Habermas's *Structural Transformation of the Public Sphere*," *Political Theory* 40, no. 6 (2012): 789–801; Susan Bickford, "Constructing Inequality: City Spaces and the Architecture of Citizenship," *Political Theory* 28, no. 3 (2000): 361, 356.

11. Gina Schlesselman-Tarango, "The Legacy of Lady Bountiful: White Women in the Library," *Library Trends* 64, no. 4 (2016): 674; Cheryl Knott, *Not Free, Not for All: Public Libraries in the Age of Jim Crow* (Amherst: University of Massachusetts Press, 2015), 30.

12. Ray Oldenburg, *The Great Good Place: Cafés, Coffee Shops, Bookstores, Bars, Hair Salons, and Other Hangouts at the Heart of a Community* (New York: Da Capo, 1999), 16. Also see Schlesselman-Tarango, "The Legacy of Lady Bountiful," 667–86; Eino Sierpe, "Confronting Librarianship and Its Function in the Structure of White Supremacy and the Ethno State," *Journal of Radical Librarianship* 5 (May 2019), 84–102; and Karla J. Strand, "Disrupting Whiteness in Libraries and Librarianship: A Reading List," no. 89 in the series Bibliographies in Gender and Women's Studies (Madison: University of Wisconsin, 2019), https://www.library.wisc.edu.

13. Wiegand, "Library as Place," 78.

14. Lyn H. Lofland, *The Public Realm: Exploring the City's Quintessential Social Territory* (New Brunswick, NJ: Aldine Transaction, 1998).

15. Ferdinand T. Day, interview by the author, September 25, 2014.

16. Donald G. Nieman, *Church and Community among Black Southerners, 1865–1900* (New York: Garland, 1994), xviii; Julia A. Hersberger, Lou Sua, and Adam L. Murray, "The Fruit and Root of the Community: The Greensboro Carnegie Negro Library, 1904–1964," in *The Library as Place: History, Community, and Culture*, ed. John E. Buschman and Gloria J. Leckie (Westport, CT: Libraries Unlimited, 2012), 81; Day, interview.

17. Sibley, *Geographies of Exclusion*, xvi, 38.

18. Ibid., 38–39.

19. Alexandria Library Company, meeting minutes, February 15, 1960, 110, records 1937– , box 98B-1, folder 1, ALSCAV.

20. Bickford, "Constructing Inequality," 355–76.

21. Alexandria Library Company, meeting minutes, March 13, 1939, 26–27, April 19, 1939, 28–29, May 8, 1939, 30–31, and June 12, 1939, 32–33, records 1937– , box 98B, folder 16, ALSCAV.

22. Cheryl Knott Malone, "Accommodating Access: 'Colored' Carnegie Libraries, 1905–1925" (PhD diss., University of Texas at Austin, 1996), 61.

23. See Gerald N. Rosenberg, *The Hollow Hope: Can Courts Bring About Social Change?*, 2nd ed. (Chicago: University of Chicago Press, 2008); Lawrence Goldstone, *Inherently Unequal: The Betrayal of Equal Rights by the Supreme Court, 1865–1903* (New York: Walker, 2011).

24. Patterson Toby Graham, "Segregation and Civil Rights in Alabama's Public Libraries, 1918–1965" (PhD diss., University of Alabama School of Library and Information Studies, 1998), 281.

25. Sarah Becker, "Residents Recall the Days of Jim Crow," *Alexandria Life*, February 18, 1999, 32.

26. Rachel Meyer, "The Rise and Fall of the Sit-Down Strike," in *The Encyclopedia of Strikes in American History*, ed. Aaron Brenner, Immanuel Ness, and Benjamin Day (Armonk, NY: Sharpe, 2009), 214, 215; Pamela Spence Richards, "Library Services and the African American Intelligentsia before 1960," *Libraries and Culture* 33, no. 1 (1998): 91–97.

27. Meier and Rudwick, *Along the Color Line*, 341, 339–42; August Meier and Elliott Rudwick, "The Boycott Movement against Jim Crow Streetcars in the South, 1900–1906," *Journal of American History* 55, no. 4 (1969): 756–75; William Hine, "The 1867 Charleston Streetcar Sit-Ins: A Case of Successful Black Protest," *South Carolina Historical Magazine* 77, no. 2 (1976): 110–14.

28. Tracy E. K'Meyer, "Building Interracial Democracy: The Civil Rights Movement in Louisville, Kentucky, 1945–1956," in *Time Longer Than Rope: A Century of African American Activism, 1850–1950*, ed. Charles M. Payne and Adam Green (New York: New York University Press, 2003), 417, 421; "Let Us in Louisville Keep Our Perspective," *Courier Journal*, [January 1942], box 2, file 12, John and Murray Walls Papers, University Archives, University of Louisville; "Negroes Ask Unrestricted Library Use," source unknown [*Courier Journal?*], [1942], clippings in box 2, file 12, John and Murray Walls Papers, University Archives, University of Louisville; "Segregation at Library Banned," *Louisville Leader*, May 22, 1948, 1; Cheryl Knott Malone, "Louisville Free Public Library's Racially Segregated Branches, 1905–35," *Register of the Kentucky Historical Society* 93, no. 2 (1995): 159–79; Rosa Parks, letter to Leona McCauley, July 7, 1948, item 020.00.00, Rosa Parks Papers, Manuscript Division, Library of Congress.

29. Howard G. Cooley, personal communication to author, February 24, 2020; William A. Elwood, "Interview with Samuel Wilbert Tucker and Otto L. Tucker, January 18, 1985," conducted for the Civil Rights Lawyers Project (Charlottesville: University of Virginia), 2006, DVD.

30. Jerry Kline, "Alexandria School Workshop: Frank Racial Questions Are Posed," *Evening Star*, August 25, 1966, B2; Jerry Kline, "Alexandria School Study: Integration Workshop Ends," *Evening Star*, August 26, 1966, C3; Perry, interview.

31. Jack M. Bloom, *Class, Race, and the Civil Rights Movement* (Bloomington: Indiana University Press, 1987); Armstead L. Robinson, "Beyond the Realm of Social Consensus: New Meanings of Reconstruction for American History," *Journal of American History* 68, no. 2 (1981): 276–97.

32. Gladys Howard Davis, interview, February 17, 2014.

33. Wiegand, "Library as Place"; Wayne A. Wiegand, "To Reposition a Research Agenda: What American Studies Can Teach the LIS Community about the Library in the Life of the User," *Library Quarterly* 73, no. 4 (2003): 369–82.

34. Elsie Tucker Thomas, interview with Spangler; Theodore Carter DeLaney, "The Sit-in Demonstration in Historical Perspective," *North Carolina Historical Review* 87, no. 4 (2010): 431–38; Florence Murray, "Alexandria Library Grows Daily in National Importance," *Washington Tribune*, September 2, 1939, 2.

35. Earl Lewis, *In Their Own Interests: Race, Class, and Power in Twentieth-Century Norfolk, Virginia* (Berkeley: University of California Press, 1991); Kenneth Kusmer, "The Black Urban Experience in American History," in *The State of Afro-American History: Past, Present, and Future*, ed. Darlene Clark Hine (Baton Rouge: Louisiana State University Press, 1986), 106.

36. John H. Bracey, Jr., August Meier, and Elliott Rudwick, eds., *Black Workers and Organized Labor* (Belmont, CA: Wadsworth, 1971); Robin D. G. Kelley, "'We Are Not What We Seem': Rethinking Black Working-Class Opposition in the Jim Crow South," *Journal of American History* 80, no. 1 (1993): 75–112; Glenda Elizabeth Gilmore, *Defying Dixie: The Radical Roots of Civil Rights, 1919–1950* (New York: Norton, 2008); Payne and Green, *Time Longer Than Rope*; Michael K. Honey, *Southern Labor and Black Civil Rights: Organizing Memphis Workers* (Urbana: University of Illinois Press, 1993); Leon Fink, *Workingmen's Democracy: The Knights of Labor and American Politics,* (Urbana: University of Illinois Press, 1985); Erik S. Gellman, *Death Blow to Jim Crow: The National Negro Congress and the Rise of Militant Civil Rights* (Chapel Hill: University of North Carolina Press, 2012); Jason Kaufman, "Rise and Fall of a Nation of Joiners: The Knights of Labor Revisited," *Journal of Interdisciplinary History* 31, no. 4 (2001): 553–79; Lewis, *In Their Own Interests*.

37. Gregg D. Kimball, "African, American, and Virginian: The Shaping of Black Memory in Antebellum Virginia, 1790–1860," in Brundage, *Where These Memories Grow*, 58; Gerald Sider and Gavin Smith, eds., *Between History and Histories: The Making of Silences and Commemorations* (Toronto: University of Toronto Press, 1997), 10–11. See also Terry Cook, ed., *Controlling the Past: Documenting Society and Institutions: Essays in Honor of Helen Willa Samuels* (Chicago: Society of American Archivists, 2010).

38. Frederick Douglass, "West India Emancipation," speech delivered on August 3, 1857, Canandaigua, NY, https://www.blackpast.org.

39. U.S. Supreme Court, *Brown v. Louisiana*, 383 U.S. 131 (1966), argued December 6, 1965, decided February 23, 1966, https://supreme.justia.com; *Brown et al. v. Louisiana*, 383 U.S. 131 (1966), argued December 6, 1965, decided February 23, 1966, https://scholar.google.com.

40. U.S. Supreme Court, *Garner v. Louisiana*, 368 U.S. 157 (1961), argued October 18–19, 1961, decided December 11, 1961, https://supreme.justia.com; U.S. Supreme Court, *Taylor v. Louisiana*, 370 U.S. 154 (1962), case not argued, decided June 4, 1962, https://supreme.justia.com; U.S. Supreme Court, *Cox v. Louisiana*, 379 U.S.

536 (1962), argued October 21, 1964, decided January 18, 1965, https://supreme
.justia.com.

41. Quoted in Carol O'Connor Wolfe, "One Brave Soldier in the Fight to Be Free,"
*Washington Post*, November 11, 1990, B8.

## EPILOGUE: TURNING THE PAGE

1. "Alexandria Circuit Court Dismisses Charges against Civil Rights Advocates at 1939
Library Sit-In," press release, October 19, 2019, https://www.alexandriava.gov;
*Commonwealth of Virginia, Petitioner, v. William Evans, Otto L. Tucker, Edward Gaddis,
Morris Murray, Clarence Strange, Defendants*, docket no. MO19001660, October 18,
2019, Circuit Court of Alexandria, VA.

2. Barbara Ann Rowan, personal communication, October 22 and 23, 2019.

3. "Alexandria Circuit Court Dismisses Charges against Civil Rights Advocates at 1939
Library Sit-In."

4. Mayor Justin M. Wilson, proclamation issued by the City of Alexandria on behalf
of the city council, Alexandria, Virginia, October 21, 2019.

5. Deborah Thomas-McSwain, interview by the author, January 19, 2020.

6. Panel discussion with descendants of the Alexandria Library sit-in protesters, October 21, 2019, Charles E. Beatley, Jr., Central Library, Alexandria, VA; Nancy Noyes
Silcox, *Samuel Wilbert Tucker: The Story of a Civil Rights Trailblazer and the 1939
Alexandria Library Sit-In* (Fairfax, VA: History4All, 2013; Arlington, VA: Noysil,
2014); Nancy Noyes Silcox, personal communication, October 27 and October 28,
2019; Patricia Sullivan, "80 Years Later, Charges from an Alexandria Sit-In Are
Dismissed," *Washington Post*, October 22, 2019, B1, B4.

7. American Library Association, "ALA News," June 8, 2020, http://www.ala.org.
Also see Kevin Dauray, "Alexandria Library Receives Prestigious Award for Program
Recognizing '39 Sit-In," *Zebra Press*, August 21, 2020, https://thezebra.org.

8. "Alexandria City Council Affirms Commitment to Racial and Social Equity for 'ALL
Alexandria,'" February 9, 2021, https://alexandriava.gov; Justin M. Wilson, memo
to Alexandria City Council, January 21, 2021, https://files.constantcontact.com.

9. Alexandria Library System, "Alexandria Library Five-Year Plan, 2015–2020," August 2,
2016, https://vdocuments.site.

10. American Library Association, "ALA Executive Board Releases a Statement That
Reinforces Commitment to Safeguarding Intellectual Freedom and Social Justice,"
August 18, 2021, https://www.ala.org; Wayne A. Wiegand, discussion, Library
History Round Table, ALA Connect, August 23, 2021; Bernadette Lear, email reply
to Library History Round Table discussion, ALA Connect, August 24, 2021; Carol A.
Leibiger, Library History Round Table discussion, ALA Connect, August 25, 2021.
See also Wayne A. Weigand and Shirley A. Weigand, *The Desegregation of Public
Libraries in the Jim Crow South: Civil Rights and Local Activism* (Baton Rouge: Louisiana
State University Press, 2018).

# INDEX

Page numbers followed by an *f* indicate a figure, *t* indicate a table.